T0114796

# TOWER OF BABBLE

## HOW THE UNITED NATIONS HAS FUELED GLOBAL CHAOS

# DORE GOLD

THREE RIVERS PRESS

NEW YORK

Published in the United States by Three Rivers Press, an imprint of the Crown Publishing
Group, a division of Random House, Inc., New York.
www.crownpublishing.com

THREE RIVERS PRESS and the Tugboat design are registered trademarks of Random House, Inc.

Originally published in hardcover in the United States in slightly different form by Crown
Forum, an imprint of the Crown Publishing Group, a division of Random House, Inc., New
York, in 2004.

Library of Congress Cataloging-in-Publication Data
Gold, Dore.
    Tower of Babble: how the United Nations has fueled global chaos / Dore Gold.
    Includes index.
      1. United Nations—History.    2. Security, International.    3. World politics—
1945–1989.    4. World politics—1989–    I. Title.
    JZ4984.5.G65    2004
    341.23'09—dc22                                                          2004014792

ISBN-13: 978-1-4000-5494-7
ISBN-10: 1-4000-5494-X

Design by Leonard Henderson

First Paperback Edition

*To my mother, Sedell Gold,*
*whose vision and values guided me in whatever I have done.*

# CONTENTS

# MAPS

*We must make sure that [the United Nations'] work is fruitful, that it is a reality and not a sham, that it is a force for action, and not merely a frothing of words, that it is a true temple of peace in which the shields of many nations can some day be hung up, and not merely a cockpit in a Tower of Babel.*

— WINSTON CHURCHILL, 1946

# The Roots of Chaos

For President George W. Bush, the crisis was much larger than just Iraq. It was global.

When the president went to the United Nations General Assembly on September 12, 2002, he faced a world that had erupted in chaos. Saddam Hussein, of course, had shown himself to be a ruthless and incorrigible dictator who had no respect for human rights or international law, and Bush was at the UN to address that problem directly. But the threats to global security were multiplying even beyond that. Nuclear proliferation had become an epidemic, as rogue regimes like North Korea, Libya, and Iran continued to actively develop the world's most dangerous arms, and countries like Pakistan, Russia, and China were only too eager to supply the technologies for their production. There was also the threat of global terrorism. The attacks on the United States just a year earlier had been the most dramatic sign that the post–Cold War world was anything but safe. A few months before the president appeared at the UN, the U.S. State Department had affirmed that at least seven governments continued to be state sponsors of international terrorism.[1]

It wasn't supposed to be this way. Twelve years earlier, almost to the day, Bush's father, President George H. W. Bush, had told a joint session of Congress that the opportunity for a "new world order" was at hand. Freed from the tensions and struggles of the Cold War, he proclaimed in his September 11, 1990, address, the world would be "freer from the threat of terror, stronger in the pursuit of justice, and more secure in the quest for peace." Bush envisioned "a new partnership of nations" emerging. Clearly, the primary instrument for maintaining this new world order would be the United Nations, according to the president, who himself was once a UN ambassador.[2] The UN, after all, was no longer paralyzed by the Cold War's superpower stalemate, so it could at last perform "as envisioned by its founders." Under the UN's leadership, it would be "a world where the rule of law supplants the rule of the jungle."[3] The UN heeded the president's call, as the UN Security Council took a unified stand against Iraq's invasion of Kuwait. After the Gulf War ended, Bush would declare that the UN had passed the "first test" facing the new world order.

For a moment, there reemerged the utopian enthusiasm that had been voiced when the UN was founded in 1945, in the wake of the Second World War. It was much like the thinking that had spawned the League of Nations after the First World War and an earlier international society, the Concert of Europe, at the end of the Napoleonic Wars, in 1815. All those postwar initiatives had been launched to try to prevent the outbreak of future conflicts. Now the UN would take the lead in the new world order, and it promised to succeed where those earlier efforts to preserve peace had failed. UN peacekeepers would be dispatched globally in unprecedented numbers. The UN would identify aggressors and act decisively to protect the world's security, just as it did in the 1991 Gulf War.

Yet when the younger George Bush went to the UN in 2002, there was more anarchy than anything else. A new crisis seemed to threaten world peace every few months. The son, in short, had not inherited any kind of stable world order from the father. George H. W. Bush had declared in 1990 that the "rule of law" would replace the "rule of the jungle," but within less than five years, the rule of the jungle had taken command. The post–Cold War order, with the UN as its centerpiece, had quickly collapsed—more quickly than either the Concert of Europe, which lasted for ninety-nine years, or the League of Nations, which was active for about twenty.

Something had gone terribly wrong. Where was the UN that was supposed to be the post–Cold War beacon for a better world? What prevented the UN from working now that the Soviet-American rivalry could no longer be blamed for the organization's inaction? Why had international conflict, and the new global terrorism, spiraled out of control in an era that was supposed to be marked by unprecedented peace?

The truth was that the UN was singularly unsuited to preserving global order. The UN had—and has—crippling flaws. The 1990s brought these flaws into sharper focus, but in fact they were there almost from the beginning. Indeed, the UN's record reflects one shocking failure after another, even in the organization's earliest days. The UN's founders created a world body based on a noble ideal: standing up to aggression, preserving international peace, and defending human rights and other fundamental principles. But it is now clear that the UN simply doesn't work.

The UN is not a benign but ineffective world body. It has actually accelerated and spread global chaos. This book examines why the UN has been such an abject failure—what flaws have prevented it from fulfilling the ambitions of its founders and of its champions, such as George H. W. Bush.

Recognizing the UN's critical weaknesses leads inevitably to this question: What must be done about the United Nations? This is not an academic question; rather, it lies at the heart of the most crucial policy debates in Washington and the world's other capitals. Many people still suggest that the UN is a panacea for the world's most difficult problems. But carefully examining the UN's past role in some of the most intractable conflicts reveals that UN involvement, in most cases, only makes matters worse.

## "THERE IS NO NEUTRAL GROUND"

President George W. Bush has often been derided by his critics as a crass unilateralist, but when he went before the UN General Assem-

bly in September 2002, he showed that he was keenly aware of the
role that the UN should be playing in international affairs. The trouble, as Bush made clear to the delegates assembled before him, was
that the UN was abdicating its responsibilities. While the immediate
issue at hand was Saddam Hussein and Iraq, the president devoted
himself as much to a forceful, revealing critique of the UN's performance as he did to the specifics of the Iraq situation. Bush began his
speech by reminding the delegates of the UN's original purpose: to
dedicate itself to "standards of human dignity" and "a system of security defended by all." The UN had been established in 1945, at the
close of the Second World War, when the horrors of Nazism had cast
a long shadow; the UN's architects had created the world body expressly to combat aggressors and to protect basic human rights. Unless the UN acted against Iraq, Bush suggested, it would fail
miserably at both. The president reiterated that the UN's "founding
members resolved that the peace of the world must never again be
destroyed by the will and wickedness of any man."

In short, the UN was born at a moment of extraordinary moral
clarity. And Bush invoked the clear vision of the UN's founders, for
he spoke in broader moral terms, not in the language of geopolitics
alone. He started not with reports about Saddam Hussein's development of biological and even nuclear weapons, but by describing
how Saddam's regime had repressed minorities, imprisoned tens of
thousands of political opponents, and systematically tortured those
whom it had arbitrarily arrested. Bush detailed the regime's tech-
niques of mutilation, electric shock, rape, and burning of its opponents. He told of how Saddam's forces had gassed forty Kurdish
villages. Even those UN members who did not accept Bush's argument that an "emboldened" Iraqi regime might in the future supply weapons of mass destruction to "terrorist allies" could hardly
deny Iraq's troubling record. Saddam's regime had trampled on
everything for which the UN stood. More specifically, the Iraqi dictator had continually violated the sixteen legally binding resolutions against Iraq that the UN Security Council had adopted since
late 1990, and had ignored at least thirty statements from the pres-

ident of the UN Security Council regarding Iraq's continued violations of those resolutions. All sixteen resolutions were the most severe kind the Security Council could adopt, falling under Chapter
VII of the UN Charter, which was reserved for cases of aggression.
Still, the UN had done virtually nothing to enforce its own resolutions. Even the Clinton administration, in 1996, had pushed the
UN to deal with the Iraqi problem, but the French, Russians, and
Chinese had used their power on the UN Security Council to repeatedly block any decisive action. Bush was now in the same position as his predecessor.

The case against Saddam Hussein was clear-cut, as President
Bush pointed out, even if members of the international community
did not want to acknowledge it. Though Saddam had said he would
honor his commitments to the UN, Bush said, "he has proven instead only his contempt for the United Nations, and for all his
pledges. By breaking every pledge—by his deceptions, and by his
cruelties—Saddam Hussein has made the case against himself."
More important, given the wide scope of Iraqi violations, especially
in the area of human rights, the president made it clear to the UN
member states that this was one of the few occasions when they were
staring pure evil in the face.

Bush was right to put the case in such stark terms. Moral judgments were a necessary prerequisite for taking any action. But they
were precisely the judgments that the UN declined to make. President Bush, in effect, threw down the gauntlet in front of the UN
member states. "We created the United Nations Security Council, so
that unlike the League of Nations, our deliberations would be more
than talk, our resolutions would be more than wishes," Bush reminded the delegates. If the UN was to avoid the fate of the League
of Nations, it would have to confront the Iraqi threat head-on. This
was, he said, "a defining moment" for the UN. "Will the United Nations serve the purpose of its founding, or will it be irrelevant?" the
president asked bluntly.

George H. W. Bush had dramatically proclaimed after the 1991
Gulf War that the UN had passed its "first test" in the post–Cold War

era. Now George W. Bush declared that "all the world faces a test"—
a new test posed by the same rogue regime.[4]

The UN failed this test. It had indeed become irrelevant, in a
sense. But it was worse than irrelevant. It was dangerous, fanning the
flames of global disorder.

How did this occur? Bush hinted at the UN's main defect in various speeches he delivered at the time: The problem was that the
UN refused to make moral judgments and thus ignored the crimes
of Saddam Hussein, among others. A year later, speaking again before the General Assembly, Bush underlined the point that ultimately the UN had to take sides: "Events of the past two years have
set before us the clearest of divides: between those who seek order
and those who spread chaos. . . . Between these alternatives there is
no neutral ground."[5]

Alas, neutral ground is precisely what the UN has repeatedly
tried to stake out when confronted with clear cases of aggression,
human rights abuse, even genocide. But in its repeated pursuit of
"impartiality," the UN actually has taken sides—in effect joining the
aggressors and the abusers. The UN has, in fact, spread global chaos.

## MORAL EQUIVALENCE

The UN's failures in the decade before George W. Bush went to the
General Assembly reveal how the world body has fueled global
chaos. Beginning with Somalia in 1993, the UN was in charge of one
peacekeeping disaster after another. These failures were linked to
some of the worst massacres of innocent civilians that the world had
witnessed in decades. In 1994 in the central African nation of
Rwanda, some 800,000 Rwandan Tutsis were murdered in a deliberate campaign of genocide—this after the UN had insisted that its
peacekeeping forces maintain strict "impartiality." It didn't seem to
matter that UN officials had been warned that the Tutsi extermination campaign was imminent. They did nothing. Then, just a year
later, UN peacekeepers stood by in the Bosnian enclave of Srebrenica as Europe's worst massacre of civilians since the Second

World War occurred: more than 7,000 Bosnian Muslims were slaughtered in a UN "safe haven" where they had sought refuge under the UN flag.

Nor was the damage from the Bosnian and Rwandan disasters confined to those specific situations. By allowing those conflicts to escalate unnecessarily, the UN sparked even broader crises. The crisis in the former Yugoslavia soon enveloped Kosovo and required a massive NATO intervention. Soon Macedonia was swept into the conflict. In the Rwandan crisis, the Hutu militants who had slaughtered hundreds of thousands of Tutsis crossed into the Democratic Republic of the Congo (formerly Zaire). Ultimately five African countries would become embroiled in the conflict, and millions would be killed in the bloodiest war in African history. The chaos was contagious.

UN officials have often blamed these disasters on the inflexible mandate the UN Security Council gave peacekeeping forces, or on inadequate budgetary resources for peacekeeping. But a deeper flaw was revealed, one that also influenced the Iraq debate. Both the Rwanda and Bosnia massacres occurred on the watch of Kofi Annan, who at the time was UN undersecretary-general for peacekeeping operations. But the Ghanaian bureaucrat was not held accountable for his office's failure to prevent those tragedies; in fact, he was elevated to the post of secretary-general in 1997. A few years later he was even awarded the Nobel Peace Prize, despite his involvement in the UN's policy of reflexive neutrality on most global disputes that had only escalated conflicts. In a devastating critique, David Rieff, who has reported on the international response to humanitarian emergencies in Bosnia and around the world, attacked Annan for his "refusal to regard the evil in the world realistically." In Iraq, Bosnia, and Rwanda, Rieff concluded in 1998, "moral judgments are not part of what he sees as his role." In Annan's "sanitized, value-neutral" diplomatic parlance, he wrote, there are no aggressors or victims of aggression, only "warring parties."[6]

This is an indictment of the entire UN, not just of Kofi Annan. Annan is the quintessential UN bureaucrat, having risen up the organization's ranks to become the first secretary-general who was not formerly an ambassador, foreign minister, or high-level official in his home country. He was intimately linked with the culture and mores of the organization itself. Annan, in fact, admitted in the aftermath of the failure in Bosnia that the UN had an "institutional ideology of impartiality even when confronted with attempted genocide."[7] Historically, this was true. For example, when the UN brokered a peace settlement in Cambodia, Secretary-General Javier Pérez de Cuéllar insisted on protecting the murderous Khmer Rouge, who were responsible for killing nearly 2 million Cambodians in the 1970s.[8] Khmer Rouge leader Pol Pot was not dragged before an international tribunal at The Hague. His deputies were not charged with genocide but instead became part of the "peace process."[9]

Diplomatic neutralism in the face of genocidal murderers is not amoral; it is *immoral*. Not intervening against those slaughtering thousands of innocents amounts to taking the murderers' side. An organization that has been dedicated to appearing "impartial" at almost any cost has far too often come down on the side of evil. Robert Kaplan accurately wrote in *The Coming Anarchy* that the UN bureaucracy worships consensus, "but consensus can be the handmaiden of evil, since the ability to confront evil means the willingness to act boldly and ruthlessly and without consensus."[10]

That inability, or refusal, to recognize and boldly confront evil is the UN's salient flaw, its Achilles' heel. It was a recurring pattern in the UN's handling of Saddam Hussein throughout the 1990s. The UN's chief weapons inspector in Iraq under Secretary-General Annan, Australian diplomat Richard Butler, sensed that Annan was giving greater credence to the claims of Saddam Hussein's regime than to those of his own inspectors in Baghdad. By 1998 Iraq was openly defying UN weapons inspectors, but still Annan tried to broker a new, softer deal for Saddam in the UN Security Council. It didn't seem to matter that his own UN monitors were expressing anguish over the Iraqi leader's repeated acts of noncompliance. The secretary-general undercut their authority and placed the Iraqi dictator's grievances on a par with the conclusions of the experts the UN itself had appointed. Butler would charge the secretary-general with "moral equivalence" for honoring the dubious complaints of a dictator who was continually violating UN resolutions.[11] Annan continued this pattern after the Iraq War began in 2003, declaring that he was "getting increasingly concerned by humanitarian casualties" emanating from U.S. operations in Baghdad, without saying a word about Iraqi abuses in the conflict.[12]

Why had the UN catered to Saddam Hussein for years even when he was openly breaking the pledges he had made to the international community? The apparent appeasement of Iraq extended beyond acceding to Saddam's requests for a weaker weapons-inspection regime. In 1995 the UN implemented an "oil-for-food" program that allowed Iraq to sell oil in order to fund purchases of food, medicine, and other humanitarian goods. The UN was supposed to control these transactions, but Saddam denied UN weapons inspectors access to many Iraqi facilities, making it impossible to ensure that Iraq was not diverting oil revenue to nonhumanitarian purposes. Nevertheless, Kofi Annan doubled the program in 1998. The UN expanded the program again in 2002, by which point weapons inspectors had been barred from Iraq for four years.

By 2004 it became apparent that this UN program had allowed Saddam Hussein's regime to pocket as much as $10.1 billion through oil smuggling and other illicit oil proceeds.[13] Worse, it seemed that Saddam had exploited the multibillion-dollar UN program to give massive kickbacks to friends and accomplices around the world. An Iraqi newspaper, *al-Mada*, published a list of more than two hundred businesses and individuals who had allegedly received black market oil vouchers for Iraqi oil; on the list was UN assistant secretary-general Benon Sevan, who had overseen the oil-for-food program.[14] As of this writing, investigations into the corrupt scheme are under way, and UN spokesmen have denied any wrongdoing.[15] But the early revelations raised serious questions about the UN's ability to deal with the most serious threats to international peace. After all, for the duration of the oil-for-food program, Iraq was supposed to be under strict UN sanctions. Was the corruption a further indication of the UN's inability to make moral choices—of determining the difference between good and evil? At least one former UN coordinator for the oil-for-food program has admitted that UN officials refused to squarely address Iraq's cynical exploitation of oil-for-food accounts because of their skewered "moral compass." This led them to feel more outrage at the United States and Britain for their sanctions policy than at the regime of Saddam Hussein.[16]

The more one probes the UN's performance, the more difficult it is to see the organization as a force for greater order, stability, or global justice. Other scandals have undercut the UN's claims for any kind of moral authority. The UN's blue-helmeted peacekeepers may have received the Nobel Peace Prize in 1988, but in the 1990s, in order to protect their own personal security, the peacekeepers or their commanders in New York often made deals under the table with states massacring their citizens or with terrorist groups whose goal was the same. Moreover, by 2000, it was clear that UN peacekeepers were spreading AIDS in Cambodia and East Timor.[17] A year later Italian prosecutors were investigating charges that UN troops from Denmark and Slovakia, monitoring the Ethiopian and Eritrean frontier, were involved in a child prostitution racket.[18] The same charges had been leveled at UN peacekeepers in Mozambique in 1996 and in Bosnia in 2002.[19]

Other developments have highlighted the defects in the UN. The UN's main human rights body, the Human Rights Commission, was founded after World War II and was chaired in its early days by Eleanor Roosevelt. But in 2003, the UN elected Muammar Qaddafi's Libya—a sponsor of terrorism and an abuser of human rights—to chair the commission. It was a fitting sign of the bankruptcy of the UN Human Rights Commission, which had also been silent about the "Killing Fields" of Cambodia, the Chinese assault on protestors in Tiananmen Square, and Idi Amin's acts of mass murder against Ugandans. Similarly, eyebrows were raised when just weeks after the 9/11 attacks, Syria—one of the main state sponsors of international terrorism—was elected to the UN Security Council for a two-year term. How could the UN Security Council take any meaningful actions against international terrorism when one of its fifteen members had been in the terrorism business for decades and gave no indication that it was about to reform?

The UN's moral equivalence affects not just its ability to enforce its resolutions or to empower its commissions and other bodies to act decisively. The resolutions themselves—whether issued by the Security Council or the General Assembly—are dripping in moral equivalence. Although UN resolutions are not, in most cases, binding international law, they play a critical role in global affairs, establishing positions on issues to which leaders and diplomats routinely refer. Even General Assembly resolutions, which are only recommendations, help determine "the norms that many countries—including the United States—would like everyone to live by," in the words of Annan spokesman Shashi Tharoor.[20] In other words, the UN is supposed to set global standards of behavior—a moral code of conduct that defines the rules of world order. But when the UN refuses to identify and encourage proper behavior, it cannot set any meaningful standards.

This problem became more apparent in the 1990s than in previous decades. During the Cold War, the competition between the superpowers had generally dictated the organizing principles of world order: the West against the Soviet bloc. But with the Cold War's end, states looked to the UN to establish the rules of the new world order. The UN has had an unusual amount of authority within the Middle East, where so much of the recent global disorder has been concentrated. Virtually every Arab state invokes the UN's decisions. Back in 1991, Syrian president Hafiz al-Assad described the UN as the source of "international legitimacy" during negotiations with Secretary of State James Baker.[21] Such a claim from an Arab leader is not to be taken lightly, for in Arabic, the word for "legitimacy" is the same as the word for "legality." Little wonder, then, that in 1999, Lebanese prime minister Salim al-Hoss, who was little more than a Syrian puppet, characterized the UN as no less than the "supreme international authority." Arab states have often elevated the UN's nonbinding resolutions to the level of international law. Even non-

Arab states in the Middle East take their political cues from the UN. The Iranian foreign minister, for instance, has called the UN "indispensable."

Of course, in turning to the "indispensable" UN for guidance, the Middle East has relied on an organization with a defective moral compass. Rather than promoting norms to combat terrorism, over recent decades the UN has become one of its primary promoters. The UN could have made a difference in that conflicted region but has only made matters worse. With no clear guidelines of behavior, various Middle Eastern leaders could be confident that they'd suffer no loss of legitimacy for their continued support of aggression, terrorism, and the abuse of fundamental human rights.

## THE SOURCE OF INTERNATIONAL LEGITIMACY?

How exactly did the UN lose the moral clarity that united its founders in 1945? The UN's architects had been united in their war against Nazi Germany, the epitome of pure evil in the twentieth century. They were determined to find a way to prevent the sort of aggression that had led to the Second World War and were firmly committed to protecting human rights, having so recently witnessed the horrors of the Holocaust. Significantly, these founders of the UN did not represent the entire global community and all its competing interests. The UN was, at base, an alliance built on shared principles. Indeed, it grew out of a military alliance, for every nation that attended the organization's founding conference in San Francisco had declared war on at least one of the Axis powers. True, the UN's founding members included states like Stalin's Soviet Union and Wahhabi Saudi Arabia, but as will be seen, these states had to acquiesce to the norms of the overwhelming majority of Western democracies and their allies. Even on human rights, they could not challenge the firm convictions of the UN's majority, even though they abused the human rights of their own peoples. (When the Universal Declaration of Human Rights came up for a vote in the new

General Assembly, the Soviets and the Saudis didn't dare vote against the measure; they merely abstained.)

That would all change, however. In the biblical story of the Tower of Babel, the nations of the world initially spoke one language but lost their unity of purpose when this changed. In the case of the UN, member states all spoke the same political language at the beginning, but as new members flooded into the organization, they brought with them their own political languages—that is, completely different values and concepts of international morality. Soon UN member states were talking past one another. The clarity of 1945 was quickly lost. As early as 1946, Winston Churchill recognized that to be effective, the UN had to preserve its unity of purpose and its ability to act decisively. Churchill expressed the hope that the UN would become "a true temple of peace in which the shields of many nations can some day be hung up, and not merely a cockpit in a Tower of Babel."[22]

The UN of the 1990s lost its ability to make clear moral distinctions because its membership had changed radically over the years. Most of the UN's original members had been inspired by the democratic leadership of Roosevelt and Churchill against the Axis powers. Yet by 1993, only a minority of UN member states, a mere 75 out of 184, were free democracies, according to the nonprofit prodemocracy organization Freedom House. At the UN's disastrous Durban Conference Against Racism in 2001, the longest ovations went to Robert Mugabe and Fidel Castro.[23]

The states that applauded Third World authoritarianism had learned years earlier how to manipulate the UN to their advantage. For example, in 1985, Soviet bloc states—including Angola, Laos, Syria, and Ukraine—introduced a draft resolution in the UN General Assembly entitled "Inadmissibility of Exploitation or Distortion of Human Rights Issues for Interference in the Internal Affairs of States." There was no subtlety here. The draft resolution's title gave away the cosponsors' intentions: to preserve their powers to abuse the human rights of their citizens. A watered-down version was adopted in 1986.[24] They preempted what in the 1990s came to be called "humanitarian intervention"; the UN would not have the authority to confront states that committed massive human rights abuses.

Despite this ugly reality, many in the West, including in the United States, continued to view the UN as indispensable for guaranteeing international peace and security. When the United States confronted Saddam Hussein in 2003, many still argued that U.S. military action in Iraq was illegitimate without a UN mandate. The UN secretary-general himself, Kofi Annan, berated President Bush: "Until now it has been understood that when states go beyond [self-defense] and decide to use force to deal with broader threats to international peace and security, they need the *unique legitimacy* provided by the United Nations [emphasis added]."[25]

But who exactly was conferring this "unique legitimacy"? Annan was essentially saying that the collective will of a group of authoritarian regimes was more legitimate than the decision of the American republic to defend itself. According to UN standards, then, a consensus of dictatorships was superior to the decision of a democracy. This reflected the fundamental problem of the UN's skewed moral judgment. If this logic was accepted, it would mean that the president of the United States and the U.S. Senate were not the final arbiters of when America needed to adopt a military option; instead the UN Security Council would have that authority over U.S. foreign policy, or the policy of any other threatened state.

In the past, U.S. presidents had not made military action dependent on UN approval when vital American interests were involved. President John F. Kennedy did not seek UN authorization to put a naval quarantine around Cuba in 1962. Instead, he relied on a "recommendation" of the Organization of American States (OAS).[26] Even in the case of the Korean War, the UN did not, strictly speaking, explicitly authorize the United States to use force against North Korea's invading army; it said only that the U.S.-led coalition could fly the UN flag. In that same war, President Harry Truman did not ask for authorization from the Security Council to dispatch U.S. forces north of the 38th parallel into North Korea; the U.S. government secured a nonbinding General Assembly resolution instead.

The United States was not alone. Annan was wrong when he indicated that it was standard practice to turn to the UN to authorize the use of force. Since the UN's founding, in fact, most countries had not gone to the Security Council before using force.[27] Leading statesmen regarded it as too dangerous to have to petition the UN before protecting their country. For example, former British prime minister Margaret Thatcher recalled, "Although I am a strong believer in international law, I did not like unnecessary resort to the UN, because it suggested that sovereign states lacked the moral authority to act on their own behalf. If it became accepted that force could only be used—even in self-defence—when the United Nations approved, neither Britain's interests nor those of international justice and order would be served. The UN was a useful—for some matters vital—forum. But it was hardly the nucleus of a new world order."[28]

True, the UN Charter severely circumscribes when it is legal for states to use force, saying that members should refrain from "the threat or use of force against the territorial integrity or political independence of any state, or in any other manner inconsistent with the purposes of the United Nations."[29] In short, wars of conquest or territorial expansion are unquestionably illegal. But how about the use of force for self-defense or in a manner that is *consistent* with the norms of the UN itself—such as using force to stop genocide? Here it is left to the member states themselves to determine whether the use of force is legitimate. States certainly must explain and justify their actions in terms laid out in the UN Charter, but ultimately they are still responsible for making decisions about their own security.[30] The UN Charter is not supposed to supersede the U.S. Constitution for Americans. Somehow, however, during the lead-up to the Iraq War, it became commonly accepted that states did not have the moral authority to make such judgments about their own security needs. This doctrine threatened to undermine the global war on terrorism, for it could give authoritarian regimes harboring terrorist groups a distinct advantage—they could deny any connection to a terrorist attack and depend on the UN to tie the U.S. military's hands.[31]

The idea that only the UN can authorize the use of force is a problem not simply because it is a threat to state sovereignty. Perhaps more troubling, the UN's moral equivalence can prevent it from defining the kind of aggression that warrants a military response. As far back as 1969, UN secretary-general U Thant confessed that the UN was having difficulty drawing distinctions between attacker and defender. Chapter VII of the UN Charter had been designed, he said, "for situations where aggressors could be easily identified and where the 'good guys' of the international world would have no moral doubts about collectively fighting the 'bad guys.' But the situation that has prevailed since the Second World War defied such simplifications."[32] As will be seen in the following chapters, the UN had many times failed to identify aggressors even in its early decades. And it would only become harder. In September 1981, just two years after the Soviet invasion of Afghanistan, ninety-three UN member states endorsed a resolution in the General Assembly accusing the *United States* of being a threat to global peace.[33] If this was the moral compass of the UN and its growing majority, why make a state's security dependent in any way on its judgments?

Serious threats to international order have often been handled outside the UN framework. State practice, in this context, is useful to review. In the 1970s the Khmer Rouge murdered millions of Cambodians, but the UN did not authorize a forceful response to this slaughter. Technically, it seemed, these massacres were not genocide, for the Genocide Convention outlawed mass murder of religious or ethnic groups but not of political opponents. The mass murder of the Cambodian people stopped only when Vietnam invaded Cambodia, for its own expansionist reasons, without going to the UN. Similarly, Tanzania ended the brutal rule of Idi Amin in Uganda without UN approval.[34] India did not ask anyone's permission to put an end to the Pakistani army's murderous campaign in East Pakistan, a conflict that gave birth to Bangladesh in 1971. Finally, President Clinton and NATO defended the Kosovars from the Serb army without a UN Security Council resolution (the Russian Federation would have vetoed such a resolution).

Were all these actions illegitimate even though they served the very moral purpose for which the UN was founded? The UN Security Council never would have approved these interventions; would it have been better to sit by and let hundreds of thousands more people die? In the book *Just and Unjust Wars,* Michael Walzer commented on the imperative to intervene without the UN when acts offend the moral convictions of ordinary people: "I don't think there is any moral reason to adopt the posture of passivity that might be called waiting for the UN (waiting for the universal state, waiting for the messiah . . .)."[35] After all, the UN might never come. It was perhaps for this reason that an independent international commission, which includes members who would normally insist on explicit UN Security Council authorization for any use of force, chose to characterize Clinton's non-UN intervention in Kosovo as "illegal but legitimate."[36]

Interestingly, although the United States had undertaken military action without explicit UN sanction before the 2003 Iraq War, the claim that only the UN could confer "legitimacy" on military action gained currency in large part because of the U.S. government. In rushing to proclaim a new world order centered on the UN, President George H. W. Bush had, according to George F. Will, "made U.S. policy subservient to the United Nations at a moment when the U.N. was pleased to be subservient to the United States." Will wrote these words in January 1992, on the first anniversary of the Gulf War. He offered this prescient warning: "There may come a time when the United States will be held hostage to a Desert Storm legacy, the idea that the legitimacy of U.S. force is directly proportional to the number of nations condoning it."[37]

A decade later, the United States would indeed encounter numerous critics who accused it of unilateralism. Yet few states would cede their right to make final judgments about their security requirements to any international organization, including the UN. They have not done so in the past and it is not likely that they will do so in the future, as the threats of global terrorism and of weapons of mass destruction intensify.[38] When a speedy response is essential, and sensitive intelligence is involved, making military action dependent on UN approval could be disastrous.

## INEPT HANDLING AND UNNECESSARY TARGETS

The UN's distorted perspective has affected vital American interests, and not just in the situation with Iraq. In the late 1990s, it was clear that the international system for curbing the proliferation of weapons of mass destruction, which included the UN's International Atomic Energy Agency (IAEA), was breaking down. Iraq, Iran, Libya, and North Korea were among those actively pursuing the world's deadliest weapons. And yet, while the UN failed to halt the spread of *offensive* weapons, it took action against *defensive* systems, as it did in a direct response to the U.S. government's plan to deploy a national missile defense system. In December 1999 the UN General Assembly adopted a resolution that called on all states to "refrain from the deployment of anti-ballistic missile systems for the defence of the territory of their country."[39] Only the United States, Israel, and Latvia voted against the Russian-inspired initiative.

In the General Assembly, it is always easier to attack the United States—explicitly or implicitly—than the Islamic Republic of Iran.

The UN has had other targets. It took stands, for example, against secessionist movements in Africa, like Katanga or Biafra, and the apartheid regimes of South Africa and Rhodesia. But the UN acted only intermittently. On the whole, the organization has had serious problems condemning any nation—except when it comes to Israel.

For decades, the UN has abandoned its normal ambivalence in global conflicts to come down against Israel. In 1975, the Soviet Union rallied the Afro-Asian bloc to support the infamous "Zionism Is Racism" resolution (Resolution 3379), attacking the very legitimacy of the only national movement that had been recognized by both the League of Nations and the United Nations. The resolution was revoked at the end of the Cold War, but it epitomized how the

UN singled out Israel but ignored the massive human rights violations of its accusers. The UN did not see fit even to comment about
human rights abuses in China or Syria, for instance, but over a
thirty-five-year period, the UN Human Rights Commission devoted
almost 30 percent of its resolutions to Israel.[40] An Israeli official
once quipped, "The UN was devoting most of its time by going after
Israel for jaywalking, while ignoring others who were engaging in
murder."

The UN's targeting of Israel did not affect the Israeli government
alone. It was, in a more subtle way, a problem for the world. The dis-
proportionate energy spent on the tiny state of Israel, where the
conflict paled in comparison to those elsewhere, was the flip side of
the UN's turning a blind eye to crises where it was urgently needed.
It all followed from the organization's endemic inability to recognize and respond to cases of real, dangerous aggression. While busy
with anti-Israeli activity, the UN gave insufficient attention to other
areas that demanded the world community's attention. For example, a civil war that raged in Liberia from 1990 to 1995 forced more
than 800,000 people—fully a third of the nation's population—into
exile in neighboring countries. Many countries were affected by
these masses of refugees from Charles Taylor's regime, but the UN
did not get involved.[41] In Sierra Leone, between 1991 and 1996,
50,000 people died and half the country's population was displaced.
Rebel forces systematically amputated the arms of political opponents—and of their children—who had used their thumbprints to
vote for the embattled government. The UN took no action. Only
years later, in 2000, did it dispatch peacekeepers to the scene.

In places where the UN did take action, its involvement was too
late. The war in the Democratic Republic of the Congo that spilled
over from the 1994 Rwandan war was the perfect example of how
the UN failed to take timely action. In 1998, five African countries
invaded the Democratic Republic of the Congo. The next year, the
UN sent a small observer force to monitor the 1999 Lusaka Peace
Accord, but the fighting persisted. There were widespread reports of
torture, mutilation of bodies, and cannibalism as a form of war-

fare.[42] By 2001, an estimated 2.5 million people had been killed in the fighting. This was an outright invasion, for several countries had crossed an international border. Where were the signatories of the 1949 Fourth Geneva Convention, who were mobilized by an Emergency Special Session of the UN General Assembly and sent to Geneva to discuss Israeli condominium construction on a barren hill in Jerusalem in 1998, the very same year as the Congo massacres? Not until 2003 did the UN actually dispatch a robust French-led force to restore order in Africa. The UN's only real success stories have come in situations in which conflicts had mostly been resolved, such as in El Salvador, Mozambique, and East Timor.

The UN's inept handling of the Israel, Rwanda, and Congo issues reveals a deeper problem in the UN: the UN has become a transparently politicized body. Rather than carefully analyzing what was actually happening in any of these crises, the UN was letting special interests dictate policy. Arab states could mobilize automatic anti-Israeli majorities on virtually any issue and were ready to press this advantage at every opportunity. In Africa, conflicting interests arrested decisive intervention. Some African states, for instance, sought to exploit the Congo's diamonds, gold, and other precious metals, while Western powers were reluctant to get involved in another peacekeeping operation. The UN was dysfunctional.

Some have argued that the UN itself cannot really be blamed for its failures, since all decisions are left up to the member states. A former U.S. official once said that blaming the UN is like blaming Madison Square Garden for a bad game by the New York Knicks. But the UN is more than a building on First Avenue in Manhattan. If its member states' political interests led to the mistakes of the 1990s, then the UN Secretariat had an obligation to produce its own independent intelligence picture of world crises and comment accordingly in the international media. The UN could create public opinion if it wanted to. There is a huge UN press corps that includes all the global wire services, from the Associated Press to Reuters to Agence France-Presse. In the late 1990s, the chief UN weapons inspector in Iraq, Richard Butler, regularly went on the *Today Show* and

*Good Morning America* to alert the American public to Saddam Hussein's ambitions (that is, until he was essentially fired by Secretary-General Kofi Annan). But the UN bureaucracy has taken moral equivalence to new heights, placing the need for "impartiality" above all other considerations. It not only placed the mass murders in Africa on an equal plane with its complaints about Israel, but it elevated its charges against Israel above nearly all of its other global grievances.

Those who argue that the UN member states ultimately make the decisions are right, to a point. The UN is not a legal body operating according to some objective legal criteria; it is a political body that reflects the sum total of the moral values of its member states. But the UN stood for certain standards at its birth, and over time it has allowed members to erode those original standards. The UN Secretariat has not stood up to establish clear standards for the international community. As result, it is virtually impossible for the UN to fulfill its most important purpose—to prevent war.

## PERPETUATING TERRORISM

In the 1920s, Winston Churchill declared that he refused to remain impartial when it came to deciding between the firefighter and the fire. The UN has ostensibly adopted a different logic: It refuses to abandon impartiality. But a UN that perpetuates judgments based on moral equivalence only tilts world order in favor of the fire, and the politicization of the UN ends up placing it far too often squarely on the side of the fire.

Today, the world confronts a raging fire: terrorism, the single biggest threat to international security. The war on terrorism is a security challenge for the entire world, not just the United States. Yet the UN has not stood up to the terrorist threat. Its moral obfuscations have prevented it from backing the firefighters.

The singling out of Israel reflects the UN's inability to confront terrorism. In recent years, for example, the UN has legitimized suicide terrorism that murdered upwards of twenty Israeli teenagers at a time as "resistance to occupation," even though the Israelis had dismantled and withdrawn their military government over the Palestinians under the 1993 Oslo Accords. True, Oslo didn't give the Palestinians an independent state. But it didn't leave them under military occupation, either; rather, it put them under the rule of Yasser Arafat's Palestinian Authority. These facts were unimportant in UN bodies, which had a strong predisposition to support violence if it was presented in the context of a struggle against foreign rule. The UN's authoritarian majority had long ago succeeded in justifying aggression and terrorist acts on the part of "national liberation movements."

So in April 2002, the UN Human Rights Commission affirmed "the legitimate right of the Palestinian people to resist Israeli occupation" just after a Hamas suicide bomber killed thirty Israelis celebrating together the Passover Seder; the resolution recalled that the UN General Assembly had reaffirmed in 1982 the "legitimacy of the struggle of peoples . . . from colonial and foreign domination and foreign occupation by all available means, including armed struggle." Some wouldn't go this far, but they have nonetheless put the Hamas suicide bomber on the same moral plane as the Israeli soldier seeking to destroy his explosives laboratory; according to this view, both are simply part of the Middle East's "cycle of violence." This moral equivalence was intended to neutralize Western criticism of the terrorism campaign against Israel and limit Israel's freedom of action to subdue it.

By refusing to condemn terrorist groups like Hamas and Hizballah—the latter of whom, as will be seen, wielded great influence among militants squaring off against U.S. troops in Iraq—the UN has only perpetuated terrorism. And by condemning Israel for responding to its opponents' repeated terrorist acts, the UN has complicated the West's ability to defend itself against the new wave of global terrorism. What would happen if Americans began to doubt their country's duty to respond to terrorism? What if they started to believe that the U.S. Air Force pilot charged with bombing an al-

Qaeda training camp was no different from the terrorist operative in the al-Qaeda camp below? In fact, already during the Reagan administration, the UN Security Council voted nine to five to condemn the United States for the 1986 bombing of Libya. Only the jointly cast vetoes of the United States, Britain, and France prevented the UN's formal adoption of the condemnation.[43]

For counterterrorism to succeed globally, moral clarity must be preserved. But the UN specializes in moral obfuscation. Thus Kofi Annan refused to condemn a Palestinian suicide bombing in the heart of Jerusalem on January 29, 2004, that killed eleven Israelis and wounded close to fifty. Instead he directed his press statement to *both* sides: "Once again I appeal, to Israelis and Palestinians alike, to rise above feelings of anger and vengeance, however natural, and to devote all their energies to negotiating a true and lasting peace." Compare that "impartial" statement to the unequivocal response to the attacks from the U.S. secretary of state, Colin Powell: "Once again, terrorists have killed innocent people."[44] The U.S. government understood what the UN did not: that the only way to deal with the worst threats to international security is to confront them directly.

## "EVIL IS PREVAILING"

Sergio Vieira de Mello, who headed the UN's humanitarian operations in Iraq before he was killed in the August 2003 bombing of UN headquarters in Baghdad, recognized that a new global crisis was emerging. Referring to the disasters of the 1990s, he said, "Recent history may suggest that evil is prevailing." It is obvious that Vieira de Mello understood the need for the UN to confront this evil, for he pointed out that "the body of international law is under severe challenge, particularly in the humanitarian sphere." Still, in his view the challenge could be overcome. "Does this mean a breakdown of these norms? I don't think so. What it means is a breakdown of respect for those norms."[45]

Vieira de Mello was overoptimistic. Those perpetrating the new global chaos actually speak in the name of the UN's norms. In the half century since the UN's birth, the high standards and hopes that the UN set for itself have been systematically eroded. That erosion is at the heart of the global disorder we know today. The UN, supposedly the protector of international peace and security, has actually undermined world order.

As this book will demonstrate, to consider the UN the "source of international legitimacy" is absurd. Only by examining the UN's record—not just its ideals, but its actual performance—can one understand how it has actually helped the world descend into such disorder. And understanding the source of today's global crises is the only way to begin to remedy the situation.

One thing is clear: The United Nations is not the answer. But before any alternatives can be considered, it is necessary to understand where this noble ideal went wrong.

# CHAPTER 1

---

# The Erosion of Standards

The United Nations was really an American idea. Indeed, as one former U.S. ambassador to the UN put it in the 1970s, "At first the UN was seen as the instrument of American ideologues."[1] The UN's founders established the organization to promote American values and principles on a global scale.

Created in the aftermath of the Allied victory in World War II, the world body had actually been conceived well before the defeat of Nazi Germany and Imperial Japan in 1945. President Franklin Delano Roosevelt had shown his enthusiasm for an international organization as early as the 1930s. The United States had never joined the League of Nations, which had been created after the First World War, but Roosevelt became the first president to send American observers to Geneva to sit in on League sessions. Roosevelt was not naïve, however. He saw the League's flaws. The organization failed to counter the rise of the Axis powers in the 1930s, the invasions of Ethiopia, Manchuria, and the Rhineland, and ultimately the outbreak of the Second World War. Thus, when Roosevelt and British prime minister Winston Churchill drew up the Atlantic Charter in August 1941—even before the United States had entered the war— they called for "a wider and permanent system of general security." It was in fact FDR who first used the term "United Nations." On January 1, 1942, less than a month after Pearl Harbor, the countries allied against the Axis powers signed the "Declaration by United

Nations," a title that Roosevelt proposed. Churchill had preferred the name "Allied Nations."[2]

Months later, according to the notes of his trusted aide Harry Hopkins, President Roosevelt explained to British foreign secretary Anthony Eden that the new international body he envisioned "should be world-wide in scope . . . but, finally, that the real decisions should be made by the United States, Great Britain, Russia, and China, who would be the powers for many years to come that would have to police the world."[3]

At 1944's Dumbarton Oaks Conference outside of Washington, FDR reiterated his conception of the new international body. Specifically he described an organization that would enforce peace through the world's "four policemen": the United States, Great Britain, China, and the USSR.[4] If an aggressor "started to run amok and seeks to grab territory or invade its neighbors," FDR explained to reporters at the time of Dumbarton Oaks, the UN would "stop them before they got started."[5] This was precisely the model the great powers drew up for the UN at the conference. As such, the UN was designed first and foremost to avoid the failures that had plagued the League of Nations. FDR was a realist, a point he drove home in an October 1944 campaign address in New York City in which, when he spoke about the UN, he reminded his listeners, "We are not fighting for, and we shall not attain a utopia."[6] For Roosevelt, the engagement of the United States and the other great powers was vital to give teeth to the organization's international security measures.

Franklin Roosevelt died on April 12, 1945, but the plan for the UN survived. In fact, within two weeks of Roosevelt's death, the UN's founding conference would convene in San Francisco, where the UN Charter would ultimately be drafted and signed. The four policemen, along with France, became the permanent members of the UN Security Council, which would eventually include ten additional rotating members. It would be responsible for safeguarding international peace and security. Yet the UN that emerged also reflected the more idealistic notions of the State Department planners who wanted the United Nations to be a community of equals that included all countries. They stressed that the new world body would be a *universal* organization, for they did not want to repeat one of the key mistakes of the League of Nations, which had never included the United States and from which Germany, Italy, and Japan had withdrawn. The UN General Assembly, separate from the Security Council, would eventually include all of the world community. While the Security Council would be the body that intervened militarily to preserve world order, the General Assembly would give voice to the values on which that order was based. It would set international standards for the future. It would also be empowered to deal with decolonization, disarmament, economics, and even development of international law.[7]

Although the UN's architects created a clear division of labor between the Security Council and the General Assembly, there was a certain built-in tension between Roosevelt's earlier idea of an exclusive great-power club and the all-inclusive international body that eventually emerged. FDR had maintained a strong conviction that small nations not be allowed to complicate the great powers' task of keeping the peace.[8] But as the Second World War had drawn to a close, wild utopian proposals were coming out of America, as many called for "world government" or a "federation of democracies."[9]

Like Roosevelt, the American commentator Walter Lippmann recognized that the United States could not rely on a broad global organization to establish peace. Near the end of World War II he had warned that the victorious powers must not delegate the responsibility for world order "to a world society which does not yet exist or has just barely been organized."[10] He had made an important point. The problem with a "world society which does not yet exist or has just barely been organized" is that it can share no common values. What joint interests would bring the diverse countries of the new UN together? What common principles would bond the UN together as its membership expanded? What would be their agenda for a better world?

Walter Lippmann had identified what would become the Achilles' heel of the United Nations and why it was bound to fail despite the high ideals of its architects.

## MORAL CLARITY

All the original UN members in 1945 shared one characteristic that might have offset the Lippmann critique: In order to be invited to the UN's founding conference in San Francisco, a state had to have declared war on at least one of the Axis powers and to have adhered to the "Declaration by United Nations" that was originally announced in January 1942. The UN's founding members, in other words, had to make choices and take a stand. The UN might have been a universal organization, but at the time of its creation it was also a military alliance, united by a common strategic purpose and by declared commitment to certain common values.

The UN's American founders assumed that it would be possible to freeze the wartime alliance of the United States, Great Britain, the Soviet Union, China, and France. Further, they believed that it could become an alliance around certain principles. Political commentators called the idea collective security. Henry Kissinger has articulated this point well: "Alliances always presume a specific adversary; collective security defends international law in the abstract."[11] For the UN's proposed notion of collective security to work, the organization would have to undertake two actions. First, the UN would have to identify that an act of aggression had indeed occurred and that some state had violated the world organization's founding principles. Second, once it determined that aggression had occurred, the UN would have to mobilize a determined response; that is, its member states would have to act as though their own vital national interests had been threatened. This revival in the Wilsonian belief that collective security around principles of world order could replace the old European balance of power, with its secret alliances, was able to come about only because of the postwar circumstances in which the UN was born.

It is impossible to exaggerate the importance of this historical context. The UN was created in a moment of extraordinary moral clarity, in which its founding members could distinguish between the aggression of the Axis powers and their own role as liberators— indeed, between evil and good. After all, the Nazis, against whom they had fought, had committed acts of mass murder unprecedented in recorded history. As the UN held its first meetings in 1946, the Nuremberg trials against Nazi war criminals were well under way. The Second World War cast a long shadow over the UN and its first covenants. Consider, for example, the UN Charter, which begins by making reference "to the need to save succeeding generations from the scourge of war" and reaffirms "fundamental human rights," something the Covenant of the League of Nations had made no reference to. Moreover, in December 1946 the UN General Assembly adopted a resolution condemning genocide and tasked a UN committee to draft a genocide convention.

One of the flaws of the early UN was that because of Stalin's wartime cooperation with Roosevelt, the organization's architects had an excessively benign, if not naïve, view of the USSR. One commentator has written of "starry-eyed Rooseveltian illusions about Great Power Unity."[12] This might be somewhat overstated, but the signing of the UN Charter did create a short-term period of euphoria that affected judgments about the USSR. Excusing Soviet behavior became common. For example, in November 1945, Secretary of State James Byrnes compared what he revealingly called the "effort of the Soviet Union to draw into closer and more friendly relations with her central and eastern European neighbors" to inter-American organizations in the Western Hemisphere.[13] This put the Iron Curtain over Eastern Europe on the same plane as the American-led Rio Treaty. The Soviets took advantage of their position to corrupt some important early UN documents. Most notably, they carved out a dangerous loophole in the Genocide Convention of 1948; the convention did not outlaw mass murder against political opponents, as distinct from religious or ethnic groups. It should also be noted that the acting secretary-general at the UN's 1945 founding conference, Alger Hiss, was probably a Soviet spy (although there is little evidence that he used his position at the conference to lobby extensively on Moscow's behalf).[14]

In those early days, the Soviet Union could not stand in the way of every important measure the UN tried to pass.[15] The USSR and its Communist allies had minimal influence because most of the UN's founding members still spoke a similar political language as allies emerging from the Second World War, and the minority of states that did not accept the prevalent values of the time were reluctant to challenge the postwar ethos. For example, one of the General Assembly's earliest acts was to adopt a Universal Declaration of Human Rights, in December 1948. The Soviets were hardly enthusiastic about the defense of personal liberties at the expense of the state, and they had sent their prosecutor from Stalin's purge trials, Andrei Vyshinsky, to the UN to argue against the declaration. But they recognized that the overwhelming majority of UN members, mostly democracies still tied together with a common sense of political purpose, supported this moral statement. The Soviets could not even bring themselves to vote against the resolution; they abstained, as did other Eastern bloc nations. The declaration passed by a vote of 48–0.

Those drafting the Universal Declaration of Human Rights understood that the General Assembly was not a "world parliament" and thus could not create binding international laws. Eleanor Roosevelt, the first chairman of the UN Commission on Human Rights, referred to the declaration as a "common standard." But this common standard could be powerful in the future: the Universal Declaration of Human Rights could provide guidelines for international conventions, or for the constitutions of newly independent states.[16] And by outlining a code of behavior expected from members of the world community, the UN General Assembly might be able to constrain the behavior of states.

The Universal Declaration of Human Rights offers a striking example of the overwhelming *political* agreement among the early UN member states. Some critics have condemned the UN in this era for its clarity of purpose, arguing that the original UN reflected only Western standards and was not a truly universal organization. Yet among the original UN members were states such as Egypt, Turkey, Ethiopia, and India—Muslims, Christians, and Hindus. Besides

Eleanor Roosevelt, the authors of the Universal Declaration of Human Rights included René Cassin, a French Jew with Orthodox Jewish training; Charles Malik, a Lebanese Christian; and P. C. Chang, a Chinese intellectual who had lectured on Confucianism and Islam. Islamic scholars had also been consulted. With the exception of Saudi Arabia, which abstained, all UN member states with large Muslim populations voted for the Universal Declaration, including Egypt, Pakistan, and Turkey. The Saudis' chief concern was that the declaration allowed for a Muslim to change his religion.[17] By 1994, Hassan al-Turabi's militant Islamist regime would argue that the UN Human Rights Commission had no standing to criticize Sudan's right to enact punishments like amputation, crucifixion, stoning, or flogging.[18]

What was the difference between the UN of 1948, in which Saudi Arabia merely abstained from voting for the Universal Declaration of Human Rights, and the UN of 1994, in which Sudan thundered about the right to behead prisoners? The fact is that the UN had become a totally different organization by the 1990s. From the original 51 member states, its membership jumped to 83 in 1959, up to 132 states in 1972, with the dissolution of European colonial empires, and to 184 by 1993. The addition of the new states posed a problem not because of race, religion, or nationality. Nor were the new Third World members added from the 1970s through the 1990s a problem because of their cultural background. Rather, the trouble related to their political systems. They were for the most part completely new states that had emerged after some struggle with former imperial powers. Many were the authoritarian offspring of the Soviet Union or the Communist Chinese. They were joined by totalitarian Islamist regimes such as the Islamic Republic of Iran or Sudan. What was emerging was a clash of ideologies, not a clash of civilizations. Many of these new states wanted international rules that would suit the needs of dictatorships rather than democracies. Even after the breakup of the Soviet bloc, only a minority of UN member states—75 out of 184—were free democracies, according to Freedom House.

Moreover, the new members had power disproportional to their actual population. Many were tiny states. By 2003, the 114 Third World states that made up the Nonaligned Movement, which voted as a bloc in the UN, at best represented a little more than a half the world's population, but it could claim nearly two-thirds of the 191 UN member states.[19] The UN had gerrymandered itself to give dozens of these authoritarian regimes a greater voice in the shape of world affairs than they deserved.

In the beginning, authoritarian regimes could not exert much influence on the machinery of the UN Secretariat. Had that political configuration survived into the 1990s, the UN could have made a considerable contribution to international security. But the states who gained so much authority in the 1990s looked at the world very differently from the way the United States did. Support for U.S. positions in the UN General Assembly continued to decline during the 1990s, despite the Clinton administration's declared support for multilateralism. In 1995 members of the General Assembly voted along with Washington 50.6 percent of the time, but by 1999 that number had dropped to 41.8 percent.[20] The United States was motivated by different political values and interests—values and interests that had helped define the UN at the outset.

Many have argued that the Cold War prevented the UN from functioning as it was originally conceived. By the late 1940s Secretary of State Dean Acheson was already describing the UN Charter as "impracticable" and the UN itself as an example of misguided Wilsonian beliefs in "the advent of universal peace and law."[21] President Truman became disillusioned with the UN as the Cold War got under way. To be sure, when the Soviet Union shifted from wartime ally to Cold War adversary, it radically changed the dynamics of the UN Security Council. The Security Council was effectively neutralized, as each superpower could exercise its right to veto resolutions authorizing military action. But if the Soviets had been the sole stumbling block to effective UN operations, then the end of the Cold War should have meant that the UN could resume the role for which it was designed.

That didn't happen.

## OPENING THE DOOR FOR AGGRESSION

American officials in the early 1990s certainly wanted the UN to reclaim its original mission. In his January 1991 State of the Union address, President George H. W. Bush laid out his vision for a "new world order," and he saw the UN as an integral part of that new order. When Madeleine Albright came to the UN as President Clinton's ambassador in 1993, she noted that for decades the paralyzed Security Council had rarely met. During her term it would convene almost daily, for, as she later explained, "the barrier to coordinated Security Council action had come down."[22] But if that barrier had fallen, it did not mean that the UN was then prepared to deal with crises that threatened international security. Too much had changed.

The problem, of course, was that the UN member states had long since lost a common sense of purpose, which had been so vital to the international body at its founding. Whereas in 1948 a tiny minority of states could do nothing but abstain from voting for the Universal Declaration of Human Rights, by the 1990s the majority Afro-Asian bloc was making assertions to the effect that " 'human rights' was an invention of Western liberalism, which had little to offer countries whose values derived from tribal wisdom or other communal traditions."[23] In 1993, for example, the UN held a world conference in Vienna on human rights. UN diplomats surrendered to demands from states like China, Indonesia, and Malaysia by drafting a final declaration that omitted any reference to individual rights such as freedom of speech or freedom of assembly.[24] The new UN majority had emptied the term "human rights" of its original meaning and hijacked it to serve its authoritarian political agenda.

The change in the UN's ethos had become evident decades earlier. The shift was quite visible in the great UN debates over decolonization in the 1960s. In December 1960, the General Assembly adopted Resolution 1514 (XV), known as the "Declaration on the Granting of Independence to Colonial Countries and Peoples." The

U.S. government had been one of the strongest advocates of decol-onization, because it would mean emancipating peoples around the world. But the Americans were concerned about this initiative, since it called for the "immediate" transfer of powers from colonial gov-ernments, regardless of the state of political preparations on the ground. The drafters of the resolution had been concerned with the "subjection of peoples to alien subjugation," but had remained silent about people's rights to representative government. The reso-lution established no mechanisms for setting up democratic rule in these newly emerging states.

Despite concerns from the United States and other democratic allies, the new Afro-Asian majority forced the resolution through. Many Afro-Asian states had been responsible for drafting Resolution 1514, in which they appropriated the UN Charter and the Universal Declaration of Human Rights to condemn colonialism. The resolu-tion passed with the support of eighty-nine states; six nations ab-stained, including the United States, Great Britain, and France. The Soviet-bloc states strongly backed the resolution, since it would po-larize relations between the West and the developing world. They would exploit this more militant anticolonial sentiment to try to force the United States and its allies to close military bases in the de-veloping world. For Moscow, this was a matter not of ideological sol-idarity but of strategic interest.

Meanwhile, many Afro-Asian states felt that the anticolonial dec-laration established a new norm for political action.[25] And just a year after the resolution passed, India attacked Goa, a small enclave on the subcontinent that was under Portuguese control. Goa was an outdated, nearly 450-year-old throwback to the colonial era, like British-controlled Hong Kong, on the Chinese coast. The Indians made no effort to negotiate Portugal's withdrawal. Instead, Prime Minister Jawaharlal Nehru, who put India's bid for Third World leadership above its reputation for nonviolence, decided to resort to armed force. To justify the action, his representatives at the UN in-voked Resolution 1514. India argued that the attack could not be considered an act of aggression because Portugal's control of Goa was illegal and its sovereignty baseless: "There can be no question of aggression against your own frontier, or against your own people, whom you want to liberate."[26]

What the Indians were saying was that the use of force was legitimate in some circumstances even when a nation was not acting in its own defense. The moral clarity of the 1945 UN was becoming obfuscated; standards for distinguishing right from wrong could not be so easily applied in the new political universe that was forming, in which aggression could be excused and morality judged in relative terms. As a result, India was beyond official reproach.

The Goa incident forced U.S. officials to take a more skeptical view of the UN. Initially, President John F. Kennedy declared his support for the UN, seeing it as a reflection of American ideals: "In supporting the United Nations, we not only support aims and ideals inscribed in our constitution, but work to convert the high goals of our own foreign policy into living reality."[27] The U.S. ambassador to the UN, Adlai Stevenson, reflected Kennedy's faith in the UN, proclaiming, "World society has to achieve the minimum institutions of order, and the only embryo of such an order is the United Nations."[28] Yet to maintain order, Stevenson felt, the UN could not abide acts of aggression like India's on Goa. When Portugal went to the UN Security Council for help after India's attack, Stevenson said to the council, "Tonight we are witnessing the first act in a drama which could end with the death of the [UN] Organization." He reminded the Security Council that the League of Nations had died because "its members no longer resisted aggressive force." The United States did not win the debate on Goa; the UN already had other concerns, and in the new political universe that it was creating, the ends could justify almost any means.[29]

India's attempt to explain away its military action on Goa was part of an ongoing struggle in the UN to redefine the term "aggression"— an issue that cut to the heart of the UN's mission. A clear-cut definition of aggression had been needed at the time of the UN's birth, since the waging of a war of aggression was one of the main charges at both the Nuremberg and Tokyo military trials.[30] Defining aggression on the basis of what happened in the 1930s may have seemed like an open-and-shut case, but everything soon became twisted. In the early 1950s the Soviets began working on more restrictive definitions of "aggression," leaving out indirect aggression—like subversion and agitating civil strife—in order to neutralize the Western response to the spread of communism.[31] The Indians were further narrowing the term to serve their purposes.

More and more, the debate about aggression reflected the conflicting interests of the various UN blocs. In 1969, Third World states insisted that any definition of aggression must not be interpreted as "limiting the scope of the [UN] Charter's provisions concerning the right of peoples to self-determination."[32] Within five years another restriction was introduced when the General Assembly adopted a definition of aggression in 1974. This time it was to protect the rights of peoples under "alien domination"—a vague term that could include anything from foreign bases to oil concessions held by Western multinational corporations.[33] Thus, one legal expert analyzing the 1974 definition could only conclude that the UN had codified "all the main 'juridicial loopholes and pre-texts to unleash aggression' available under preexisting international law."[34]

In short, over the years the General Assembly introduced enough exceptions into prohibitions against aggression to give a pass to states that initiated armed conflict. (When the UN sponsored the Rome Conference in 1998 to establish the International Criminal Court, an agreed definition of "aggression" still eluded those who attended; the crime of aggression will be under the court's jurisdiction only when a common definition is reached in the future.)[35]

It is telling that the UN could not even reach a working definition of the very thing that it had been created to prevent.

## CONDONING TERRORISM

In October 1970, the UN held a special commemorative session on the tenth anniversary of its 1960 anticolonial declaration. The General Assembly adopted language during that October meeting that made reference to "freedom fighters" and the need for the UN to invite "representatives of [national] liberation movements." Before the close of the fall session, the General Assembly crossed a moral Rubicon, adopting on December 14, 1970, Resolution 2708 (XXV), which went far beyond the 1960 anticolonial declaration. The new resolution explicitly stated that the UN "reaffirms its recognition of the legitimacy of the struggle of the colonial peoples and peoples under alien domination to exercise their right to self-determination and independence *by all the necessary means at their disposal* [emphasis added]."[36]

This was a historic shift in the UN General Assembly, and it occurred at a time when international terrorism was on the rise, with the world facing a new wave of airplane hijackings. The UN's new position could only be understood by those who regarded themselves as members of "national liberation movements" as a license to commit murder in the name of the cause of self-determination. The UN, in other words, had taken the first step toward legitimizing global terror.

Just four years later, in 1974, PLO chairman Yasser Arafat was invited to speak before the UN General Assembly for the very first time. Arafat was the leader of a terrorist organization: a year earlier his Black September units murdered the U.S. ambassador to Sudan, Cleo A. Noel, and a year before that they had conducted their massacre at the 1972 Munich Olympics. He arrived at the UN wearing a military uniform and carrying a pistol in a holster under his jacket. Nevertheless, Arafat was treated with all the diplomatic protocol accorded to a head of state. For example, on the General Assembly podium he was provided with the ceremonial leather armchair that is reserved only for world leaders (though he was asked to not sit in it).

Arafat had to be extremely careful about how he expressed himself in his first address on the world stage. Nonetheless, given the new ethos at the UN, he felt comfortable enough to state, "We are also expressing our faith in political and diplomatic struggle *as complements, as enhancements of armed struggle* [emphasis added]." He explained to the UN ambassadors seated below him that he had been able to come to New York because the UN itself had changed. "The United Nations of today is not the United Nations of the past," he said. "Today's United Nations represents 138 nations, a number that more clearly reflects the will of the international community." And the new United Nations, he argued, was "more capable of implementing the principles embodied in its Charter and in the Universal Declaration of Human Rights." Arafat was co-opting these fundamental UN documents to justify his movement's continuing reliance on violence as a political instrument to advance its cause.

Arafat universalized his message, allying himself with peoples of the world still "gripped by armed struggles provoked by imperialism and racial discrimination." These struggles, he said, were "legitimate and just," and he declared it "imperative" that the "international community should support these peoples in their struggles." Over the years the PLO has developed intimate ties with Cuba, North Vietnam, East Germany, revolutionary African groups, and the Sandinistas of Nicaragua; these are the sorts of "legitimate and just" struggles Arafat and the PLO align themselves with.

When Arafat finished his speech, the majority of UN delegates gave him enthusiastic applause, and many rose to their feet to cheer him. The UN's original clear concept of human rights and noble postwar efforts to protect the freedom of individuals had now been changed. The new concept was of collective national rights protected by self-appointed militant groups, who were fully prepared to trample on individuals' human rights. Any moral restraints on terrorism that might have existed in the world community were now stripped away.

Arafat was right: The UN had changed. Moral clarity had given way to moral relativism.

Sure enough, a year after Arafat received his warm reception at the UN, the General Assembly gave a standing ovation to Ugandan dictator Idi Amin, who would ultimately murder some 300,000 of his people.

The new set of values that dominated the broadened membership of the UN clearly limited the organization's ability to set out
clear political standards banning terrorism and political violence. In
1979, the General Assembly approved an exception to the international convention against taking hostages. The exception applied to
cases "in which people are fighting against colonial occupation and
alien occupation and against racist regimes in the exercise of their
right of self-determination."[37] The General Assembly continued
along this path in 1982, when it adopted Resolution 37/43, which
stated that the UN "reaffirms the legitimacy of the struggle of peoples for independence, territorial integrity, national unity and liberation from colonial and foreign domination and foreign occupation
by all available means, including armed struggle." Rather than out-
lawing terrorism, the UN was finding ways of condoning it as a legitimate form of political expression.

This trend has continued for more than two decades. In
February–March 1997, the UN convened an ad hoc committee on
"Terrorist Bombings and Nuclear National Terrorism." Not surpris-
ingly, a group of Arab states led by Saudi Arabia, Syria, and Egypt
contributed a joint statement that condemned "attempts to stigma-
tize legitimate resistance as terrorism." The much larger Nonaligned Movement, which at the time embraced nearly 120 of the
184 UN member states, similarly affirmed "the legitimacy of the
struggle of peoples under colonial or alien domination." Such a
struggle "did not constitute terrorism," this massive bloc of UN
members argued.[38]

Two years later, the same argument came from Syria, a nation
that the U.S. State Department has long recognized as a state sponsor of terrorism. In a letter to Secretary-General Kofi Annan dated
March 24, 1999, Syria's ambassador to the UN ironically lamented
the lack of international standards for formulating a precise definition of "terrorism": "The Syrian Arab Republic has called for the establishment of internationally agreed standards that clearly
distinguish between terrorism, which must be condemned and com-
bated, and the legitimate national struggles against foreign occupa-

tion which must be supported."[39] George Orwell could not have drafted a better document. Within a year Syria would be voted in as a nonpermanent member of the UN Security Council, charged with safeguarding international peace and security.

## BEYOND A "TALK HOUSE"

Was all this just the unimportant noise of the politicized UN General Assembly? A former U.S. ambassador to the UN, Richard Holbrooke, has called the General Assembly a "talk house . . . which simply has no importance except as a forum for speeches."[40] But to consider the General Assembly an innocuous debating society— annoying, perhaps, but harmless—ignores the significant influence the UN's General Assembly can have. True, from a strictly legal standpoint, UN General Assembly resolutions do not create binding international law. Yet these resolutions have a much broader political impact that goes beyond their legal status. Indeed, if the UN General Assembly's resolutions had no real value, then why did members of the Nonaligned Movement make such efforts to get the UN to adopt their positions? What were they trying to achieve? They undoubtedly understood that the entire UN system was affected by the value structure that the General Assembly was erecting.

In the late 1970s and early 1980s, for example, Third World nations waged a campaign to force the UN to modify the 1949 Geneva Conventions on the laws of war in order to elevate the legal status of "national liberation" groups. They obtained some of these modifications in 1977. In 1984, they worked through the Sixth Committee, the committee that helped the General Assembly prepare resolutions relating to its responsibility to "encourage the progressive development of international law." According to a 1984 Pentagon memorandum, these nations sought to put armed combatants from these "national liberation movements" on the same plane as ordinary civilians—something that would have made it much more difficult for the United States to prosecute the current war on terrorism. For example, if armed combatants were only soldiers in uniform or those who actually fired their weapons, then what would be the status of a terrorist mastermind, dressed in civilian clothing, who was organizing attacks on New York or London from a country willing to give him sanctuary? The Pentagon warned that making this modification might sweep away "hundreds of years of law and morality."[41] By eroding international humanitarian law and complicating the West's ability to defend itself against terrorist attacks, the UN General Assembly was having far more impact than just another debating society would have.

Moreover, UN General Assembly resolutions have fed into decisions taken by other UN bodies. In 2002, for instance, Israel was confronted with a surge in suicide bombing attacks by Hamas. The worst of the attacks came on March 27, 2002, with the Passover Massacre at Netanya's Park Hotel; the bomb, which went off just as the Israelis sat down to commemorate the Passover Seder, left 30 dead and 140 wounded. In response, Israel launched Operation Defensive Shield in order to root out Hamas and other terrorist groups in West Bank cities. The UN Human Rights Commission in Geneva took up the subsequent military escalation in its deliberations. Instead of condemning the terrorist attacks on Israeli civilians, the UN Human Rights Commission blasted Israel's self-defense operations and "the military siege imposed on Palestinian territory." Worse still, it declared that it "affirms the legitimate rights of the Palestinian people to resist the Israeli occupation."

In taking this position, the Human Rights Commission explicitly relied on UN General Assembly Resolution 37/43, the 1982 resolution that reaffirmed the right of peoples to engage in "armed struggle" against "colonial and foreign domination." Troubled by the implied support that the UN Human Rights Commission would be providing to suicide terrorism, Britain and Germany, which might normally abstain in such cases, voted against the resolution. (The United States could not vote because in May 2001 it had been voted off the Human Rights Commission, a move the notorious human rights abuser Communist China had reportedly lobbied extensively for.) Although this vote came just months after 9/11, the West was by no means united in the fight against terrorism: Austria, Belgium, and France voted *for* the resolution. The measure passed by a vote of 40–5, with seven nations abstaining.[42] The whole episode demonstrated how the international norms that the UN General Assembly created, including those that provided the moral underpinnings for something as evil as international terrorism, could seep into the rest of the UN system and disrupt allied solidarity.

The UN General Assembly affects other parts of the UN in one other important way. Its resolutions many times have "entrusted" the secretary-general to remain "seized" of issues that it raised in its resolutions. That is, the General Assembly's decisions provide political guidance to the secretary-general, for UN resolutions set out the terms of reports that the secretary-general and his staff are commissioned to prepare. Even if a secretary-general personally disagrees with the content or spirit of UN resolutions, he has no authority to ignore them. He is their conduit to the huge UN bureaucracy, which he oversees from the thirty-eighth floor of the blue-green Secretariat tower in New York City. His policies inform the political orientation of thousands of UN staff members on the floors below and the positions of those belonging to the UN's specialized agencies, such as the UN Development Program (UNDP) or the UN Educational Scientific and Cultural Organization (UNESCO). The politics of the General Assembly influence the entire UN. As early as the 1950s, René Cassin of the Human Rights Commission complained about the "scandalous politicization" of the UN's specialized agencies.[43]

The General Assembly's resolutions have influence far outside the UN as well. As the chief spokesman for the UN, the secretary-general promotes the UN General Assembly's resolutions to the entire international community. In his public speeches and television interviews, he has to be careful not to contradict the content of these resolutions. This is the case no matter what the topic is; in recent years, for example, we have seen Secretary-General Kofi Annan honor the General Assembly's resolutions when speaking about terrorism, Iraq, or weapons of mass destruction.

Finally, the UN General Assembly's resolutions often serve as recommendations that states can adopt when they are codifying new treaties.

The influence of these resolutions is far-reaching and must not be underestimated.

## FAILURE

President George H. W. Bush imagined the UN would play a pivotal role in protecting the "new world order" after the 1991 Gulf War. But Bush and other U.S. officials did not recognize the flaws in the UN that doomed its ability to secure international peace and thus doomed the new world order.

World order requires moral clarity to distinguish aggression from legitimate acts of self-defense. It requires a mandate to combat terrorism against innocent civilians rather than efforts primarily aimed at excusing violence by blaming it on "underlying" political or economic causes. And it requires a commitment to defend individual human rights, and not an effort to systematically change their meaning to the defense of "national rights," which has allowed regimes to abuse their citizens with impunity.

Rather than draw the new UN member states to accept the ideals that its founders had advocated, the United States and its allies for the most part let the states of the Nonaligned Movement set the agenda and political program that the UN would adopt. The old UN was born in the shadow of the Holocaust; the new UN did nothing in the 1970s and 1980s as mass murder was conducted in Cambodia, Burundi, Uganda, and Syria, and finally when Iraq attacked the Kurds with chemical weapons.

Of course, the UN's failure to deal with pressing conflicts was nothing new. Indeed, almost immediately after the organization's founding, it failed to resolve the most pressing conflicts that emerged: the first Arab-Israel conflict in 1947–48 and the first war between India and Pakistan over Kashmir in 1948. Failure has been a recurring theme in the UN's history.

# CHAPTER 2

---

# Failure Foreshadowed

*The First Tests for the UN in Israel and India*

The invasion of Palestine by the Arab states was the first armed aggression which the world has seen since the world war. The United Nations could not permit such aggression to succeed and at the same time survive as an influential force for peaceful settlement, collective security, and meaningful international law."[1]

That is how the first UN secretary-general, Trygve Lie, summarized the challenge the UN faced on May 14, 1948, as the British withdrew from what had been since 1922 their League of Nations Mandate over Palestine. Israel proclaimed its independence, and five armies from the Arab League—Egypt, Syria, Lebanon, Transjordan, and Iraq—with the addition of token units from Saudi Arabia and Yemen, invaded the nascent state the day it was born. Lie did not mince words. In his view, a clear case of aggression had occurred. But how would the UN respond?

The secretary-general concluded that nothing less than the credibility of the UN as a security organization was at stake. The day after the Arab invasion, Lie warned the UN Security Council of the gravity of the situation, explaining how Egypt had cabled the UN to declare that its forces were engaging in an "armed intervention" in Palestine. The Arab states' actions that day only reinforced the secretary-general's conviction that the military strike constituted an act of aggression. Egyptian air force planes bombed Tel Aviv, and the Arab League issued a statement confirming that its forces were advancing into Palestine. The secretary-general of the Arab League also announced, "This will be a war of extermination and a momentous massacre which will be spoken of like the Mongolian massacres and the Crusades."[2] In other words, the Arab states made no effort to hide their aggression and intent.

The pressure on the UN to do something was enormous. Lie wrote to the Security Council that this was "the first time since the adoption of the [UN] Charter that Member States [of the UN] have openly declared that they have engaged in armed intervention outside their own territory." At the end of May, the U.S. representative to the UN, Warren Austin, commented on the Arab League's pronouncements about its invasion, "Their statements are the best evidence we have of the international character of this aggression." Even on the Soviet side, Andrei Gromyko admitted, "What is happening in Palestine can only be described as military operations organized by a group of states against the new Jewish state," and he characterized the formation of Israel as a "national liberation movement." He added that the states "whose forces had invaded Palestine have ignored the Security Council's resolution."[3]

At that time there was complete moral clarity as to who was the aggressor and who was the defender in the unfolding conflict. Even the rival superpowers agreed. So what would the UN do? This was a critical question, for if the UN's collective security system was to work, first aggression had to be identified, and then UN member states had to undertake defensive measures in response.

Trygve Lie already saw from the opening discussions at the UN Security Council on May 15 that "prompt and effective action will not be forthcoming." He admitted that failure to address the attack would "result in the most serious injury to the prestige of the United Nations."

Lie had good reason to be so concerned. The Palestine issue was one that the UN had been dealing with throughout its short history. In fact, it had inherited the issue from the League of Nations, which had confronted the Palestine situation in the wake of the First World War.

The geographic area that became British Mandatory Palestine had been a group of imperial districts of the Ottoman Empire since 1517; the British army conquered it during the First World War and turned to the League of Nations to resolve its final disposition along with that of other captured territories. During the war, to convince Sharif Hussein of Mecca, the leader of the Hashemite clan of the Hijaz in Arabia, to break away from the Ottoman Empire, Britain had committed itself to supporting the establishment of a great unified Arab state covering what is today the Arabian Peninsula, Iraq, parts of Jordan, and Syria. Yet the British were careful to exclude Palestine, and in 1917 their foreign secretary, Lord Balfour, declared Britain's support for a Jewish national home in Palestine. When in 1920 the Ottoman Empire renounced sovereignty over its Asiatic territories, including Palestine, it appeared that the Arabs would obtain a huge state covering most of the Middle East and the Jews would receive a relatively small wedge of territory in Palestine. (After 1922, the British insisted that the League of Nations' provision for a Jewish homeland would not apply to eastern Palestine, which became Transjordan.)

This almost became the basis for an early Arab-Jewish understanding, between the Hashemites and the Zionist movement. But once France received British backing for its territorial share of what was to become the Syrian and Lebanese Mandate, the Arab side felt it had been double-crossed by the European powers. Regardless, the 1922 League of Nations Mandate for Palestine endorsed the Balfour Declaration by recognizing both "the historical connection of the Jewish people with Palestine" and "the grounds for reconstituting their national home in that country." The mandate system represented a compromise between nineteenth-century European colonialism and American insistence on various peoples' right to self-determination. It allowed the British and the French to retain control of large parts of the Middle East until the peoples of the region were, in the eyes of the League of Nations, ready to exercise their rights to obtain statehood.

When the UN was formed in 1945, the UN Charter committed the new organization to the obligations undertaken by the League of Nations after World War I. Specifically, Article 80 of the UN Charter upheld the existing rights of states and of "any peoples." Backers of Jewish statehood had lobbied for this provision at the UN's founding conference in San Francisco in order to reaffirm the Jewish right that the League of Nations had recognized more than two decades earlier. Thus from its founding the UN had assumed responsibility for the dispute over Palestine.[4]

In April 1947, an exhausted British postwar government asked the UN to make recommendations for the future of Palestine. In response, the General Assembly formed a UN Special Committee on Palestine (UNSCOP), which issued a majority report advocating the partition of Palestine into a Jewish state and an Arab state. In November 1947, the UN General Assembly adopted this UNSCOP report through Resolution 181; among the resolution's thirty-three supporters were the United States and the Soviet Union. In addition to recommending the partition of Palestine, the resolution called for the internationalization of Jerusalem. Resolution 181 stated, "The City of Jerusalem shall be established as a *corpus separatum* [a separate entity] under a special international regime and shall be administered by the United Nations." Jewish authorities had reluctantly acquiesced to this provision only when they realized that without Jerusalem's internationalization, mostly Catholic states in South America might join the Arab bloc in the UN and reject partition. (Ironically, the case for Jewish sovereignty was actually strongest in Jerusalem, for a Jewish majority had been restored in the ancient Jewish capital back in 1864—more than a half century before the arrival of the British and the promulgation of the Balfour Declaration.) Although a clause in Resolution 181 held that after ten years the residents of Jerusalem could call for a referendum on modifying the UN regime, Jerusalem was at that point supposed to be a UN responsibility.

Resolution 181 was a nonbinding recommendation of the General Assembly—that is, the UN did not create the State of Israel. Thus, Israel did not owe its legal existence to the UN Partition Plan.[5] According to international law, UN resolutions do not create states;

rather, when political communities meet certain minimal standards—having a permanent population under the control of a government, a defined territory, and a capacity to enter into relations with other states—then a state can be said to have emerged that is entitled to be recognized by other states.[6] But the UN Partition resolution was significant even though it was nonbinding, because it meant that, like the League of Nations, the UN had acknowledged the Jewish people's preexisting right to a state. That formal recognition would be included in Israel's own Declaration of Independence in 1948.

The Arab states announced that they would not be bound by what the UN had decided and then walked out of the General Assembly. The next day the *New York Times* summarized their position with this headline: "Arabs See U.N. 'Murdered.' "

No wonder the whole issue made the UN secretary-general nervous.

The Arab League refused to accept a Jewish state, declaring the Balfour Declaration "legally void" and calling the Arab inhabitants of Palestine the "lawful owners of the country." The Arab states also argued that the UN "cannot be treated as the successor of the League of Nations insofar as the administration of mandates is concerned."[7] Implicitly, they sought to nullify the Jewish people's rights to their ancestral homeland, which had been recognized by the international community after the First World War and reiterated by the UN itself.

Almost immediately, Palestinian Arabs resorted to military force to try to overturn the UN resolution. Backed by thousands of volunteers from Arab countries, mainly from Syria, Palestinian Arabs conducted large-scale attacks against isolated Jewish villages and against cities with mixed populations. Transjordan's Arab Legion was already encamped in Palestine, under the command of British officers, and was receiving weapons from departing British troops. Jerusalem was a primary target for this first wave of armed Arab groups. By early April 1948, David Ben-Gurion, who would become Israel's first prime minister, would remark, "The Jews of the Old City of Jerusalem have been under siege for several months. Jewish Jerusalem as a whole is almost completely cut off from the rest of the country and is under constant threat of starvation." Out of a total population of 160,000, a population of 100,000 Jews was at risk. Arab forces were working on plans to cut off the city's water supply, and on May 12, Arab forces would shut off water-pumping stations for Jerusalem.

According to Resolution 181, the UN was responsible for Jerusalem, and Jewish authorities appealed to the UN Security Council to honor the commitments that the world body had undertaken with respect to the Holy City. On April 1, 1948, the future foreign minister of Israel, Moshe Sharett, asked the Security Council to intervene: "We consider that the United Nations is solemnly bound to avert catastrophe by assuming responsibilities in Jerusalem."

The specific points of debate regarding Palestine—a debate that went back decades—were not the key issue confronting the UN. Rather, the issue was how to deal with the Arab use of force. Article 2 of the three-year-old UN Charter explicitly stated that all UN members "shall refrain in their international relations from the threat or use of force against the territorial integrity or political independence of any state." Yet the UN Security Council did not condemn the Arab aggression. Instead, on April 17, 1948, it called on "all persons and organizations in Palestine" to "cease all activities of a military or para-military nature." In other words, the Security Council drew no distinction between attacking and defending armies. Under such circumstances it was not surprising that the Arab combatants ignored the UN.

Instead, on May 14, the Arab coalition launched its full-scale invasion. The Arab Legion of Transjordan joined the siege of the Arab irregulars from the north, east, and west of the city. One prong of the two-pronged Egyptian invasion force tried to break through in Jerusalem from the south, in the area of Kibbutz Ramat Rahel. Syrian and Iraqi volunteers operated in the neighborhood of Katamon. On May 22, the UN Security Council adopted a resolution calling for a cease-fire, but the Arab states rejected it. They would ignore three further appeals.[8] The very foundations of the UN were threatened.

On May 28, the Old City of Jerusalem fell; its Jewish residents were evicted. Fifty-seven synagogues and academies in the Old City were either destroyed or desecrated, including the synagogue of the great scholar Nachmanides, which had been erected in 1267.[9] Where was the UN as this devastation occurred? Would the UN now defend its own resolution? Would the UN protect Jerusalem and its antiquities from further destruction?

Had the UN General Assembly asserted UN authority in Jerusalem the moment the British withdrew on May 14, further hostilities might have at least been deterred. The Arab states might not have wanted to challenge the UN so directly by invading UN-controlled territory. But no such assertion of UN authority followed. As Israel's first ambassador to the UN, Abba Eban, noted, "It was not a passive default, but rather an active relinquishing of responsibility in a critical hour."

The UN General Assembly had concluded that in order to provide a legal basis for UN jurisdiction in Jerusalem, it would have to act before the British Mandate expired. But the UN did not put its flag in Jerusalem by that deadline, which pleased the Arab states, who rejected Jerusalem's internationalization just as they opposed Palestine's partition.[10] When the mandate expired at 6 P.M. New York time, Iraq's UN representative cheered, "The game is up." The General Assembly had lost its right of succession in Jerusalem.[11]

With no UN forces deployed to defend against the Arab states' invasion, the only armed forces that came forward to lift the siege of Jerusalem and to save the city's Jewish residents were the underground Jewish units that were united under the Israel Defense Forces (IDF) Responsibility for protecting armored convoys of supplies to Jerusalem fell to the Harel Brigade under the command of Yitzhak Rabin, which belonged to the Palmach, the elite prestate Jewish strike force. In April 1948, these troops had taken the Kastel, the hilltop position that dominated the previously closed-off road connecting Jerusalem to Tel Aviv. Days later, with the siege broken,

131 supply trucks carrying 500 tons of food could reach Jerusalem.[12] Within twenty years, Rabin would become chief of staff of the IDF.

The moral significance of what had occurred was not lost on Israeli prime minister David Ben-Gurion: The UN had not lifted a finger to defend the Jews of Jerusalem from the invasion of the Arab states. Only Israel had provided for their defense. Ben-Gurion concluded in 1949, at the end of the first Arab-Israeli War, "But for our successful stand against aggressors acting in defiance of the United Nations, Jewish Jerusalem would have been wiped off the face of the earth. The whole Jewish population would have been annihilated and the State of Israel would never have arisen. We cannot today regard the decision of 29 November 1947 as being possessed of any further moral force since the United Nations did not succeed in implementing its own decision. In our view, the decision of 29 November about Jerusalem is null and void."[13]

## REWARDING AGGRESSION

After the UN failed to prevent the outbreak of the first Arab-Israeli War, it proceeded to make diplomacy more difficult as well. If it was clear to the UN secretary-general, as well as to the ambassadors of the United States and the Soviet Union, that the Arab states had committed an act of aggression against Israel, in defiance of repeated UN Security Council resolutions, then it might have been reasonable to expect that the UN would reflect this conclusion in its diplomatic initiatives. At the end of the Second World War, Germany, as an aggressor state, lost territories to neighbors like Poland. This principle could have been applied to the Arab states. To reverse the principle, and penalize the victim of an outright attack while rewarding the aggressor, would only assure that aggression would be repeated in the future. Nonetheless, this is precisely what the UN did.

Chapter VII in the UN Charter holds that in cases of "aggression" the UN can resort to military force to end conflicts. The Security Council brokered its first fragile truce on May 29, 1948, when it threatened to undertake Chapter VII action if either party rejected the call for a truce. The threat worked. The imposed truce lasted for four weeks. For the nascent State of Israel, the UN cease-fire provided a vital break in the fighting that allowed the Israel Defense Forces to recover militarily and to go on the offensive in subsequent stages of the war. But on the diplomatic side, the UN's intervention would prove to be highly problematic. In order to enforce its truce, the Security Council recommended that Count Folke Bernadotte, a Swedish diplomat who had already been appointed as the UN mediator in the Palestine conflict, be dispatched to the Middle East.

Bernadotte arrived in Israel and issued his own peace plan on June 28, 1948. Rather than proposing solutions for Jerusalem that took into account the lessons of the recent fighting, or even just accepting the original idea of internationalizing Jerusalem in accordance with the 1947 Partition Plan, Bernadotte now proposed that Jerusalem be placed under completely Arab sovereignty, with municipal autonomy for the Jews (who, it should be remembered, were the majority population in the city). He envisioned further Israeli territorial concessions in the southern Negev region as well, in exchange for some Israeli land acquisitions in the Galilee.

The Israeli government rejected the Bernadotte Plan, and in September 1948 Bernadotte was assassinated in Jerusalem by Jewish terrorists belonging to Lehi (the Stern Gang).[14] His tragic end somewhat obfuscated the difficult legacy that he left for resolving the Arab-Israeli conflict: He had reversed the usual expectations of the defeated party—in this case, the Arab states—regarding the contours of any future territorial settlement.

Despite the devastation Jerusalem suffered during the Arab armies' assault, the UN General Assembly continued to call for the internationalization of the city and for its administration by the UN. The General Assembly adopted a resolution to this effect on December 9, 1949. Again the UN was sending a message that was completely divorced from what had happened on the ground during 1948. Just four days later, however, Ben-Gurion announced that Israel was moving its seat of government to Jerusalem. Then, in April

1950, Transjordan annexed the entire West Bank, which it had invaded during the war, and changed its own name to Jordan. Only Pakistan and Great Britain recognized Jordanian sovereignty over the West Bank, although Britain's recognition explicitly did not apply to Jerusalem.

The UN was notably silent about subsequent Jordanian abuses in Jerusalem. Jews were denied access to the Western Wall and other holy sites, in violation of the 1949 Armistice Agreement. Moreover, the Jordanians destroyed thousands of tombstones in the ancient Jewish cemetery on the Mount of Olives and used them for paving roads and providing latrines for the Jordanian army. By 1965, Christian institutions were prohibited from buying land in and around Jerusalem.[15] It was not surprising that the Christian population on the Jordanian side plummeted during the nineteen years of Jordan's rule, from 25,000 in 1949 to 11,000 in 1967.

The UN also complicated efforts to reach a solution for the very difficult issue of Palestinian refugees. The UN had developed its own mechanisms for dealing with refugee disasters around the world since the Second World War, which created tens of millions of displaced people. The practical preference of refugee organizations at that time was refugee resettlement over repatriation.[16] This also required certain operational definitions about who exactly was to be defined as a refugee. According to the 1951 Convention Relating to the Status of Refugees, a refugee was someone who was unable or unwilling to live in the country of his former "habitual" residence and did not have any other nationality. Yet in the case of the Palestinian Arabs, the UN agreed to unique definitions of what a refugee was and removed them from the definitions contained in the global convention.[17]

First, Palestinian Arabs could keep their designation as refugees even if they acquired a new nationality—for example, if they became Jordanian or Syrian citizens. Second, the UN erased the requirement of "habitual" residence in the refugee's previous country; instead, it defined an Arab refugee as one whose residence was Palestine "for a minimum of two years preceding the conflict in 1948." The UN was thus taking into account many recent Arab immigrants into Palestine even if they would not be seen as being Palestinian according to general criteria that the UN had established in other instances. This was not an academic issue of legal fine points, but involved potentially huge numbers of people. Back in 1939, President Franklin Roosevelt had observed, "Arab immigration into Palestine since 1921 has vastly exceeded the total Jewish immigration during the whole period."[18] Finally, the UN determined that the direct descendants of refugees were also eligible for refugee status.

All other cases of refugees in the world came under the jurisdiction of the UN High Commissioner for Refugees (UNHCR); for the Palestinian Arabs, the UN established a completely separate agency, the UN Relief and Works Agency (UNRWA).[19] The agencies had different missions.[20] UNHCR was supposed to find permanent homes for refugees and thus solve refugee crises. In contrast, UNRWA was designed only to support the Palestinian refugees within the refugee camps that the Arab states created. UNRWA also made the Palestinian refugee problem far more difficult to solve, in part because the Arab states seized on the UNRWA's redefinition of refugee status to assert that the Arab-Israeli War had created 900,000 Palestinian refugees. By Israel's count, however, the figure was closer to 520,000,[21] and Bernadotte, the UN mediator, had come up with an even lower number, 330,000.[22]

Moreover, because UNRWA offered no incentive for Arab governments to absorb the refugees, Arab diplomats could thwart any plan to resettle the refugees in the surrounding Arab states. Indeed, in December 1948 the Arab states voted against Resolution 194, which recommended that Palestinians be repatriated only if repatriation was a refugee's wish and he was prepared to live in peace. And when, for example, the UN General Assembly earmarked $200 million for UNRWA refugee resettlement in 1952, the Arab League refused to cooperate with any such resettlement scheme.

The Arab states' rigid approach to the refugee issue became a particular problem because the UN acquiesced to that approach. UNRWA's commissioner-general would even write reports that betrayed sympathy for the perspective that the UN itself was responsible for the plight of Palestinian refugees, since it was the UN that had proposed the partition of Palestine and the creation of a Jewish state.[23] According to that logic, the UN, out of a sense of guilt, would fund Palestinian relief and not press for alternatives that would lead to the dismantling of UNRWA-supported camps.

But despite the Arab states' approach to the Palestinian refugee issue, overwhelming evidence indicated that it was the Arab states themselves that had been most responsible for displacing Palestinians. This much was clear at the time of the first Arab-Israeli War. Sir John Troutbeck, the head of Britain's Middle East Office in Cairo, reported that Palestinian refugees had declared to him that "their Arab brothers" were the ones who "persuaded them unnecessarily to leave their home."[24] Syria's prime minister in 1948–49 confirmed this conclusion in his memoirs: "Since 1948 we have been demanding the return of the refugees to their homes. But we ourselves are the ones who encouraged them to leave."[25]

Thus it is clear that the refugee problem was a direct result of the Arab states' aggression, which launched the first Arab-Israeli War. Had they not attacked in 1948, there would have been no Palestinian refugees. Of course, there would have been no Jewish refugees either. Both the Arab states and UNRWA focused on the Palestinian refugee problem, which obscured the fact that there were more than 570,000 Jewish refugees from the Arab states—roughly the equivalent of the number of Palestinian refugees.[26] In effect, an exchange of population had taken place as a result of the first Arab-Israeli War. Yet the UN twisted the issue in such a way that the victim of aggression was penalized rather than its perpetrators.

The UN did not make the Arab-Israel conflict any easier to resolve; it left an extremely difficult legacy that almost assured the outbreak of future wars in 1956, 1967, 1973, and 1982.

## FAILING ANOTHER TEST

Around the same time that the first Arab-Israeli War was heating up, the UN faced another clear test of its ability to preserve international

## THE KASHMIR DISPUTE

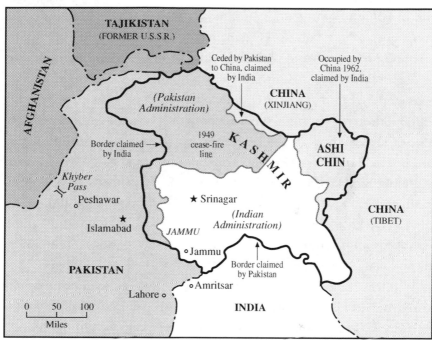

security. The UN was a brand-new organization, and many still had high hopes for its ability to prevent the sort of conflict that had characterized much of the twentieth century to that point. Unfortunately, just as it could not honor its commitments in Palestine, the UN failed the early test it faced with a conflict between India and Pakistan.

Although the UN did not have a role in the partition of British India as it had with British Mandatory Palestine, it nevertheless had a stake in the conflict that eventually broke out. On June 3, 1947, the British government published a plan for the partition of the Indian subcontinent that provided for the independence of India and Pakistan on August 15. It would be inaccurate to say that partition separated South Asia into Hindu and Muslim states. True, Pakistan was established on the basis of the idea that its Muslim population constituted a distinct nation, whose rights could be guaranteed only in a Muslim state. India, however, was based on an entirely different kind of idea of secular nationalism that guaranteed the rights of its religious minorities, including tens of millions of Muslims.[27]

Conflict arose because the partition of India did not resolve the fate of some 584 princely states, most of which had Hindu populations, but about a half dozen of which had mostly Muslim residents. The appointed viceroy of British India, Lord Mountbatten, urged the princely states to decide whether to join India or Pakistan; he discouraged them from opting for independence. The question of which nation to join proved particularly problematic for the princely state of Jammu and Kashmir. Kashmir, which bordered both Pakistan and India, had a mostly Muslim population but was ruled by a Hindu, Maharaja Sir Hari Singh. The maharaja faced a tribal rebellion in southwestern Kashmir in early October 1947. The Pakistani army moved quickly to aid the rebels with manpower, arms, and transport. This Pakistani-reinforced rebellion reached the outskirts of the Kashmiri capital, Srinagar, where rebels cut off the electrical power.

With his back against the wall, the maharaja appealed to the Indian government for military help. Prime Minister Jawaharlal Nehru of India, who himself came from an aristocratic Kashmiri family, made such assistance contingent upon Kashmir's merging with India. He also insisted that Kashmir's decision to join India have the support of the Kashmiri Muslim leader, Sheikh Mohammad Abdullah, who had been under Nehru's influence since the 1930s and had actually opposed the accession of Kashmir to Pakistan. The maharaja agreed to Nehru's terms, and on October 24, 1947, he signed an Instrument of Accession that made Kashmir part of India.[28] Indian forces were airlifted to Kashmir, where they managed to stop the rebel offensive. Direct battles between the Indian and Pakistani armies followed. The Indians were unable to dislodge the Pakistani-backed rebels from about one-third of Kashmir, an area that the Muslims would call Azad Kashmir (literally, "free Kashmir"). Indian-Pakistani clashes in Kashmir continued into 1948.

This was more than a territorial dispute. In a meeting with President Harry Truman in October 1949, Prime Minister Nehru frankly admitted that determining the fate of Kashmir "on a religious basis" would be destabilizing for India, for it "would have a deeply unsettling effect upon the Moslems living in India."[29] Nehru recognized that if Kashmir was excluded from India simply because it had a

Muslim majority, Indian Muslims would experience doubts about the government's commitment to secularism. In short, the Kashmir dispute touched on the very foundations of the Indian state as a secular nation.

The Pakistani government undoubtedly had similar considerations, for the Pakistani state was founded on the basis of the principle that Indian Muslims needed their own political entity. But Pakistan also had a very practical problem as it waged an ongoing war with India: If Kashmir went entirely over to the Indian side, Pakistan would have no buffer zone to protect its major cities. Islamabad, the Pakistani capital, was only thirty miles away from Kashmir, while Lahore was about eighty miles away.

Since Pakistani forces were involved in a conflict on Indian territory, Nehru considered expanding the confrontation into a full-scale counterattack against Pakistan. But Lord Mountbatten persuaded him to go to the UN instead. He convinced Nehru that the UN would promptly direct Pakistan to withdraw the raiders who had invaded Kashmir. So on January 1, 1948, India turned to the UN Security Council.

At the UN, the Indians charged that "such a situation exists between India and Pakistan owing to the aid which invaders, consisting of nationals of Pakistan and of tribesmen from the territory immediately adjoining Pakistan on the North West, are drawing from Pakistan for operation against Jammu and Kashmir, a State which has acceded to the Dominion of India and is part of India." In short, India accused Pakistan of outright aggression. Further damning was the Indian claim that many of the 19,000 "invaders" who had entered Kashmir were Pathan tribesmen from the area of North West Frontier Province, near the Afghan border, who had been transported across all of Pakistan in order to reach Kashmiri territory. The Indians insisted that the Security Council call on Pakistan to stop these attacks, warning that the situation in Kashmir was a "threat to international peace and security with which it is pregnant if it is not solved immediately."

Press reports at the time supported India's charge. For example, the *Times* of London wrote on January 13, 1948, "That Pakistan is unofficially involved in aiding the raiders is certain. Your correspondent has first hand evidence that arms, ammunition and supplies are being made available to the Azad Kashmir forces. A few Pakistani officers are also helping direct their operations." The *New York Times* carried similar claims by independent observers on January 29.[30]

Pakistan countered the Indian charges at the UN and flatly denied that it had provided any assistance to the tribesmen who had invaded Kashmir. Pakistan's skilled foreign minister, Sir Mohammed Zafrullah Khan, questioned the validity of Kashmir's accession to India, though India's representative had promised the Security Council that the Kashmiri people would have a plebiscite to ratify the accession. Khan also accused India of conducting a genocidal policy against Muslims in general.[31] He adeptly converted India's charges of a militant Muslim insurgency into a general problem of "alien" elements that included Sikh bands from India. This way Pakistan could put itself on an equal footing with India: Each had forcefully intervened without authorization, according to this view. The Pakistani representative suggested that all foreign forces needed to be withdrawn from Kashmir. Clearly there were divergent views of what had occurred in Kashmir.

The UN Security Council adopted a policy of strict evenhandedness in its treatment of both India and Pakistan. On January 20, 1948, the UN passed a resolution establishing a three-member Commission on India and Pakistan (UNCIP) to travel to Kashmir and determine the facts of what exactly had happened. The resolution said nothing about a Pakistani insurgency or the "tribesmen" that appeared in India's complaint. India had brought what it felt was a clear-cut case of aggression to the UN and come up empty-handed, with the UN's only response being to form a committee. This was hardly the decisive action Lord Mountbatten had promised.

At the UN, Indian officials felt, Pakistan "had succeeded, with the support of the British and American members, in diverting the attention from that complaint [of Pakistani aggression] to the problem of the dispute between India and Pakistan over the question of

Jammu and Kashmir." As a result, "Pakistan's aggression was pushed into the background." Sardar Patel, the Indian official responsible for the States Ministry, which guided Indian policy toward the accession of new states, concluded that by referring the Kashmir issue to the UN, India had unwittingly prolonged the dispute and obscured the merits of its case.[32] Indeed, the conflict appeared to be escalating after the UN's first engagement. In short, for India, going to the UN was a mistake.

What went wrong for India at the UN Security Council? Didn't the Indians have an open-and-shut case of Pakistani aggression against their territory? It turned out that Mountbatten's suggestion to Nehru that he would get a fair hearing at the UN had been somewhat disingenuous. British foreign secretary Ernest Bevin wrote to Prime Minister Clement Attlee that London had to be very careful about siding with India at the UN, given the tensions that had arisen in the Islamic world over Palestine.[33] Against this background, one can see how it would have been difficult for India to get a fair hearing in the UN Security Council. The British, as well as the Americans, who followed their lead, had greater interests in Pakistan, which was immediately contiguous to the Eurasian landmass and could, therefore, provide strategic bases to the West in the emerging Cold War. These military interests, and not any abstract principles about aggression, would determine their approach to the Indian complaint at the UN.

On April 21, 1948, the UN Security Council adopted another resolution on Kashmir, this one expanding UNCIP's membership to five states and stating that "tribesmen and Pakistani nationals not normally resident therein" needed to withdraw from Kashmir. With Resolution 726 it looked as though the UN was slowly beginning to acknowledge aggression. But the resolution did not suggest strong and immediate steps to remedy what had occurred, and it also called on India to reduce its forces in Kashmir "to the minimum strength required" for maintaining law and order. Moreover, it very carefully balanced its call for Pakistan to withdraw insurgents with a call for India to hold a plebiscite on Kashmir. It was as though both states were equally at fault: Pakistan for promoting an insurgency in Kashmir, and India for delaying the plebiscite that, in fact, it had originally proposed.

The UN created a kind of false symmetry between the fundamental grievances of each side and placed them on the same moral plane. Indian leaders felt that the UN had failed to brand Pakistan as the aggressor state; unless Pakistan's aggression was recognized and condemned, they argued, little progress could be made in resolving the Kashmir problem.[34] The Indian government ultimately rejected the UN's latest intervention, arguing that Resolution 726 made India look like a "co-accused" with Pakistan.[35]

Visiting Karachi, Pakistan, in July 1948, the UNCIP members were shocked to hear that Pakistan's denials of official involvement in the Kashmiri conflict were completely untrue. The Pakistani foreign minister, Sir Mohammed Zafrullah Khan, admitted that three Pakistani brigades had been involved in the fighting since May. Josef Korbel, the Czech chairman of UNCIP (whose daughter, Madeleine Albright, would become the U.S. secretary of state nearly five decades later), called the news of Pakistani involvement a "bombshell."[36] Even with this Pakistani admission to Korbel's team, however, the UN retained its carefully balanced approach. In August, UNCIP did state that "the presence of troops of Pakistan in the territory of the State of Jammu and Kashmir constitutes a material change in the situation," but little else changed in terms of what the UN was proposing to do in its previous resolutions.[37]

Very shortly, it became clear that the earliest phases of the Kashmir war were not just a spontaneous revolt by strictly indigenous forces against the maharaja's rule. Rather, Pakistan had directly intervened right from the start, as India had asserted. In his memoirs, Major General Akbar Khan disclosed that he had written the plan for Pakistani involvement in the Kashmir crisis, "Armed Revolt in Kashmir."[38] Referring to the Azad movement, he explained, "As open interference or aggression by Pakistan was obviously undesirable, it was proposed that our efforts should be concentrated upon strengthening the Kashmiris internally—and at the same time taking steps to prevent the arrival of armed civilian or military assistance from India into Kashmir." Pakistan's Kashmiri allies, he explained, needed "plans, advice, weapons, ammunition, communications, and volunteers." Akbar Khan was by no means the only senior Pakistani official involved in plans to infiltrate Kashmir; other military officers, such as the director of intelligence, played key roles, and the Pakistanis also deployed ground and air forces.[39] And Pakistani leader Mohammed Ali Jinnah approved of the plot to infiltrate Kashmir, according to the 1997 testimony of a Pakistani regional minister on the BBC. British commanders in the Pakistani army were reportedly kept in the dark, however.[40]

When UNCIP prepared its first interim report, it finally recognized Pakistan's direct involvement in Kashmir: "The Azad movement, which constitutes an organized political and military body, is assisted by the Pakistani High Command and is engaged in active revolt against the existing [Kashmiri] government. This movement has cooperated since October 1947 with the invading tribesmen and individual Pakistan nationals."

Despite the fact that the UN commission had substantiated India's charges against Pakistan, the UN still was not willing to determine that aggression had occurred and to take measures accordingly. India was concerned that UNCIP's August resolution might provide the basis for recognizing the Azad Kashmir government, which would tighten Pakistan's grip on the portion of Kashmir that it occupied. For example, UNCIP proposed that any Kashmiri territory evacuated by Pakistan be administered by "local authorities," precluding the insertion of India's administration. And by continuing to recommend a reduction of Indian forces in Kashmir, as Resolution 726 first suggested, the UN was, in the Indian view, robbing India of its ability to protect Kashmiri territory from external aggression.[41] Clearly, rather than being punished by the UN for its aggression, Pakistan was deriving distinct territorial and strategic advantages.

Indeed, Pakistan sent an urgent communication to UNCIP in November 1948 alleging that India was reinforcing its troops in

Kashmir. Again the UN became active, proposing through UNCIP a truce to be followed by a plebiscite. To monitor the cease-fire, in early 1949 the UN dispatched twenty military observers, the United Nations Military Observer Group in India and Pakistan (UNMOGIP). In July 1949, the UN got India and Pakistan to sign the Karachi Agreement, which formally established the cease-fire line based on the positions the armies of India and Pakistan had established on the ground. In other words, the UN did not resolve the conflict, it merely froze the two antagonists in their positions. Even its peacekeeping force, as the UN secretary-general would later explain, did not have the mandate to provide for any security along the mountainous, 500-mile cease-fire line: "Because the role of UNMOGIP appears frequently to be misunderstood, it bears emphasis that the operation has no authority or function entitling it to enforce or prevent anything, or to try to ensure that the cease-fire is respected."[42]

Given that this force, according to the UN secretary-general, exercised "the quite limited function of observing and reporting," it had a highly constrained role in stabilizing the Indian-Pakistani frontier.[43] In fact, in subsequent years the UN would see its role in Indian-Pakistani affairs shrink even more.

A second Kashmir War broke out in August 1965. At the request of the UN Security Council, Secretary-General U Thant flew off to Pakistan and India in order to mediate. He achieved nothing.[44] The fighting spread beyond Kashmir to the international border between the two countries. The UN Security Council passed five resolutions between September and December 1965, calling on the parties to observe their cease-fire, but to no effect. The UN looked impotent. The deadlock between the two warring countries was finally broken by Soviet premier Alexei Kosygin, who invited the leaders of India and Pakistan to Tashkent, where they reached a new cease-fire agreement in January 1966. Soviet diplomacy had succeeded where UN diplomacy had failed.

The UN failed again in the early 1970s, after the third Indian-Pakistani war, which led to the dismemberment of East Pakistan and the establishment of Bangladesh. After the war, Prime Minister Indira Gandhi of India met with President Zulfikar Ali Bhutto of Pakistan at the former British-Indian colonial summer capital of Simla.[45] Pakistan had been badly defeated militarily. To a large extent, the Simla Agreement, which was signed on July 2, 1972, reflected the interests of the victor, India. The Simla Agreement made no mention of previous UN Security Council resolutions on the conflict between India and Pakistan. It did not even contain a clause about UN peacekeeping forces.

In fact, the Simla Agreement had a distinctly antimultilateralist clause that could only be interpreted as an effort to keep the UN out of any postwar diplomacy: "The two countries are resolved to settle their differences by peaceful means through bilateral negotiations or by any other peaceful means mutually agreed upon between them." The agreement gave India a veto over any Pakistani move to turn to any other multilateral forum for assistance, including the UN, and it transformed the previous cease-fire line into a more permanent "line of control." Now that India had the upper hand, it no longer recognized the UN monitoring authority that it had agreed to in the 1949 Karachi Agreement. The UN observers in UNMOGIP looked superfluous, though the UN secretary-general argued, weakly, that only the UN Security Council could terminate the presence of the UN force in Kashmir.[46] India had brought the Kashmir issue to the UN in the first place, but it wanted the UN out. While India would remain active in UN affairs as a leading member of the Nonaligned Movement, it was completely disillusioned with the world organization when it came to the protection of its vital national interests in the defense of Kashmir.


## THE LEGACY OF EARLY FAILURES

The UN's failure to deal with conflicts in Israel and Kashmir had a profound impact. These tests came almost immediately after the organization's formation, and by failing to take a firm stand against well-documented cases of aggression, the UN betrayed the vision of its founding fathers. In each case it was not difficult to establish that a country had been the victim of armed attack. The natural tendency of UN diplomats was to accept the arguments of warring parties equally, rather than penalizing the aggressor, rewarding the defender, and thereby deterring armed attacks in the future. It is no wonder that India eventually regretted that it had turned to the UN in the first place. The UN not only "internationalized" the issue of Kashmir's fate, which from India's perspective was an internal matter, it also prolonged the conflict with Pakistan, which led to at least two more full-scale wars on the Indian subcontinent. It repeatedly created a false equivalence between those who tried to work within the norms of the UN and those who rejected them.

The UN's failures with Israel and India were particularly problematic because these cases set precedents. Throughout the process of decolonization, as newly emerging states were consolidating their territories, cases in which states made conflicting claims of sovereignty often arose. Article 2 of the UN Charter prohibited the use of force against the "territorial integrity" of another state. Many states, disputing the borders of their neighbors, could argue that this fundamental UN prohibition was not applicable in their case, because their military incursion did not violate their neighbor's territorial integrity.[47] Dozens of states with irredentist claims could exploit this loophole, leading to worldwide anarchical conditions. Why rely on the caveats of the UN Charter when Pakistan had moved into Kashmir and was not condemned? Why shouldn't they follow that lead?

Communist China was one nation that took advantage of the UN's failures. In October 1950, a half million People's Liberation Army soldiers invaded Tibet to assert China's territorial claim. Tibet had argued that it had declared its independence from China in 1911, just as Nepal had, and therefore was a fully sovereign state under the Dalai Lama.[48] The Chinese invasion forced tens of thousands of Tibetan refugees, including the Dalai Lama, to escape to India, and ultimately the Communist government settled 4 million Chinese immigrants in eastern Tibet.[49] The El Salvadoran govern-

ment issued an appeal to the UN on behalf of the Tibetan government, but the UN took no measures. Only in 1959 did the General
Assembly adopt a resolution regarding Tibet, but this resolution,
like others that followed in 1961 and 1965, only deplored the violation of human rights in Tibet. The UN did not address Communist
China's use of force. The question of whether the status of Tibet was
an internal Chinese affair or a matter of international dispute had
been settled by overwhelming force.

The problem wasn't that the Chinese specifically examined the
cases of India or Israel and then decided that they could grab Tibet
with impunity. The problem was that the UN's failure to act decisively had made it difficult to discern a clear and broadly applied UN
doctrine against aggression. Stopping aggression was one of the
main purposes for which the UN had been founded, yet even in the
few years since it was born, aggression was spreading. In June 1950,
just before the subjugation of Tibet, a massive force from North
Korea had invaded South Korea.

The absence of a firm norm against aggression plagued the UN
in subsequent decades as well. As noted in Chapter 1, India took the
law into its own hands in 1962, when it overran the tiny Portuguese
colony of Goa. India could argue that since the UN had not openly
condemned Pakistan's invasion of Kashmir, India also had a right to
use force, especially against an outdated colonial outpost whose legitimacy, it would argue, the new global consensus in the General
Assembly did not accept.

The use of force to consolidate new states became the norm in
the Third World. Indonesia moved into North Borneo, into
Sarawak, and ultimately into the Portuguese colony of East Timor.
The UN did condemn the invasion of East Timor by a vote of 72–10,
with forty-three nations abstaining, including the United States,
which had its own Cold War interests in bolstering Indonesia.[50] But
it would take more than twenty years for Indonesia to respond.

If states could attack the territories of disengaging colonial powers, then what about colonial legacies? Syria refused to appoint a
resident ambassador to Lebanon, since it believed that French im-

perialism had torn that region out of the original Syrian patrimony. The Syrian occupation of Lebanon became the inevitable result of a diplomatic doctrine that refused to accept the legitimacy of lines drawn by colonial powers. In 1975, beleaguered Lebanese Christians invited Syria to intervene in the Lebanese Civil War against the Sunni Muslims, but within a few years these same Christian militias would be fighting the Syrians themselves. The most notable assault on a colonial legacy was the 1990 Iraqi invasion of Kuwait, a state that after all existed only because the British Empire had turned this formerly Ottoman territory into a British protectorate in the late nineteenth century.

The international community did not have a clear and consistent response to these acts of aggression. Because of the poor reputation of Portuguese dictator Antonio Salazar, the international community was not quick to condemn attacks on Lisbon's possessions.[51] When Argentina, ruled by a military junta, tried to invade the Falkland Islands in the 1980s in order to consolidate its control over these disputed territories, it could not muster international support in a struggle with democratic Britain. Saddam Hussein sought to build on the resentment toward the oil-rich Kuwaiti emirate in poorer parts of the Arab world, and thereby undercut Kuwait's legitimacy as well as its right to have its independence restored. The Iraqi leadership miscalculated, however, and the UN Security Council charged Iraq with aggression. But the decisiveness of 1991 was rare.

The UN was designed to fill a unique role. It was supposed to create international standards that would help shape a more stable world order. The UN Charter specifically empowered the UN Security Council to determine whether an act of aggression had taken place (Article 39). The mandate was clear, but unfortunately the UN has not been able to follow that mandate consistently. The problem is that the UN Security Council is not a court that determines the guilt or innocence of states by trying to use objective legal criteria. It is first and foremost a political body, and it has been grossly inconsistent in judging cases of aggression. Moral relativism was an inevitable by-product of the UN's work; often the attacker was not treated very differently from the victim of aggression.

As early as the 1940s and 1950s, the UN did not meet its responsibility to respond to acts of aggression, and therefore it did not advance the sense that there was an agreed basis for a new world order. Instead, what held the international community together was the alliance system created by the Cold War.

**THE KOREAN WAR**

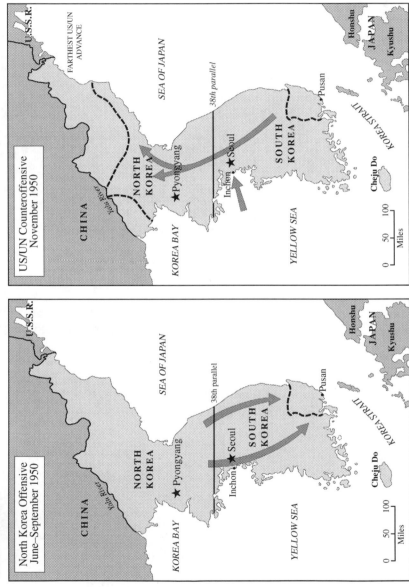

North Korea Offensive
June–September 1950

US/UN Counteroffensive
November 1950

# CHAPTER 3

# The Cold War Freeze

*From Korea to Cuba*

**W**hen North Korean troops invaded South Korea in June 1950, what followed looked exactly like the kind of crisis for which the UN was created. It was, after all, a case of bald aggression.

And this was precisely how UN secretary-general Trygve Lie saw it. The Norwegian refused to assume a neutral position between the warring parties, for as he would later recall, the North Korean surprise attack reminded him of "the Nazi invasion of Norway."[1] It was beginning to seem as though the moral clarity of 1945 had returned. If the UN was established to prevent the sort of conflict that led to the Second World War, here was its opportunity.

The UN had in fact been focused on the Korea situation well before the invasion, almost from the organization's founding. Korea had been divided into two occupying zones after the Second World War. The Soviets controlled the northern zone, above the 38th parallel, which they seized eight days before the Japanese surrender; the Americans, the southern zone. Japan had occupied Korea in 1905 and annexed it five years later, converting it into a Japanese colony from 1910 until 1942. During the Second World War, in 1943, the United States, Britain, and China had jointly declared that "Korea shall become free and independent." But the deadlock between the Soviets and the Americans was such that by the fall of 1947, the United States decided to place the Korean issue before the UN. Two weeks before the UN General Assembly proposed the partition of Palestine, it adopted a resolution calling for all-Korea elections.

Plans for a unified Korea soon collapsed, however. In September 1948, the Soviets officially recognized the North Korean government of Communist Kim Il-sung, and five months later the United States recognized South Korea, whose government the pro-Western UN General Assembly had declared to be "lawful." In 1949, South Korea acquired the status of an observer mission at the UN (like the Vatican).

On June 25, 1950, well-armed North Korean forces poured across the 38th parallel and into South Korea. The Korean War had begun.

The Truman administration turned immediately to the UN Security Council. It secured approval of Resolution 82, which "determined" that an "armed attack" had occurred and that the North Korean action constituted a "breach of the peace." The resolution also called for "the immediate cessation of hostilities" and "the withdrawal of the North Korean Forces to the 38th parallel." The resolution in addition called on member states "to render every assistance to the United Nations" in the execution of the resolution. Two days later, with the adoption of UN Security Council Resolution 83, the UN urged all members to "furnish such assistance to the Republic of Korea as may be necessary to repel the armed attack and restore international peace and security."

The North Koreans didn't stop, however. As a result, President Truman ordered U.S. air and naval forces to give cover to South Korea's retreating troops. A little over a week later, the UN adopted yet another resolution, this one putting the whole UN military effort against North Korea under U.S. command and authorizing that force to fly the UN flag. Truman appointed General Douglas MacArthur the commander of UN forces. Seventeen countries eventually provided military aid; the largest non-American forces came from the United Kingdom and the British Commonwealth—as would be the case with the coalition that fought Iraq in 2003. Echoing some of the utopian UN rhetoric of 1945, Truman would call the American-led UN force a "landmark in mankind's long search for a rule of law among nations."[2]

The mobilization and deployment of UN forces took time, and by the end of July the North Korean army had driven the South Koreans into an enclave in the southeastern corner of the Korean peninsula, around Pusan. Nevertheless, the UN deployment was significant because it marked the first time the world body had responded quickly to aggression without much debate. The UN appeared to be functioning as a tight alliance, as its architects had intended, rather than as a universal organization incapable of decisive action because of its diverse opinions.

Yet the UN had not suddenly become a well-oiled machine with well-defined objective criteria for defining aggression. Rather, the UN was able to come to agreement so quickly mainly because the Soviet Union had withdrawn its representative from the Security Council. On January 13, 1950, five months before the North Korean invasion, the Soviets had boycotted to protest the fact that the UN still recognized the Nationalist Chinese government even though the Communists had consolidated their rule on the Chinese mainland. Thus, as the UN Security Council debated the Korean situation and then adopted resolutions, there was no Soviet veto to protect North Korea. The rest of the Security Council was pro-Western, so when the council voted, only Yugoslavia abstained. In short, the UN of 1950 worked because it was more like NATO than like the UN of 2003.

What might have the Soviets said had they sat on the Security Council? In the Soviet view, the North Korean invasion wasn't an open-and-shut case of aggression, as the Western powers thought it was. According to UN resolutions, Korea was supposed to become one united country. The Soviet and American military sectors were in the process of becoming states, each with claims to the other half. The United States and the Soviet Union had withdrawn their armies from Korea in 1949. Thus, from Moscow's viewpoint, the war between North Korean forces and those of the South was essentially a civil war, and not the invasion of one sovereign state into the territory of another state. The UN, from the Soviet perspective, had no jurisdiction to become involved. The Chinese would use the same sort of argument for their 1950 invasion of Tibet—it was strictly an internal issue.

Although the UN did move quickly to counter the North Korean aggression, in a sense the UN had already failed when the Korean War broke out. The UN had not deterred North Korea from taking offensive action in the first place. Clearly, the strong, principled position against aggression laid out in the UN Charter had had no impact on North Korean leaders, or on their Soviet backers. If the North Koreans and the Soviets had understood that the norms the UN had fashioned against aggression would be backed by force, then they might not have launched the invasion to begin with. Perhaps they had witnessed the UN's failure to act decisively in Palestine and Kashmir and had decided they would strike quickly, before the UN could muster a sufficient response. Alternatively, the North Koreans might have thought that by adopting the Soviet argument that this was just an internal war, they could obfuscate their aggression and get away with it.

U.S. actions before the invasion also signaled to the North Koreans and the Soviets that the Americans would not respond forcefully to an attack on South Korea. After the United States withdrew its forces from the Korean peninsula in 1949, leading American spokesmen actually said that Korea was beyond America's defense perimeter in Asia. General MacArthur, for instance, stated in March 1949 that the U.S. line of defense in the Pacific ran through the chain of islands at the fringes of the Asian coastline. On January 12, 1950, Secretary of State Dean Acheson announced that the United States could not guarantee the security of any areas on the Asian mainland, which of course included Korea.[3] The United States seemed to be declaring that Korea was not a vital interest for which it might go to war.

The UN Security Council might have operated efficiently because the Soviet Union withdrew its representative, but that situation would not last long. On August 1, 1950, the Soviets returned to take up their seat on the Security Council once again. They made their presence felt immediately; it was their turn to assume the presidency of the Security Council, which rotated every month. They vetoed an American draft resolution that would have insisted that all states refrain from assisting North Korea. Then Moscow undertook its own initiatives, calling for the withdrawal of all foreign troops from Korea—meaning U.S.-led forces. The Soviets outrageously alleged in the Security Council that the United States was engaging in mass exterminations of Korean civilians.

The United States did begin to make progress on the battlefield. MacArthur's counterattack began in the middle of September, when he landed a huge American force behind North Korean lines at Inchon and recaptured nearby Seoul. The North Korean army was routed. Suddenly the United States and the UN had to decide whether it was sufficient just to recapture the area of South Korea, below the 38th parallel, or if it was necessary to drive north and eliminate the Communist regime. Nonetheless, with the USSR back on the Security Council, the Americans could not think solely about military strategy. How could the United States keep the UN supportive of its military operations against North Korea with a Soviet veto in the Security Council hovering overhead?

## AMERICA TAKES THE LEAD

The Cold War had created a complete Soviet-American deadlock in the Security Council. Accordingly, the Truman administration devised ways of making its UN strategy compatible with the realities of Soviet countermoves in the Security Council. Secretary of State Dean Acheson conceived of a way of skirting the USSR by empowering the General Assembly. His "Uniting for Peace" resolution of November 3, 1950, stated, "If the Security Council, because of lack of unanimity of the permanent members, fails to exercise its primary responsibility for the maintenance of international peace and security in any case where there appears to be a threat to the peace, breach of the peace, or act of aggression, the General Assembly shall consider the matter immediately." The resolution specified that the General Assembly could be convened in an Emergency Special Session and could recommend the use of armed force.

Acheson's measure was not an idealistic expression of confidence in world government. Rather, it was a pragmatic move, demonstrating that the United States could not rely on the main UN institution designed to protect international peace and security—the Security Council. Washington preferred using the UN General Assembly, where it could wield its political weight to muster an anti-Soviet coalition.

The maneuver worked. Ten days after the Uniting for Peace resolution was approved, the United States pushed a British draft resolution in the General Assembly recommending that "all appropriate steps be taken to ensure conditions of stability throughout Korea." That was diplomatic shorthand, albeit somewhat ambiguous, for backing the U.S. decision to lead UN forces across the 38th parallel and into North Korea.[4] The resolution received overwhelming support, passing by a vote of 47–5.

Acheson had pulled off a brilliant move—in the short term. It enabled the United States to secure UN cover for MacArthur's offensive toward the Korean-Chinese border. But the Uniting for Peace resolution would serve American interests only as long as the majority of UN members remained pro-Western. Within a short number of years, as decolonization progressed and the number of new anti-Western states in the UN grew, Acheson's resolution would boomerang back against American interests. The UN General Assembly would evolve into an instrument for the Soviet Union and its allies to bypass the U.S. veto in the Security Council. Thus, by June 1967, it would be the USSR convening an Emergency Special Session of the General Assembly, in this case in opposition to the United States and Israel.

Acheson's resolution opened a Pandora's Box in the UN system, as it would lead to repeated attempts to erode the Security Council's authority. The UN Charter specifically assigned the Security Council "primary responsibility for the maintenance of international peace and security" and stipulated that the General Assembly "shall not make any recommendation" regarding a dispute already under consideration in the Security Council. These clauses were intended to protect the supremacy of the UN Security Council and to avoid situations in which the Security Council made one recommendation while the General Assembly recommended an entirely different, perhaps even contradictory, approach.[5] Acheson's resolution undercut the UN Charter and created numerous problems down the road. In 1989, for example, Cuba and Nicaragua managed to initiate a discussion in the General Assembly about Panama, against the wishes of the United States and Great Britain, which preferred to keep the issue in the Security Council, where they could exercise their veto.[6]

The United States saw the unintended consequences from Acheson's strategy even during the Korean War. Although the UN General Assembly had supported MacArthur's advance into North Korea, it proved unreliable once the fortunes of the U.S.-led coalition changed. U.S. forces had reached Pyongyang, the North Korean capital, by late October, but in late November, more than a quarter million Chinese soldiers crossed over into North Korea and joined the war. MacArthur's army was forced to retreat to the 38th parallel. The Truman administration wanted to bring the Communist Chinese intervention in Korea to the General Assembly in December 1950. Suddenly UN members, including American allies, were concerned about an expanded war.[7] With China now involved, the UN General Assembly no longer acted swiftly and decisively. The United States tried to get the General Assembly to employ economic measures against China, but this rather modest proposal was adopted only after a long delay. And it took the United States two months just to get the General Assembly to determine that the People's Republic of China had "engaged in aggression" in Korea. The only practical steps the General Assembly recommended in response to the aggression was boycotting trade of strategic materials with China and North Korea. Having seen the UN General Assembly's failure to remedy conflicts, states that were themselves victims of aggression could hardly be comfortable with Acheson's idea.

Secretary Acheson's resolution created another problem: The General Assembly could make all sorts of recommendations, but it was not empowered actually to dispatch armed forces. This limitation exposed a corresponding weakness in the entire UN involvement in Korea. Even the UN Security Council resolutions of June and July 1950, which were the cornerstones of the U.S. military campaign against North Korea, were worded as "recommendations." The UN's authorization of the use of force was, at best, implicit.[8] In the 1991 Gulf War, in contrast, the UN Security Council actually "authorized" UN member states "to use all necessary means" to evict Iraq from Kuwait. The Gulf War resolution was adopted under Chapter VII of the UN Charter, which made its contents legally binding under international law.

This was not just a matter of semantics. The UN actually empowered states to fight Saddam Hussein, but it empowered no one to beat back the North Koreans. In 1950, the only step the UN formally "authorized" was the unfurling of the UN flag. A similar situation would arise more than a half century later, when in November 2002 the UN Security Council passed Resolution 1441, which referred to Iraq's "material breach" of UN resolutions and warned of "serious consequences" for continued Iraqi noncompliance. This resolution set the stage for the use of U.S. power to disarm Iraq but did not formally authorize it. For that reason, European states in 2003 insisted on a second resolution explicitly authorizing the use of force before they would support President Bush's decision to go to war; by comparison, no one insisted that President Truman receive formal authorization to use force.

In essence, it wasn't the UN Security Council resisting North Korean aggression back in 1950—it was the United States and a coalition of its allies. President Truman, like President George W. Bush fifty-three years later, took the lead. The UN did not obligate states to join the war effort in either Korea or Iraq, but in both cases its resolutions provided justification for action. Thus, the legal basis for the Korean War wasn't much different from the legal basis for the Iraq War.[9]

Had the Truman administration not taken forceful measures in June 1950, the UN probably would not have done much against North Korea. Even with the Soviets absent from the Security Council, securing a multilateral consensus for swift action would have been extremely difficult. What the UN provided was legitimacy for the Truman administration's military campaign. The UN provided moral sanction, which was particularly important for U.S. public opinion.

When a reporter asked Truman in a press conference on September 21, 1950, if he had decided whether U.S. military action would spread into North Korea itself, the president responded, "No, I have not. That is a matter for the United Nations to decide. . . . It will be worked out by the United Nations and I will abide by the decision that the United Nations makes."[10] But in reality, Truman's Joint Chiefs of Staff, under instructions from the National Security Council, had spent the previous three weeks making plans to cross the 38th parallel. It didn't matter that the UN secretary-general had not backed the strategy, or even that America's British allies were concerned that moving into the north would provoke Chinese intervention or a Chinese countermove against the British colony of Hong Kong.[11] The United States was in the driver's seat.

## "WHAT IS THE UNITED NATIONS DOING?"

The whole Korean War episode demonstrated how difficult it was for the UN to stop aggression during the Cold War, especially aggression that emanated from Soviet expansionism. Perhaps out of recognition of the UN's limitations, Trygve Lie's successor as UN secretary-general, Dag Hammarskjöld, tried to make the UN a "third force" defending smaller nations. In the Congo in 1960, he pioneered the idea of deploying UN forces to head off a U.S.-Soviet scramble for hegemony. Hammarskjöld injected troops to support the Congo's beleaguered prime minister, Patrice Lumumba. In doing so, however, he drew the UN into an internal war over the right of the Congo's mineral-rich Katanga province to declare independence.

By shuttling back and forth between Lumumba and the Katangan leader, Moise Tshombe, the UN accorded diplomatic standing to the breakaway Katanga province—a luxury not afforded to other areas of the Third World that had far deeper historical claims to independence, from Biafra in Nigeria to Iraqi Kurdistan to Tibet. Hammarskjöld's support for Katanga quickly got him in hot water with the Lumumba government and its Soviet backers. In September 1961, Hammarskjöld was killed in a plane crash during one of his Congo missions; Soviet intelligence reported to the Kremlin that he had been killed by forces loyal to the late Lumumba, who had died earlier that year.[12]

Hammarskjöld's poor relations with Moscow were surprising, for he had intended to avoid getting drawn into Cold War politics as his predecessor had. The Soviets had refused to recognize Trygve Lie, so even though his term as secretary-general had been extended, he resigned his post in November 1952. In the words of his aide Brian Urquhart, Hammarskjöld "welcomed the demise of the illusion that the UN could enforce peace and resolve all conflicts." He spoke about the UN as "a body where ideologies are permitted to clash inside the wider framework of a fundamental unity of purpose for peace."[13] These intellectual acrobatics meant that the UN became more of a meetinghouse of ideas than a force to contend with aggression and defend human rights.

The strongest example of the UN's Cold War impotence was provided during the Hungarian Revolution of 1956. As mass demonstrations against Hungary's Communist government spread in late October 1956, Budapest invoked the Warsaw Pact treaty and called for Soviet troops to restore order. Rebel forces nonetheless fought on. On October 30, a new Hungarian national government was formed, under Imre Nagy, which announced that the Soviet Union had agreed to withdraw all its forces from Hungary. But two days later, fresh Soviet forces poured into Hungary. Nagy appealed to Hammarskjöld, for the new leader had withdrawn Hungary from the Warsaw Pact, meaning that Moscow had no legal basis for its intervention. This was now a case of Soviet aggression.

Nagy wanted the great powers to guarantee Hungary's neutrality to prevent the Soviet military from forcing Hungary to stay within the Eastern bloc. He asked the secretary-general to put the Hungary issue on the UN General Assembly's agenda. Given the certain Soviet veto in the Security Council, Acheson's Uniting for Peace resolution was invoked and an Emergency Special Session of the General Assembly was convened. Within twenty-four hours of Nagy's request, Soviet troops had encircled Budapest. On November 4, 1956, just as Radio Budapest went off the air with cries of "Help Hungary!—Help us!" the General Assembly adopted a resolution calling on the secretary-general "to investigate the situation caused by foreign intervention in Hungary." He was to prepare a report to the UN "at the earliest moment."

The UN worked at a snail's pace, however. As Soviet tanks entered Budapest and crushed the revolt, the UN General Assembly continued to discuss the Hungarian situation. Free Hungarian radio stations—those that could still broadcast—appealed to the world, asking, "What is the United Nations doing?" The Italian ambassador to the UN commented, "While the Secretary-General studies, investigates, and reports, the Hungarian people is being massacred."[14] The General Assembly discussions continued through November 10, by which point the Soviets had taken over the country.

At the very same time that the UN was doing nothing about the Soviet invasion of Hungary, it condemned the joint operation of Britain, France, and Israel against Nasserist Egypt. The UN's condemnations proved effective, as these nations withdrew all their forces from Egyptian territory. The UN was an important institution for these countries, because they were democracies, where public opinion mattered. The UN could have substantial influence on foreign policy in democracies, since it could provide moral sanction for military action or it could undercut foreign policy with its criticisms. But as the Hungary situation revealed, the UN had only a minimal impact on the totalitarian regimes of the Soviet bloc and their Third World supporters. Public opinion was irrelevant for dictatorships. UN resolutions were not a prerequisite for military action, and UN condemnations did not make any impression on dictators.

Under such conditions, a UN charting a more neutralist course during the Cold War was doing far worse than encouraging moral equivalence between the East and the West. Because it could often check the assertion of Western power and the freedom of action of democracies, it could serve as a powerful tool in the hands of the Soviet Union. This was not lost on the Soviet Union, which in the 1960s tried to forge a bloc of states in the General Assembly that would condemn Western policies.

After Korea and Hungary, the United States would be careful about turning to the UN in order to deal with its vital interests. In August 1959, Laos requested UN observers to monitor the assistance that North Vietnam was providing to the government's Pathet Lao opposition. After the UN issued several inconclusive reports, the Kennedy administration took the Laos question out of the hands of the UN and convened a Geneva Conference in May 1961.[15] Both the Kennedy and the Johnson administrations decided not to take the Vietnam War to the UN in the 1960s as the Truman administration had done with the Korean War in the 1950s.

In the Cold War stalemate, the UN did not have much authority; it mainly had propaganda value for the two superpowers. It could not be ignored, but it also could not be relied on to resolve key international disputes. That became evident in 1962, with the outbreak of the Cuban Missile Crisis.

## THE CRISIS IN CUBA AND UN INACTION

When Ambassador Adlai Stevenson went to the UN Security Council in 1962 to present U.S. aerial photographs of Soviet ballistic missiles deployed in Cuba, his action seemed to emphasize the importance of the UN, even under Cold War circumstances. In truth, however, the UN became part of the Cuban Missile Crisis relatively late.

On October 16, 1962, President Kennedy was informed that American U-2 reconnaissance aircraft had photographed the deployment of Soviet SS-4 medium-range ballistic missiles in Cuba. The SS-4 could strike targets that were 1,020 nautical miles from

## THE CUBAN MISSILE CRISIS:
## RANGE OF SOVIET SS-4 BALLISTIC MISSILES

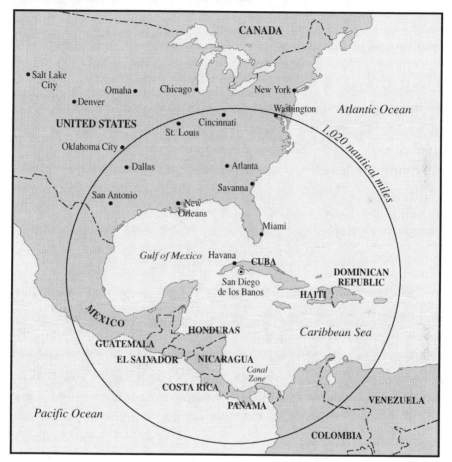

Cuba—meaning that Dallas, St. Louis, Cincinnati, and worst of all Washington, D.C., were within range of its three-megaton nuclear warheads. The CIA concluded that eight missile launchers with sixteen missiles were deployed at two launch sites in western Cuba; they required a preparation time of eighteen hours to be ready.

Kennedy made the crisis public in an address to the American people on the evening of October 22. He spoke about "unmistakable evidence" that Soviet missiles were being put into Cuba. In the speech he disclosed that the U.S. Navy would impose a "strict quarantine" on all offensive military equipment bound for Cuba.[16]

Kennedy already had read fresh reports that new launch sites were being prepared near Havana for the Soviet SS-5 missile, which had an even greater range (2,200 nautical miles). These sites would be operational by December 1962. There was no time to waste. The U.S. Navy's quarantine got under way almost immediately. Fifty-six American warships encircled Cuba.[17]

Ambassador Stevenson did not go before the UN Security Council to unveil America's U-2 photographs until October 25—well after the U.S. Navy had begun to implement President Kennedy's quarantine order for Cuba. The United States had gone to the Security Council on October 22, even though the Kennedy administration knew that the Soviets would veto any resolution. The United States had already secured support for possible military action from the Organization of American States (OAS) through its Rio Treaty. This was not a substitute for a UN resolution, but during an October 22 National Security Council meeting, Secretary of State Dean Rusk had made it clear to President Kennedy that invoking the Rio Treaty would provide the best legal basis for the U.S. "blockade action." By going to the OAS, the United States could argue that it was acting in accordance with the UN Charter, which recognized the role that regional organizations would play in maintaining international peace and security.[18] Formally, an OAS "recommendation" was no substitute for the UN Security Council, but this was the best the Kennedy administration could do. The State Department did not want to argue that the quarantine of Cuba was an act of self-defense under Article 51 of the UN Charter, since that would open the door for Soviet military action against U.S. forward-deployed forces in countries encircling the Soviet Union.

Clearly, the United States was not waiting for a conclusion of the UN proceedings or any decisive UN authorization before using force. At best, Washington could construct arguments showing that it had implicit authorization to act. Indeed, Kennedy had already taken action without obtaining even the most minimal UN approval. He was not going to wait for a UN Security Council resolution before initiating naval operations. These operations might be re-

garded as an act of war, even if they were done for the most
justifiable defensive reasons: to protect the American people from
the threat of a Soviet nuclear attack. Nor did the United States in-
voke Acheson's Uniting for Peace resolution to convene an emergency session of the General Assembly.

The UN acquired a totally different kind of importance in the
Cuban Missile Crisis. Still revered in American public opinion, the
UN received enormous American network television coverage. It
had a huge press pool. It was a place where the Kennedy adminis-
tration could make its case yet again to the American people and at
the same time to the world. The latter was particularly important.
The Kennedy administration notified U.S. allies about Cuba on
October 21, a day before Kennedy addressed the American people.
British prime minister Harold Macmillan expressed doubts about
America's ability to muster UN support.[19] The Canadian leadership
spoke about the need to provide credible evidence before UN
members.[20]

The Soviets also understood the potential impact of the UN on
world public opinion, even if the Security Council would not take
any specific actions. Normally, a debate in the UN Security Council
does not make good drama. Ambassadors carefully read their prepared texts while sitting, not veering a syllable from the language
that was approved by their superiors in their home capital. Often
these speeches have a tediously slow cadence to allow for simultane-
ous translation. The October 25 debate was different. Moscow's UN
ambassador, Valerian Zorin, played for a wider audience. He
charged the United States with falsifying its intelligence reports on
Soviet missiles in Cuba: "Falsity is what the United States has in its
hands—false evidence." To make matters worse, the Soviets sat in
the chair of the rotating president of the Security Council that
month, which allowed them to control the procedural aspects of a
Security Council meeting.

Adlai Stevenson responded to Zorin that evening, just hours
later. He opened his remarks by confronting the Soviet ambassador
directly: "All right, sir, let me ask you one simple question: Do you,

Ambassador Zorin, deny that the USSR has placed and is placing medium- and intermediate-range missiles and sites in Cuba? Yes or no—don't wait for the translation—yes or no." Zorin refused to answer, saying he wasn't on trial: "I am not standing on the dock of an American court and I shall not answer at this stage."

Stevenson then provided his famous response. After telling Zorin that he was, in fact, in "the courtroom of world public opinion," Stevenson retorted, "I am prepared to wait for my answer until hell freezes over, if that is your decision." Using his powers as president of the Security Council, Zorin recognized the right of the ambassador of Chile to speak. Yet he too asked Zorin to answer Stevenson's question. Only then did Stevenson display the U-2 photographs and explain their content.[21] At 7:25 P.M., the Security Council adjourned; it would never meet again to deal with the Cuban Missile Crisis. Stevenson's interrogation of Zorin constituted the greatest diplomatic theater that the UN had ever witnessed. But it did not lead to any specific resolutions or any other measures by the Security Council.

Secretary-General U Thant, who had replaced Hammarskjöld, tried to intervene in the crisis. He proposed to both President Kennedy and Soviet premier Nikita Khrushchev a suspension of Soviet arms shipments and of the American quarantine of Cuba for three weeks in order to defuse the crisis and provide time for diplomacy. Unable to take sides in a superpower dispute, the secretary-general could only use the UN as an evenhanded third party. He put the United States and the Soviet Union on the same plane.

The problem here was not one of moral equivalence alone. Kennedy had no patience for this UN role. He complained about U Thant's input in the crisis.[22] The president's advisers were concerned that by focusing on ways to achieve a "standstill" in the military situation, U Thant had forgotten that America's purpose was to achieve the removal of all offensive Soviet missiles from Cuba. According to U Thant's proposal, the Soviets could continue work on the missiles they had already delivered to Cuba. Freezing the crisis would have given the Soviets a victory—the successful militarization of Cuba with nuclear weapons. Clearly doubting U Thant, Secretary Rusk cabled Stevenson in New York to remind the secretary-general yet again of fundamental U.S. goals.

Khrushchev accepted U Thant's appeal.[23] This was significant, for it provided the first indication to Washington that the Soviets were looking for a way out of the crisis. Nevertheless, Kennedy felt that Khrushchev had not conceded much at this stage; after all, the Soviets had no ships in the area to hold back.[24] Moreover, despite the intervention of the UN secretary-general, the Soviets were still building up their missile sites in Cuba, as U.S. officials had anticipated.[25]

U Thant still pressed Stevenson to get Kennedy to match the Soviet move and "publicly suspend the quarantine" of Cuba. He also hoped that the United States would halt its U-2 reconnaissance flights over Cuba while he visited Havana.[26] Kennedy wanted to reject U Thant's proposals outright and prepared a letter to this effect, but it was held up at the last minute largely because of State Department input.

Then, on October 28, while U Thant was urging Stevenson to make new concessions in New York, the Soviets suddenly folded. The Moscow Domestic Service announced that Khrushchev had decided to dismantle the missiles in Cuba and return them to the Soviet Union.[27]

U Thant's diplomacy did not get the Soviet missiles out of Cuba. What ended the Cuban Missile Crisis was the ultimatum that Attorney General Robert Kennedy delivered to the Soviet ambassador in Washington, Anatoly Dobrynin. Unless the Soviets removed their missiles, the attorney general said, U.S. forces would have to bomb them. The implication was clear: The United States was prepared to attack Cuba. Khrushchev would later admit that his decision to capitulate was based on a simple calculation: A Soviet-controlled Cuba without missiles was better than a U.S.-occupied Cuba.[28] The administration added face-saving elements to the Soviet concession: an American pledge not to invade Cuba and the withdrawal of obsolete Jupiter intermediate-range missiles from Turkey. Robert Kennedy requested only that the removal of U.S. missiles from Turkey not be depicted as a quid pro quo in any way. With that, the nuclear show-down ended.

The United States had resolved the Cuban Missile Crisis—not the UN.

The UN was involved in the aftermath of the Cuban Missile Crisis in one important way: The Kennedy administration needed a way to verify that Khrushchev had indeed followed through on his commitments and pulled out the Soviet missiles from Cuba. In this early stage of the Cold War, Moscow had not accepted the idea of on-site inspections by Americans, so the UN secretary-general became the intermediary who would establish the rules of verification. The U.S. government, recognizing the importance of continuing aerial surveillance of Cuba, offered technical assistance if the UN chose to fly planes with its own markings. But the UN Secretariat did not seem interested in the American offer. Instead, U Thant put forward a Soviet proposal that representatives of the International Red Cross inspect Soviet ships going to Cuba. Moscow did not want trained officers from Western states allied with Washington gaining intelligence on Soviet missiles. But the United States had doubts about the Soviet-UN proposal, seeing that the inspectors it called for did not have sufficient technical proficiency to verify the removal of Soviet missiles. General Curtis LeMay, former head of the U.S. Strategic Air Command, commented, "Jesus Christ, what in the hell do a bunch of gray ladies know about missiles."[29]

## THE TURN AWAY FROM AMERICA

The UN actually did nothing to achieve peace and security in the Cuban Missile Crisis, aside from serving as a stage for Stevenson's verbal battle with Zorin. Had President Kennedy needed to order an air strike of Cuba, he would not have waited for UN authorization. Although the Kennedy administration balked at U Thant's proposals, Washington was careful not to openly criticize the UN or its secretary-general, for in 1962 the UN still retained its aura from

1945. But the U.S. government had good reason to object to the UN's handling of the situation. U Thant's diplomacy demonstrated a recurrent UN problem: In trying to defuse the crisis, he treated the aggressor (the USSR) and the defender (the United States) as equals, sometimes even preferring the Soviet position on specific diplomatic details. Khrushchev summarized the Soviet view of the UN secretary-general years later: "U Thant wouldn't allow the UN to do anything detrimental to the interests of the Soviet Union, the socialist countries, and those countries that were unaligned to military blocs."[30] To Khrushchev, U Thant was a real friend of the Soviet bloc.

U Thant's position as an intermediary between the superpowers, even one whom Khrushchev saw as being pro-Soviet, was an inevitable by-product of the Cold War situation. He had seen how the Soviets had cut off diplomatic contact with his two predecessors, including Dag Hammarskjöld, who had intended to be evenhanded with the superpowers. To U Thant's mind, he had no choice but to carefully maneuver diplomatically between Moscow and Washington and avoid taking sides. This inevitably eroded the moral force of the secretary-general, as he appeared to be wedded to a posture of strict neutrality. Thus the Cold War crippled the authority not only of the Security Council but also of the UN secretary-general. Only with the end of the Cold War in 1991 would it be possible to determine whether UN bodies, as well as its Secretariat, could take an indisputable stand against aggression instead of adopting the muddied positions for which they had become infamous.

Despite the UN's failures during the Cuban Missile Crisis, the United States ended 1962 with an optimistic view of its position in the world body. Summarizing America's standing in the UN as the General Assembly's annual meeting came to a close, Secretary of State Dean Rusk wrote to President Kennedy, "The damage which the Cuban missiles did to the credibility of Soviet statements was pervasive. By contrast, it helped to increase confidence in the words, and the actions, of the United States." Rusk felt the American position in the UN was stronger than it had been in years, with one reservation: "Colonialism is the only area in which we emerged with a spattering of egg on the face." He explained that the United States was still caught between the African states and NATO allies like Portugal and Britain that continued to have colonies in Africa. Still, Rusk felt that "as the number, if not the intensity, of colonial issues declines, the Soviet empire stands out more and more prominently on the horizon."[31] That is, he believed the anticolonialist campaign would begin to focus on Moscow, which had its own empire in Asia.

Dean Rusk might have been confident in America's position in the UN, but he did not recognize the significance of changes that were occurring. Already the UN had been proven to be incapable of taking action against aggression if one of the superpowers was involved. The United States had tried to work around that problem by employing Dean Acheson's strategy of circumventing the Soviet veto in the Security Council and going straight to the General Assembly. But new problems emerged that made Acheson's strategy untenable. In the 1950s, a majority of UN members had sided with the United States in the Cold War. In the 1960s, Moscow made it a priority not to allow that situation to continue. As a result, the UN would become increasingly hostile to American interests.

# CHAPTER 4

# Igniting War, Undermining Peace

## *The Six-Day War and the Struggle over Resolution 242*

It was bad enough that the UN had so often failed to prevent the outbreak of conflicts. But what if it actually ignited them?

The Cold War Middle East had all the ingredients to make it one of the world's most combustible regions. From the vantage point of President Lyndon Johnson, after the United States consolidated its strategic position in Western Europe through NATO and blocked Soviet expansion in Turkey as well as Iran, the USSR became more determined than ever to penetrate beyond this strategic barrier by gaining footholds in the Mediterranean, the Middle East, and the Indian Ocean.[1] A new leadership took control in Moscow in 1964 and, trying to recover from the diplomatic blow dealt during the Cuban Missile Crisis, made its naval squadron a constant presence in the Mediterranean. The UN had been active in the Arab-Israeli sector of this volatile zone since the 1948–49 war, but it failed to either prevent the outbreak of conflict or pave the way to a lasting peace. It was about to face another critical test in the Arab-Israeli crisis of 1967—a crisis that the UN, through its bungling, actually enabled.

At the end of the first Arab-Israeli War, the UN had sponsored the negotiations that led to the Armistice Agreements of 1949, which drew lines separating the warring parties. The UN chaired the Mixed Armistice Commissions, which were set up to oversee the implementation of the agreements, but already by the mid-1950s the armistice arrangements were breaking down. Israeli prime minister

## THE SEQUENCE OF EVENTS LEADING TO THE 1967 SIX-DAY WAR

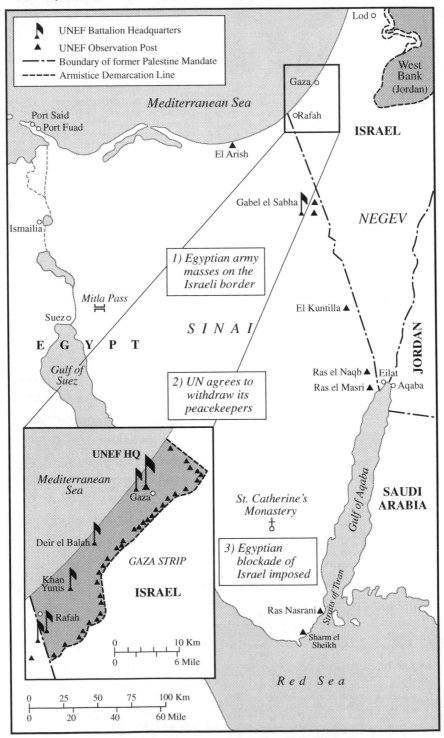

David Ben-Gurion complained in October 1956, after repeated hostile incursions into Israel, "We demanded week after week that UN representatives take substantial steps to ensure that the Arab countries put an end to these murderous attacks and legally observe their cease-fire obligations. All our insistence was in vain."[2] Problems only worsened when the Syrians pressed their claims to the Sea of Galilee, Israel's only freshwater lake, which the armistice had established was entirely within the territory of Israel.[3] Declaring that a belt of 250 meters of the lake was within Syrian territorial waters, Syria intensified artillery attacks on Israelis from atop the Golan Heights.[4] After 1964, Syria even tried to divert the waters feeding the Sea of Galilee. Israeli-Syrian clashes followed, but the UN refused to take action.

The situation deteriorated further in April 1967, when Syria, emboldened by a new defense treaty with Egypt, escalated its shelling of villages in northern Israel. The Israelis responded to the unusually heavy Syrian artillery barrages by launching fighter aircraft, which shot down six of Syria's Soviet MiG fighters. Syria's armed infiltrations of Israel increased. The chief of staff of the Israel Defense Forces, Lieutenant General Yitzhak Rabin, warned the Syrians in public that continued provocations would lead to a firm Israeli response that could endanger the Syrian regime.[5]

Israel was trying to deter the Syrians from further exploiting their topographical advantage on the Golan Heights to shell Israeli civilians, but the Soviet Union exploited this situation to spread rumors about Israel's plans and inflame the Arab world. The Soviets warned Egypt that Israeli armed forces were preparing a major offensive against its Syrian military partner. Israel vociferously denied the charge. Prime Minister Levi Eshkol invited Soviet envoys to inspect Israel's northern positions, but the Soviets refused the offer, as they had their own agenda: expanding their military presence along NATO's southern flank. The UN did nothing to stop this international crisis from escalating. It did not even challenge the Soviet reports to Egypt. The Egyptians prepared for war. Indeed, by May 18, 1967, President Gamal Abdel Nasser of Egypt had massed 80,000 soldiers and 550 tanks on Israel's southern border.[6]

As the crisis unfolded, the UN's peacekeeping forces were directly challenged. On May 16, Egypt's military liaison to the United Nations Emergency Force (UNEF) ordered that the UN partially withdraw its peacekeepers from along the border between Israel's southern Negev Desert and Egyptian Sinai, where UNEF had been stationed since the end of the 1956 Sinai War. UNEF had been the pride of the UN—the first full-fledged UN peacekeeping force ever put on the ground. Now Egypt was conveying its aggressive intentions by demanding that the UN pull its peacekeepers back. One of the UN's observation posts was at Ras Nasrani, just north of Sharm el-Sheikh, where huge Egyptian artillery guns overlooked the narrow Straits of Tiran—a vital shipping lane that Israel depended on for access to the Red Sea and ultimately the Indian Ocean.

The Egyptian call for withdrawing UNEF troops should have gone directly to the UN General Assembly. Back in 1957, Israel had withdrawn from Sinai and the Gaza Strip on the understanding that it had a solid commitment from the UN secretary-general at the time, Dag Hammarskjöld, that any Egyptian request to withdraw UNEF in the future would have to go through the General Assembly. The American secretary of state, John Foster Dulles, had confirmed Israel's understanding of this UN commitment.[7] But Hammarskjöld's successor, U Thant, ignored this promise. He tried to call the Egyptians' bluff about the UN peacekeepers by ruling that their request for a partial UNEF pullout was unacceptable. Explaining to Egypt's UN ambassador that UNEF "cannot be asked to stand aside in order to enable the two sides to resume fighting," he said that "a request for the temporary withdrawal of UNEF would be considered tantamount to a request for the complete withdrawal of UNEF from Gaza and Sinai." With this "all or nothing" approach, U Thant expected Nasser to fold. It was a bad miscalculation. The Egyptians came back on May 18 with a formal request signed by their foreign minister "to terminate" the UNEF presence altogether.

U Thant went ahead and ordered UNEF's withdrawal. It was like lighting matches in a gas station. The UN secretary-general himself had predicted what would happen if UNEF were withdrawn when, just months earlier, on September 7, 1966, he reported to the Security Council, "Relations between peoples on opposite sides of the line are such that if the United Nations buffer should be removed, serious fighting would, quite likely, soon be resumed." When confronted with his own report by Israel's UN ambassador, Gideon Rafael, U Thant said he had forgotten that he had authored these conclusions.[8]

Although U Thant had ignored Hammarskjöld's earlier assurances to Israel and refused to take the issue to the General Assembly, he did not take the UNEF decision alone. He had the full support of his UN staff, including Undersecretary-General for Political Affairs Ralph Bunche, the African-American diplomat who had been instrumental in past Arab-Israeli diplomacy.[9] In other words, the UNEF failure was not just a deficiency of this particular secretary-general; it was a broader UN failure.

U Thant still felt he could deal with Nasser personally and decided to fly to Egypt to launch a new diplomatic initiative. But on May 22, as the secretary-general's aircraft was en route from New York to Cairo, Nasser announced that he was closing the Straits of Tiran, thereby enacting a blockade against Israeli shipping. It was an act of war.

Nasser had been a pan-Arab savior since the withdrawal of the British and the French from the Suez Canal in 1956. He had intervened in the politics of Algeria, Lebanon, Syria, Jordan, and Yemen, where he dispatched a huge expeditionary army in 1962. Nasser's air force even bombed Saudi border towns close to the Yemeni border as he sought to extend his power within the oil-rich Arabian Peninsula. The Egyptian leader was also being courted by Moscow; in 1964 he had been designated as a "Hero of the Soviet Union."[10] Soviet admirals were making regular pilgrimages to Egypt at this time, seeking naval and air bases to counter the U.S. Sixth Fleet. Nasser would not stand down from a confrontation with Israel. The UN secretary-general mistakenly felt that the Egyptian leader could be dealt with. Nasser did not need to be understood; he needed to be deterred.

Once in Cairo, U Thant did not take a forceful stand against the blockade. In Egypt, he came up with a proposal that was hauntingly reminiscent of his failed personal diplomacy with the Soviets during the Cuban Missile Crisis. Engaging in the same moral equivalence, he suggested to Nasser that Egypt lift its blockade of Israel for two weeks and in exchange he would ask the Israelis to stop using the Straits of Tiran for the same period of time—which would have the same effect as the Egyptian blockade.[11] Thus, U Thant was comparing Egypt's right to engage in an act of war with Israel's right to use international waters for peaceful commerce. He had undermined the UN's goal of advancing international principles that protected a world order based on peaceful relations between states. And the appeasement effort didn't even work. Nasser declined the offer, and the secretary-general left Cairo empty-handed.

The UN Security Council did not convene to discuss the Egyptian-Syrian crisis until the morning of May 24, at the initiative of Canada and Denmark. The Soviet representative made it immediately clear that the USSR would block further UN action: "The Soviet delegation deems it necessary to stress that it does not see sufficient grounds for such a hasty convening of the Security Council and for the artificially dramatic climate fostered by the representatives of some Western powers."[12] One UN ambassador after another from the Soviet bloc or the Afro-Asian group repeated the Soviet line. Even France, which since 1956 had been a loyal ally of Israel, now turned against the Jewish state, as its ambassador suggested that the UN needed more time for "careful study" of the issues involved— "careful study" being a synonym, in the words of the Israeli ambassador, for "doing nothing."[13] Israeli foreign minister Abba Eban later cynically summarized the main thrust of the UN Security Council debate: "The mere imminence of war was no reason for convening the tribunal charged with the preservation of peace."[14]

President Lyndon Johnson's administration watched the UN's inept diplomacy and tried to launch a last-minute initiative of its own to solve the Middle East crisis. Although leaders of the Senate Foreign Relations Committee still called for a "multilateral" solution when Secretary of State Dean Rusk appeared before the group in late May, President Johnson was more realistic. The president told his advisers, "I want to play every card in the UN, but I've never re-

lied on it to save me when I'm going down for the third time."[15] The
U.S. ambassador to the UN, Arthur Goldberg, characterized U
Thant as "weak-kneed" in his treatment of Nasser; the National Se-
curity Council felt it was necessary to "stiffen his spine."[16]

Ultimately, however, the Johnson team took few measures. Looking to go outside the UN, Johnson explored the possibility of the
United States joining with other maritime powers to form a naval
force that could reopen the Straits of Tiran. The United States ap-
proached eighteen maritime nations to send ships. Only Australia
and the Netherlands agreed. Even the British went soft.[17] With the
failure of this idea for international intervention, it became clear
that Israel was alone.

## WAR

The UN's failure to provide even the most minimal signal that
Nasser's aggressive moves were unacceptable encouraged other
Arab states to join forces with Egypt against Israel. Syria did not need
any encouragement to mass its army in the Golan Heights to Israel's
north. But in early June, even Jordan's King Hussein, who had been
a pro-Western rival of Nasser, flew to Cairo and placed his armed
forces under Egyptian command. Hussein then agreed to allow other
neighboring states to put their troops in Jordan, whose territory was
geographically closest to Israel's main cities. Two Egyptian com-
mando battalions joined nine Jordanian brigades that were poised to
strike Israel from the Jordanian-controlled West Bank. And one-third
of the Iraqi army traversed Jordanian territory and was positioned to
cross the Jordan River by the morning of June 5, 1967.

Nasser had unveiled his intentions before an Arab Trade Union
Congress on May 26: "The battle will be a general one and our basic
objective will be to destroy Israel."[18] By early June, the combined
force ringing Israel's borders had grown to 250,000 troops, more
than 2,000 tanks, and 700 front-line aircraft.[19] The Israeli air force
had only a few airfields, while the Arab states had many more spread

out over the Middle East. Israel could not absorb the first blow; it had no strategic depth, with Jordanian forces massing in the West Bank, only nine miles from the coastal city of Netanya and just two miles from Israel's international airport. As time went on, more and more Arab expeditionary forces—mostly from Iraq—reached the front lines. The UN did nothing to halt this buildup.

Surrounded, Israel decided to preempt the expected assault from the coalition of Arab armies. Still, Israel initially acted only against Egypt, which had already engaged in an act of war through its blockade of the Straits of Tiran. So on the morning of June 5, some two hundred Israeli aircraft headed for Egypt's airfields and destroyed the Egyptian air force on the ground.

Israel hoped that by concentrating its relatively small military forces against one adversary alone, it could keep Egypt's war partners out of the fighting. In fact, the same morning that it launched its preemptive strike on Egypt, Israel passed a message to Jordan's King Hussein through General Odd Bull, the UN Truce Supervision Observer force commander in Jerusalem: If Jordan maintained the cease-fire along the 1949 armistice lines, then Israel would not attack Jordan.[20] Using the UN as a conduit for such a delicate message was extremely problematic; indeed, General Bull resented the message he was asked to deliver, arguing that it was "a threat, pure and simple" and adding that the UN should not be involved in passing on threats from one state to another.[21] Again a senior UN official was judging a state under siege more harshly than it was judging a state that had joined a coalition dedicated to an aggressive assault against a UN member state.

The fighting quickly escalated, as the Jordanian leadership ignored Israel's communication and picked up the fight against Israel. More than a thousand Israeli civilians were wounded in the Jordanian assault, but Israel held its fire until Jordanian ground troops crossed into Jerusalem and actually seized Government House, the UN headquarters in Jerusalem.[22] Syria, meanwhile, sent bombers to attack Israel's oil refineries in Haifa Bay. In response, Israel launched air strikes that destroyed two-thirds of the Syrian air force.[23] Finally, Iraqi bombers attacked Israel, prompting an Israeli counterstrike. In each case, the Israeli military was clearly responding to prior acts of war initiated against it.

By June 10, 1967, the map of the Middle East had changed. Israel had captured the Gaza Strip and the Sinai Peninsula in its entirety right up to the Suez Canal, destroying the Egyptian military that had threatened a mass invasion just a week earlier. Israeli forces had also captured the West Bank from Jordan and dismantled its military potential in that territory completely. They recovered the Old City of Jerusalem, from which Jewish worshipers had been denied access since the city fell to the Arab Legion in 1948. Finally, Israel took over the Golan Heights from Syria, clearing away Syrian artillery and armor that had shelled northern Israeli villages for more than a decade.

The UN, whose acts of omission and commission had ignited the 1967 Six-Day War, quickly shifted its focus from the military situation on the ground to deciding the terms of any postwar diplomacy. The UN role in the conflict up until this point had been a dismal failure: it had directly contributed to Egypt's planned invasion, enabled the outbreak of the war, and then stayed largely passive once the armies engaged, even after its Jerusalem headquarters had been overrun by the Jordanians. By contrast, the UN would take a far more active role in determining the terms of the postwar settlement. Even here, however, it would undercut its own achievements.

## RESOLVING THE CONFLICT

The UN position after the Six-Day War was shaped by the diplomatic clash between the superpowers. The Soviet Union pressed the UN Security Council to link any cease-fire resolution to a call for Israel's withdrawal to the lines that were in place on June 4, 1967, before the war. President Lyndon Johnson firmly opposed any such linkage, however, and the Security Council adopted just a call for a cease-fire.[24] A Soviet draft resolution in the Security Council on June 14 condemning Israel's "aggressive activities" additionally failed, receiving only four votes out of fifteen.[25]

Perhaps because of the U.S. stance in the Security Council, Moscow shifted the debate on the Six-Day War to an Emergency Special Session of the General Assembly, convened on June 19, 1967. Here, then, was Dean Acheson's Uniting for Peace resolution being turned against the United States and its allies. Soviet premier Alexei Kosygin came from Moscow to lead the Soviet delegation. He condemned Israel as the aggressor. Establishing Israel as the aggressor was important for the Soviet diplomatic agenda, which was to restore the prewar situation. In particular, the Soviets wanted Israel to immediately withdraw all its forces from the territories it had captured. In exchange, the Soviet ambassador to Washington, Anatoly Dobrynin, worked out a formula that struck the Israeli ambassador to the United Nations, Gideon Rafael, as only "a vague and noncommittal undertaking" by the Arab states to halt their hostility.[26] As Secretary of State Dean Rusk put it, the Soviets were trying to trade "a horse for a rabbit."[27]

The United States and most of its Western allies preferred to use the new situation to bring about a negotiated settlement of the Arab-Israeli conflict. But it was also important for Washington to defeat the Soviet diplomatic onslaught, since the superpowers were in a strategic struggle for influence in the Middle East. Following the Six-Day War, the Soviet Navy tripled the size of its Mediterranean fleet and began flying surveillance missions over the U.S. Sixth Fleet from Egyptian airfields.[28] (Years later the Soviets would convert the Syrian port of Tartus into the primary base for their Mediterranean fleet's submarines. Airfields in Syria and Libya, not only in Egypt, came to host Soviet Naval Aviation.) Moscow retained a strong interest in the Suez Canal as a means to reinforce its positions in the Indian Ocean and Persian Gulf and as a supply line to North Vietnam.[29]

President Johnson was aware of this new struggle and tried to check Soviet advances. The Israeli army had defeated Soviet arms on the battlefield. It was now up to American diplomacy to decisively beat back Soviet initiatives at the UN. On June 19, the same day that

the Emergency Special Session of the UN General Assembly convened, President Johnson gave a major speech outlining U.S. policy.
First, he said that Israel should not withdraw its forces to the prewar
armistice lines: "This is not a prescription for peace, but for a re-
newal of hostilities." Second, Johnson spoke about the need for
peace agreements. The agreements that had ended the Sinai War in
1957, when Israel withdrew from Sinai, had not ensured peace; they
had only set the stage for a renewed round of warfare ten years later.
Third, Johnson addressed the need to respect the territorial integrity and political independence of all states in the Middle East.
Therefore he was rejecting the legitimacy of the prewar threats to
destroy Israel. The president's speech also touched on maritime
rights, justice for refugees, and the interests of all three great reli-
gions in Jerusalem.[30]

It was no surprise, then, that the Soviets had chosen to go to the
General Assembly. That strategy allowed them to circumvent the
American veto in the Security Council. Just as important, the Soviets
were convinced that the combined strength of the Soviet bloc and
the Third World states would push their political agenda through
the General Assembly. Despite what the United States and its Western allies maintained, the Soviets wanted to condemn Israel as the aggressor in the conflict. And so they drafted a resolution for the General Assembly that stated that Israel was "in gross violation of the
Charter of the United Nations" and had "committed a premeditated
and previously prepared aggression."

Yet while the General Assembly in the mid-1960s was already
stacked against Israel, the Soviets ultimately failed to achieve their
goal. Their resolution was not adopted. The UN Emergency Special
Session on the Six-Day War deliberated for close to two months. In
the end, the overwhelming majority of the international community
recognized that Israel could not be considered the aggressor in the
Six-Day War. Even though the Israelis had fired the first shot against
Egypt on the morning of June 5, 1967, that had come in response to
Egypt's blockade of the Straits of Tiran two weeks earlier, an act of
war against Israel. And along other fronts, with Syria, Iraq, and Jor-

dan, Israeli military operations began only after Israel's opponents opened fire. The facts spoke for themselves. For that reason, the repeated efforts to brand Israel as the aggressor in 1967 simply failed.[31]

This perception of Israel as a victim of aggression also affected the debates in the UN Security Council. After the Six-Day War, the Security Council began drafting a resolution that would become the foundation of the Arab-Israeli peace process for the next thirty-five years. Resolution 242, which was adopted in November 1967, would provide the agreed basis for the 1979 Egyptian-Israeli Treaty of Peace, the 1991 Madrid Peace Conference, the 1993 Oslo Accords, and the 1994 Treaty of Peace between Israel and Jordan. Every word and phrase in Resolution 242 was carefully crafted. The resolution ultimately reflected the Western view that Israel was not the aggressor in the Six-Day War but rather had waged a war of self-defense.

In the Security Council's debate, the resolution's withdrawal clause became the key issue. Under international law, legal rights to captured territory after a war sprang from the circumstances in which it was lost and gained by a disputant. Three years later, in 1970, a seminal article on the status of the territories Israel captured in the Six-Day War came from Stephen Schwebel, who would serve as a legal adviser to the U.S. Department of State and later as a judge on the International Court of Justice in The Hague. Writing in the *American Journal of International Law,* Schwebel argued, "Where the prior holder of territory had seized that territory unlawfully, the state which subsequently takes that territory in the lawful exercise of self-defense has, against that prior holder, better title."[32]

The U.S. government did not wholeheartedly adopt this position at the time of the debates on Resolution 242, but even as its UN delegation suggested that peace depended on an Israeli withdrawal, it stipulated that this withdrawal must be to "secure and recognized boundaries." In addition, the United States was careful not to make any "quantitative judgment on the scope of the withdrawal or of the territorial change."[33] The British agreed. Foreign Secretary George Brown told Israeli foreign minister Abba Eban that Britain would advocate Israeli withdrawal only in the context of a permanent peace, to secure recognized boundaries that Israel determined were satisfactory for its security.[34]

One reason the Western allies were so concerned with secure boundaries was that the old armistice lines from 1949 were not recognized international borders. Though these boundaries would come to be known in political shorthand years later as the 1967 borders, they were simply lines separating armies that had fought one another back in 1948. This was especially true of the Israeli-Jordanian armistice lines. The armistice agreement that both sides reached specifically stated, "No provision of this Agreement shall in any way prejudice the rights, claims, and positions of either Party hereto in the peaceful settlement of the Palestine question, the provisions of this Agreement being dictated exclusively by military considerations." This clause was put into the armistice at the insistence of Jordanian negotiators. In short, the previous lines separating Israel from the recently captured West Bank and Gaza Strip had no international political standing.

Furthermore, key elements of the previous territorial status quo had been illegal. After all, Jordan had invaded the West Bank and part of Jerusalem in 1948 in what UN secretary-general Trygve Lie had called at the time an act of aggression. True, the UN Security Council took no special action against Jordan, but the international community did not treat the West Bank as Jordanian sovereign territory either. Jordan's annexation of the West Bank was recognized by only two countries, Great Britain and Pakistan—the former adding that its recognition did not extend to East Jerusalem. Moreover, Egypt had invaded the Gaza Strip in 1948. The Syrians had grabbed small but strategically significant pockets of Israeli territory from 1949 and 1967. Was this land to be returned? To force Israel back to the prewar 1967 lines would be rewarding the aggression undertaken by the Arab states in 1948 and years afterward.

There was also the special case of Jerusalem. According to the UN Partition Resolution of 1947, Jerusalem was supposed to become a separate internationalized city. The UN failed to create that regime, but to ask Israel to withdraw from East Jerusalem and turn the Old City over to the Jordanians would not create a situation any more satisfactory than Israel ruling the city by itself. To restore the *status quo ante* in Jerusalem would mean accepting a situation in which Jews were prevented from praying at their holy sites and Christian rights were circumscribed. These historical dilemmas would be reflected in the language that eventually went into Resolution 242.

The British ambassador to the UN, Lord Caradon, took the lead. On November 16, 1967, he produced a new draft resolution that took into account various drafts that nonpermanent members of the Security Council had submitted in October, as well as the language the United States was considering.[35] The British proposal called for "withdrawal of Israeli armed forces from territories occupied in the recent conflict" and balanced this clause with another that recognized the right of all states in the Middle East to live within "secure and recognized boundaries." In the preamble Lord Caradon included a phrase that many Third World countries had advocated: "the inadmissibility of the acquisition of territory by war." The placement in the preamble was significant, for it removed the language from the operative part of the resolution, the part that states were supposed to implement. In any case, the phrase did not preclude the acquisition of territory by means other than war—such as negotiation.

The Arab states did not like the British use of the term "recognized boundaries," as they still refused to recognize the State of Israel. Then the Soviets objected to the lack of the definite article before the word "territories," claiming that this ambiguity would allow Israel to withdraw from some but not all of the territories it had captured. The Soviet representative thus insisted that the word "all" be placed before "territories" ("withdrawal of Israeli armed forces from *all* the territories occupied in the recent conflict [emphasis added]"), but Lord Caradon adamantly rejected the Soviet ambassador's effort to amend Britain's careful wording.[36]

The British prevailed at the UN, with America's help. What looked like diplomatic nitpicking to an outsider became the basis for a drama between the United States and the Soviet Union over the word "the." On November 21, 1967, the Soviet leader, Alexei

Kosygin, sent a message directly to President Johnson insisting once more that the definite article "the" be placed before the word "territories." The Soviet premier still maintained that Israel was the aggressor. Johnson firmly rejected Moscow's last-minute effort and deflected any Soviet initiatives to get him to change his mind.[37]

On November 22, the UN Security Council adopted Resolution 242, which preserved the British language in the withdrawal clause. Even the Soviet Union voted for the resolution, despite the fact that it called for Israeli withdrawal only from "territories," not from "the territories" or "all the territories." The Security Council, in fact, unanimously adopted the resolution. Resolution 242 did not call for reestablishing the former armistice agreements in exchange for any Israeli withdrawal; rather, it emphasized the need to terminate the state of belligerency between Israel and its neighbors.

Arab diplomats argued that Israel had achieved only a partial victory by getting the definite article "the" dropped from Resolution 242's withdrawal clause, because the French text of the resolution still called for withdrawal and stipulated *des territoires.*" This was a legal stretch, since in the idiomatic translation of English into French, frequently what appears in English as indefinite is rendered definite in French, with no change in the meaning of the original term; in fact, the French ambassador to the UN at the time insisted that the French text was "identical" to the original English text.[38] At best, Arab diplomats could argue that there was some ambiguity in the French version. But even this discrepancy between the English and French versions of Resolution 242 would be somewhat overstated, since according to international practice, in cases of conflicting texts the original text serves as the authoritative point of reference.

This practice would be warranted particularly in the case of Resolution 242, since it was drafted by the British, who best understood the intent behind the language that they chose. And the entire negotiation over Resolution 242 was conducted with reference to the English text. (British foreign secretary George Brown would clearly summarize that intent in 1970: "The proposal said 'Israel would withdraw from territories that were occupied,' not 'from the territories,' which means that Israel will not withdraw from all the territories.") In any event, ten of the fifteen members of the UN Security Council in 1967 were English-speaking countries and only three were French-speaking.[39] In short, it was clear that the UN did not require Israel to withdraw to the 1967 lines.

Even the Soviet Union seemed to have thrown in the towel and accepted that Resolution 242 did not imply a full Israeli withdrawal. The language left open the possibility of modifying the previous armistice line, which the Soviets' deputy foreign minister, Vasily Kuznetsov, admitted when he said, "There is certainly much leeway for different interpretations that retain for Israel the right to establish new boundaries and to withdraw its troops only as far as the lines it judges convenient."[40]

Securing passage of Resolution 242 was a great victory for the United States and its Western allies. For decades afterward the United States preserved the letter and spirit of Resolution 242's territorial clauses, as Washington reinforced the understanding that the resolution did not compel the Israelis to withdraw to the 1967 lines. For a short while in 1969, Secretary of State William Rogers was willing to speak only about "insubstantial alterations" in the pre-1967 lines, but subsequent secretaries of state never repeated this language.[41] President Ford wrote to Prime Minister Yitzhak Rabin in September 1975 that the United States "would give great weight" to the idea of Israel "remaining on the Golan Heights." President Ronald Reagan took what had been quiet diplomatic assurances and made them part of a public address to the American people on September 1, 1982: "In the pre-1967 borders, Israel was barely ten miles wide at its narrowest point. The bulk of Israel's population lived within artillery range of hostile Arab armies. I am not about to ask Israel to live that way again." Reagan's secretary of state, George Shultz, continued this line by declaring emphatically on September 16, 1988, "Israel will never negotiate from or return to the lines of partition or to the 1967 borders." In the Madrid Peace Conference of October 1991, President George H. W. Bush did not call for a full Israeli pullout; he put forward a vision of a peace settlement based on "territorial compromise." President Clinton's secretary of state, Warren Christopher, maintained that tradition on January 17, 1997, when he wrote a letter of assurances to Prime Minister Benjamin Netanyahu stating that Israel was entitled to "defensible borders."

Finally, President George W. Bush brought all those assurances together in his April 14, 2004, letter to Prime Minister Ariel Sharon, in which he wrote, "Israel must have secure and recognized borders, which should emerge from negotiations between the parties in accordance with UNSC Resolutions 242 and 338. In light of new realities on the ground, including already existing major Israeli population centers, it is unrealistic to expect that the outcome of final status negotiations will be a full and complete return to the armistice lines of 1949." The president also included the term "defensible borders."

Another aspect of Resolution 242 reflected the strong influence of the United States: It did not mention Jerusalem at all. Years later, the U.S. ambassador to the UN at the time the resolution was adopted, Arthur Goldberg, explained that "this omission was deliberate," as the U.S. government did want to describe Jerusalem as "occupied territory." According to Goldberg, President Johnson and the Department of State had ordered this policy directly. With this omission, the U.S. delegation tried to draw a distinction between the status of Jerusalem and that of the rest of the West Bank.[42]

Thus, despite the haggling involved in arriving at Resolution 242, in the end the UN did what it what was supposed to do: It articulated the principles for resolving a conflict. Unfortunately, in the years ahead it would undermine its own principles.


## REGRESSION


Resolution 242 was an important achievement for the UN, which had failed so miserably when U Thant agreed to pull out UNEF peacekeepers. The UN had not been coaxed into rewarding aggression, as Soviet diplomats had hoped it would be. It had come up with a flexible and realistic model for peacemaking that would provide an agreed framework for future negotiations between Israel and its neighbors.

But in fact, this achievement was not really a reflection of the UN's ability to resolve international conflicts. Rather, it was the direct result of the determined and coordinated efforts of the United States and its allies. Indeed, during the framing of Resolution 242, the Johnson administration had been directing U.S. actions at the highest level, and it forced Moscow to adopt Washington's language for resolving the conflict. The United States had skillfully outmaneuvered the Soviets.

Absent the strong and principled vision that the United States and Britain championed, the UN reverted to form. U Thant appointed Gunnar Jarring, Sweden's former UN ambassador, as his special representative to promote an agreement between Israel and the Arab states in accordance with Resolution 242. On February 8, 1971, Jarring took it upon himself to submit an aide-mémoire to Israel that reinterpreted Resolution 242 as requiring a full withdrawal.[43] In its February 25 response to Jarring, the Israeli government wrote, "Israel will not withdraw from the pre–June 1967 lines," thereby reasserting its legal rights under Resolution 242.

Over the next three decades, the UN General Assembly would adopt resolutions that contradicted the essence of what had been written in Resolution 242. For example, on December 5, 1975, the General Assembly adopted Resolution 3414, which stated that "a just and lasting settlement" of the Arab-Israeli conflict must be based on "the total withdrawal from all the Arab territories occupied since June 1967."[44] The General Assembly was trying to rewrite Resolution 242, which made clear that parties to the Arab-Israeli conflict would have to reach a peace settlement among themselves that identified the borders to which Israel would withdraw. In the 1990s, after Jordan declared that it had disengaged from the West Bank and the Palestinians assumed its role, the UN General Assembly described both the West Bank and East Jerusalem as "occupied Palestinian territory."[45] On December 2, 1998, the General Assembly adopted a resolution calling for "the withdrawal of Israel from the Palestinian territory occupied since 1967." Finally, in response to President George W. Bush's April 2004 letter to Prime Minister Sharon describ-

ing a "full and complete" withdrawal as "unrealistic," the UN General
Assembly asserted the exact opposite. The resolution adopted on
May 7, 2004, called for "two viable, sovereign, and independent
states, Israel and Palestine, based on its pre-1967 borders."

With this language, no room was left for territorial compromise.
It appeared that the Security Council was saying one thing about Israel's borders and the General Assembly was saying something entirely different. Clearly the General Assembly's statements conflicted
with the Security Council's Resolution 242, which created the possibility that Israel could retain part of the West Bank or Gaza Strip territory so that it would achieve "secure and recognized boundaries."
Despite what the Security Council's resolution had outlined, the
General Assembly was prejudging any future negotiation by approving language that already assigned the entire territory to the Palestinian side.

UN secretary-general Kofi Annan also degraded the achievement
made in Resolution 242. On March 12, 2002, Annan declared that
Israel had to terminate its "illegal occupation" of the West Bank and
the Gaza Strip: "To the Israelis I say: you have the right to live in
peace and security within secure internationally recognized borders.
But you must end the illegal occupation."[46] But again, Resolution
242 clearly showed that the borders to which Israel would withdraw
had to be defined in peace treaties involving Israel and its neighbors. Israel was never expected just to pick up and pull back to the
pre-1967 lines, for Resolution 242 was not self-enforcing. In regard
to West Bank and Gaza Strip territory, Israel needed to reach a negotiated agreement with a Palestinian peace partner.

Essentially, Annan was undercutting a Security Council resolution with his own politicized view of Israel's legal responsibilities.
Additionally, Resolution 242 linked Israel's withdrawal from territory to the end of the state of belligerency on the Arab side. Annan
demanded that Israel "end the illegal occupation" but did not say a
word about the requirement that the Palestinians, or other Arab
parties, make peace. Later, Annan's spokesman, Fred Eckhart, explained that the secretary had been speaking "politically," not

"legally." Yet Eckhart admitted that this was the first time that Annan had called the Israeli presence in the West Bank and Gaza Strip illegal.

Annan's statement completely undermined future peacemaking efforts, and it did not go unnoticed. It was all over the media. The *New York Times,* for example, featured his remark as its "Quote of the Day" on March 13, 2002. A week later, Professor George P. Fletcher of Columbia Law School wrote in the *New York Times,* "A new provocative label of 'illegality' is now out of the chute and running loose, ready to wreak damage. The worst prospect is that Palestinians will dig in with a new feeling of righteousness and believe that the international community will force Israel to withdraw from its 'illegal occupation.' "[47]

The entire episode with Resolution 242 and its aftermath revealed the flaws in the UN. While the UN could successfully resolve conflicts, at the same time it could undermine its own achievements. In 1967, it was as clear as day who the aggressor was—the Nasserist-led Arab state coalition—and who the victim of aggression was: Israel. Thirty years later those historical facts remained unchanged. Yet the UN erased this original context and altered the terms of its own original resolution.

Significantly, the problems could not be blamed on Cold War tensions alone. After all, the UN Security Council adopted Resolution 242 despite Soviet-American tensions, which were high in 1967. But the UN eroded Resolution 242, and the flaws that caused that erosion were intrinsic to what the UN had become: With its Third World majority and the amoral ethos followed by members of its Secretariat, it could not defend the principles on which it was founded or even the resolutions its own Security Council adopted.

Many observers missed the signs, however. As a result, when the Cold War ended, many believed that the UN would finally meet the expectations that Roosevelt and Truman originally had for the organization back in 1945—that it would stop aggression, assure world peace, and prevent the crimes against humanity that had occurred in the Second World War.

# CHAPTER 5

# The Return of the UN?

*The 1991 Gulf War Victory and the Lead-up to Another War*

**A**t first glance, the victory in the 1991 Gulf War looked like a harbinger of the UN's return to playing a vital role in international security. After all, the UN had responded swiftly to a case of naked aggression: The Security Council had authorized the use of force against Iraq after Saddam Hussein's unprovoked invasion of Kuwait. This was precisely the role the UN's founders had intended the organization to play.[1] The reason the UN was working at last, it seemed, was that the end of the Cold War had eliminated the American-Soviet tensions that had gummed up the UN machinery for so long. Indeed, instead of neutralizing each other in the Security Council, the United States and the USSR (which would not dissolve until August 1991) actually worked together on Iraq. Brian Urquhart, the right-hand man of past UN secretaries-general, would call the Gulf War "the first exercise in the unanimous collective security that we've been talking about since the days of Woodrow Wilson."[2]

UN advocates like Urquhart were euphoric that the organization had returned to center stage in world politics. There were good reasons for this enthusiasm. First, the UN had worked quickly. The Security Council convened just eleven hours after the first Iraqi troops crossed the Kuwaiti frontier on August 2, 1990; that same day, the council adopted a resolution condemning the invasion and calling on Iraq to withdraw. Second, the key UN members had worked, for the most part, in unison. Each of the five permanent members of the Security Council—the United States, the Soviet Union, the United Kingdom, France, and China—condemned the attack. Third, the UN had clearly and repeatedly condemned Iraq's action. Every UN resolution on Iraq invoked Chapter VII of the UN Charter, which deals with cases of aggression. Finally, with Resolution 678 the UN explicitly "authorized" member states "to use all necessary means to uphold and implement" its earlier call for Iraq to withdraw—that is, it authorized the use of force. This language was even clearer than the wording the UN had used in the Korean War.[3]

But missed amid all the excitement were the significant faults in the UN that the Persian Gulf crisis had exposed. Few stopped to ask whether the UN could have prevented the Iraqi attack on Kuwait in the first place. The UN had in fact had opportunities to take action against Iraq earlier. For example, when Saddam Hussein ordered the Iraqi army to invade Iran on September 21–22, 1980, it was no less an act of aggression than his conquest of Kuwait ten years later. Why hadn't the UN responded then?

Despite the clear case of aggression in 1980, the UN Security Council did not condemn Iraq. The problem wasn't simply the Cold War, for when the Iraq-Iran War broke out, the superpowers were largely in agreement that they would remain neutral; only in mid-decade did Kuwait draw in the United States and the USSR to take a position against Iranian air attacks on Kuwaiti oil tankers.[4] In 1980, Saddam had political immunity, because it was difficult to mobilize an anti-Iraqi consensus. One issue was that some nations did not want to jeopardize their lucrative arrangements with Iraq. France, Germany, and the Soviet Union were among the countries making money off of Iraqi oil and by supplying arms to Saddam's regime. The Soviets had supplied Iraq with 180-mile range Scud-B missiles, and French and German companies made fortunes extending the range of those missiles to nearly 400 miles—long enough to strike Tehran to the east and Tel Aviv to the west. Moreover, Iraq had the backing of key Arab partners at the time, like Kuwait and Saudi Arabia, who had influence in the West. Finally, to the Carter administration, Iran was a pariah state, for it had taken Americans hostage.

The UN was supposed to defend the principles of the UN Charter and not just reflect the sum total of its members' interests. But UN secretary-general Kurt Waldheim didn't try to prod members of the Security Council into taking a more forceful position against Iraqi aggression.[5] He offered his "good offices" to both Iran and Iraq to settle their conflict by peaceful means. He was carefully balanced, not fixing any blame on the aggressor, Saddam Hussein.[6] Thus, even though Waldheim himself brought the Iraq-Iran War to the attention of the Security Council on September 23, 1980, defining it as a threat to "the maintenance of international security," the Security Council just backed the secretary-general's evenhanded offer of "good offices." Five days later it finally adopted Resolution 479, calling on both Iran and Iraq "to refrain immediately from any further use of force."

Essentially, the UN was calling for a cease-fire without demanding that Iraqi forces withdraw from Iranian territory.[7] Meanwhile, the Iraqi attack force was advancing rapidly into Iran; the Iranian city of Khorramshahr, in the oil-rich province of Khuzistan, had already fallen to the Iraqi army. The UN's moral equivalence was yet again rewarding aggression. As a result, Iran adamantly refused to have anything to do with the UN Security Council for years, until the final phases of the war.

The 1991 Gulf War also revealed how the UN had failed to deal with the spread of weapons of mass destruction. The International Atomic Energy Agency (IAEA), which was under the aegis of the UN, was supposed to verify that states were complying with the 1968 Nuclear Nonproliferation Treaty, whose objective was to halt the spread of nuclear weapons. Iraq was a party to the treaty and even served on the IAEA's Board of Governors from 1980 through 1988 and again from 1989 through 1991. Yet there were signs that the Iraqis were not honoring their commitments. The first was their Osiraq nuclear reactor, which Jacques Chirac, as French prime minister in the 1970s, had been instrumental in supplying to Iraq. The IAEA stated that the Iraqis were not using the reactor for a nuclear weapons program, but Israel refused to rely on IAEA safeguards. In 1981 an Israeli bombing raid destroyed Saddam's French-supplied Osiraq reactor. The UN

Security Council immediately condemned Israel for this action. A decade later, however, it would become clear how important the raid had been; after the Gulf War, the U.S. secretary of defense, Richard Cheney, thanked the Israelis for the strike.

After the Gulf War, the IAEA learned that the Iraqis had been completing a secret nuclear weapons program right under its inspectors' noses. The IAEA inspectors had been duped. The agency's director-general, Swedish diplomat Hans Blix, would admit, "It's correct to say that the IAEA was fooled by the Iraqis."[8]

Right up until the Gulf War the IAEA had averred that Saddam Hussein was adhering to the Nuclear Nonproliferation Treaty. The entire episode demonstrated that this critical UN body had failed to detect what the Iraqis were doing and to deter Saddam from violating the nonproliferation treaty. Incidentally, the weakness of the IAEA system would be exposed again in 2003, when Iran's and Libya's secret nuclear programs came to light; both states had been Nuclear Nonproliferation Treaty signatories and been under IAEA scrutiny for years.

Remarkably, when the UN needed to find a new head weapons inspector for Iraq in 2000, it settled on the man who had overseen the IAEA's failures in the 1980s, Hans Blix. He was chosen because the Russians and the French wanted someone who would not be "too aggressive" with the Iraqis. The problem with Blix, and the UN more generally, was that he usually accepted Iraq's declarations. He did not approach Iraq as an evil regime that had systematically violated its international legal obligations. Instead, he many times spoke about the need to "show respect" for those his team was dealing with. His inspectors were given "cultural sensitivity" courses. As a result, he was easily misled. In his multilateral universe, it was important to treat all states that signed the Nuclear Nonproliferation Treaty in a similar fashion, whether they had a record of aggression or not.

Perhaps the greatest fault of the UN was that it stood by while genocide occurred. The UN had been established in 1945 with two recent historical experiences in the background: the Nazi aggression against Europe and the horrors of the Holocaust. And if the UN was to fulfill the purpose its founders had envisioned, it not only had to counter aggression effectively but also had to become assertive when there was the threat of genocide. The UN failed to live up to this latter mission with regard to Iraq, both before and after the 1991 Gulf War.

In the 1980s Saddam Hussein launched an offensive against Iraq's Kurdish minority. The most notorious assault against the Kurds was the March 16, 1988, chemical attack on Halabja, in which five thousand Iraqi Kurds were immediately killed. Thousands more were injured in the three days of attacks. It was known immediately that the Iraqi armed forces used mustard gas and nerve gases like sarin and tabun, while later analyses indicated that they also used VX nerve agent and aflatoxin, which causes liver cancer in its victims after five to seven years.[9] In some cases, the Iraqi chemical weapons caused genetic damage to the Kurds that manifested itself in children born years later.

But the Iraqi assault on the Kurds went far beyond the Halabja attack alone. The attacks had begun in March 1987 with the appointment of Saddam's cousin General Ali Hasan al-Majid, who came to be called "Chemical Ali," as governor of Northern Iraq. During what Baghdad called the Anfal campaign of 1988, between 100,000 and 200,000 Iraqi Kurds were killed, many in mass executions.[10] Kurdish sources charged in February 1988 that about 1.5 million Kurds had been forcibly uprooted from their homes; thousands of Kurdish villages were leveled. Kurdish leaders sought international intervention: Jalal Talabani, who headed the Patriotic Union of Kurdistan, formally accused Saddam's regime of genocide, while Masud Barzani, the head of the Kurdish Democratic Party, appealed to the UN to deter the ongoing chemical attacks.[11]

The Kurds needed international protection, as they did not have a state of their own. At the end of the First World War, the Principal Allied Powers supported Kurdish independence in the 1920 Treaty of Sèvres. But Turkey, Iraq, Iran, and Syria, where the Kurds resided, all opposed the creation of an independent Kurdish state in the decades that followed. Thus by the 1980s, approximately 25 million Kurds were spread over several Middle Eastern states.

Still, the UN response to the suffering of the Iraqi Kurds was belated and, at best, tepid. In July 1987, the UN adopted a resolution calling for a cease-fire in the Iraq-Iran War. Secretary-General Pérez de Cuéllar focused on getting the parties to implement its terms, which required that he maintain an impartial image.[12] Delving into Iraqi wartime atrocities would have undercut this effort. The calculus remained unchanged even after the March 1988 chemical attack on Halabja. The UN Security Council did not adopt a resolution condemning the use of chemical weapons until August 26, 1988, *after* it had achieved the Iraq-Iran cease-fire. Halabja and other Kurdish towns had been gassed five months earlier. It was too little and too late.

Formally, the UN had an excuse. Its officials could argue that the Kurdish issue was an internal Iraqi matter and that therefore the UN had no standing to get involved. Yet Saddam's Kurdish campaign was already an international issue, since it generated 60,000 refugees who sought asylum in Turkey and 150,000 refugees who entered Iran.

The UN had failed to address these problems in the years leading up to the Gulf War, but at war's end in 1991 it would have a second opportunity to demonstrate whether it could protect the human rights of the Iraqi Kurds.

## IGNORING GENOCIDE—AGAIN

The U.S.-led coalition liberated Kuwait and completed its 100-hour land war against Saddam Hussein on February 27, 1991. Within a week a popular rebellion exploded throughout Iraqi Kurdistan. On March 19, Kirkuk, the oil-producing center of Iraqi Kurdistan, fell to Kurdish rebels. Another revolt broke out among the Shiites in southern Iraq. Saddam Hussein would not allow this to continue without a military response, so at the end of March he launched a full Iraqi counteroffensive using heavy weaponry and airpower. As many as a quarter of a million Shiites were probably killed by Saddam's regime.[13] The situation for Shiites in Iraq's southern marshes was particularly severe. The Baath Party newspaper, *Al-Thawra*, claimed in April 1991 that the "Marsh Arabs" were not real Iraqis and it described them as a "monkey-faced" people. It thus set the stage for the ethnic cleansing of the marshes, which included not just straight military attacks but apparently the use of toxic chemicals in the marsh waters. This became evident from the large-scale deaths of animals and birds in the area as well.[14] In the north, the Iraqi army killed some 20,000 Kurds and Turkomans and again forced the Kurds to run for Turkey or Iran—this time more than 1.5 million people. Turkey did not want to give the Kurds asylum; the Kurds feared for their lives and wouldn't return to Iraq. Tens of thousands of Iraqi Kurds were clinging to the frozen mountaintops between the two countries. The situation had exploded into a full-fledged international refugee crisis. And this time the UN could not so easily disavow responsibility. Whereas the Iraq-Iran War had involved the UN only at the very end, with the cease-fire negotiations, the 1991 Gulf War had been authorized by the UN Security Council.

Nevertheless, the UN's action on the Kurdish refugee crisis was decidedly weak. On April 5, 1991, the Security Council adopted Resolution 688. It condemned "the repression of the Iraqi civilian population in many parts of Iraq, including most recently in Kurdish-populated areas." Beyond this declaration, however, it contained extremely watered-down demands. True, it insisted that Iraq allow humanitarian organizations immediate access to the region. But elsewhere the resolution only expressed "the hope that an open dialogue will take place to ensure that the human and political rights of all Iraqi citizens are respected." Finally, it suggested that the secretary-general make another mission to the region and report back to the Security Council. Though the Kurds were being exterminated, the UN was not taking action; it was merely calling for "open dialogue" and reports.

The UN was not about to authorize the use of military force to protect the Kurds. Unlike all the other UN resolutions on Iraq, Resolution 688 contained no reference to Chapter VII of the UN Charter and therefore had no teeth. And even this relatively weak resolution barely passed in the Security Council, achieving just one more than the minimum nine votes required for passage.[15] The Soviet Union had been wary of the resolution because it tended to suspect UN human rights initiatives as a Trojan horse for encouraging hostile minority populations to resist the continued rule of authoritarian regimes. It agreed to vote for Resolution 688 only after a clause was included "reconfirming the commitment of all Member States to respect the sovereignty, territorial integrity and political independence of Iraq."

China, which did not want the UN to try to loosen its hold on Tibet, took a harder line than the Soviets and abstained. India abstained as well. But Third World states like Cuba, Yemen, and Zimbabwe voted against Resolution 688, largely because they were concerned that it set a precedent for the powerful states of the West to intervene inside weak developing countries on humanitarian grounds, ignoring their sovereign rights. To these authoritarian regimes, the Kurds' human rights—including their right to be protected from Saddam Hussein's genocidal policies—were worth sacrificing in order to preserve the absolute rights of state sovereignty.

Resolution 688 did not empower the UN to forcibly enter Iraqi territory to relieve the Kurds, who were dying at a rate of a thousand a day. But the United States and Great Britain decided they could not wait for the UN; they acted by themselves. When President Bush launched Operation Provide Comfort on April 16, 1991, and deployed 12,000 U.S. soldiers in northern Iraq to create a "safe haven" for the Kurds, he did so without any authorization from the UN. Allied military forces led the relief effort, for the UN lacked the emergency capabilities to get to the Kurds quickly.[16] Under U.S. leadership, coalition air forces created a no-fly zone over the Kurdish-populated parts of northern Iraq, again without the approval of the Security Council.

Nongovernmental organizations did a great deal more than the UN to provide a detailed study of Iraqi atrocities against the Kurdish people. Human Rights Watch concluded after an eighteen-month study that genocide had indeed occurred. The organization sought the assistance of several states to press genocide charges against Iraq in the International Court of Justice in The Hague, whose judges were selected by the UN General Assembly and Security Council. Two states agreed to press ahead with the suit against Iraq, but only if at least one European country joined them. Human Rights Watch could not obtain the support of a European state to join the suit.[17] Another UN institution had failed to protect the human rights of the Iraqi Kurds.

## CORRUPTION AND APPEASEMENT

The failure of the UN to address Iraqi human rights abuses against the Kurds was not the only tragedy to break the new image of the UN as a serious contributor to international security after the Cold War. In the 1990s, the UN also managed to erode one of its greatest achievements coming out of the Gulf War—the creation of the weapons-inspection team known as the UN Special Commission (UNSCOM).

On April 3, 1991, with the full involvement of the United States, the UN Security Council had adopted Resolution 687—the Gulf War cease-fire resolution—requiring Iraq to destroy, remove, or render harmless all nuclear, chemical, and biological weapons, as well as missiles with a range greater than 90 miles. To begin this process, Iraq had to disclose the amount of weaponry it still possessed or had destroyed. UNSCOM's job was to inspect Iraqi facilities to confirm that Iraq's declarations were true. The UNSCOM inspectors were also supposed to supervise the destruction of any remaining prohibited materials.

The new inspections were far more robust and intrusive than those the IAEA had conducted in the past. Iraq had easily circumvented those earlier inspections, because they had been limited to designated locations and had always been preannounced. After the Gulf War, however, UNSCOM conducted many inspections without giving prior notice, and the IAEA and UNSCOM were even empowered to dig into the files of Iraqi intelligence agencies.

Under pressure from continuing UN economic sanctions, Iraq destroyed huge quantities of prohibited weapons, many times without any UNSCOM supervision. UNSCOM itself was destroying more weapons than the coalition forces had managed to reach during the Gulf War. It eliminated 690 tons of chemical agents, as well as forty-eight missiles and fifty missile warheads.[18] UNSCOM was a huge success story. And when it became clear that Saddam Hussein had created a huge program to hide his remaining weapons of mass destruction, UNSCOM created a "Concealment Unit" in order to find this missing weaponry. Using careful analysis of captured Iraqi documents, interviews with defectors, and U-2 aerial surveillance photos, UNSCOM showed the Security Council just what illegal weapons Iraq was probably retaining.[19] This was not the UN of U Thant, which had been timid about conducting aerial surveillance missions over Cuba in 1962 in order to verify that the Soviets had withdrawn their missiles.

What many observers of the Iraq situation would forget years later was that the UN put the burden of proof squarely on Iraq for disclosing what had happened with its weapons of mass destruction—not on the inspectors. UNSCOM's job was to determine whether the Iraqis were telling the truth. But whether UNSCOM could continue to conduct the kinds of thorough inspections envisioned in Resolution 687 would depend on the political will of the UN Security Council. And that is where the UN fell down. Indeed, what brought about the demise of UNSCOM was not just the obstructionism of Saddam Hussein, or his French and Russian supporters, but mainly the UN itself.

In particular, the problem was Secretary-General Kofi Annan. The Ghana-born Annan had risen to the top of the UN bureaucracy in January 1997, after the Clinton administration waged a campaign against Secretary-General Boutros Boutros-Ghali. The administration hoped that Annan, a career UN employee, would serve as a force for UN reform, making the organization more acceptable to the

Republican-controlled Congress. But rather than build on UNSCOM's success to show that the UN could cope with post–Cold War international security problems, Annan evolved into UNSCOM's adversary.

After Annan became secretary-general, he appointed Australian diplomat Richard Butler as head of UNSCOM. The former Australian ambassador to the UN had years of arms control experience. Though the secretary-general appointed him, Butler reported to the UN Security Council itself.[20] But to many UN bureaucrats, Butler was an outsider, since he wasn't formally a UN employee (he received his salary from the Australian government). The UN had a built-in interest to encroach on his turf. This may have been exacerbated by the fact that the UNSCOM leadership looked as though it represented the West—Butler was Australian and his deputy, Charles Duelfer, was American—whereas most UN bureaucrats came from Third World countries. Whatever the case, Butler had to deal with interference from the Office of the Secretary-General that his predecessor at UNSCOM, Rolf Ekeus, had not faced.

Annan obstructed Butler in several ways. Most important, he undercut the UN's own attempts to pressure Iraq by greatly expanding a program that allowed Saddam Hussein to circumvent UN sanctions. Back in 1991 the UN Security Council had imposed economic sanctions on Iraqi oil sales abroad because prior to the Gulf War, Iraq had used its oil sales to fund arms purchases and the development of weapons of mass destruction. But then in 1996 the UN had implemented an oil-for-food program, which allowed Saddam's regime to sell oil in order to be able to purchase food and other humanitarian items. The UN was supposed to strictly control these transactions and monitor how the Iraqis used the oil revenue—some $67 billion from 1997 through 2002. By 1998, however, Iraq was openly defying UNSCOM inspectors, refusing to comply with UN resolutions. Without the ability to inspect Iraqi facilities, UNSCOM could not ensure that Saddam Hussein was adhering to the terms of the oil-for-food program; the Iraqi dictator could possibly divert money to nonhumanitarian purposes. Amazingly, on February 1, 1998—precisely at the time when Iraq was defying UNSCOM—Kofi

Annan appeared before the Security Council and recommended more than doubling the oil-for-food program.[21] Why Annan was doing this was unclear. Perhaps he sought to buy Saddam Hussein's goodwill, in anticipation of his own diplomatic initiatives, which would follow shortly. But all he did was give Saddam a huge windfall of income and make Iraqi compliance with UNSCOM's demands even less likely.

In 2004, it would become clear just what Annan had wrought by expanding the so-called oil-for-food program. The U.S. General Accounting Office (GAO) estimated that from 1997 through 2002, Saddam's regime pulled in $10.1 billion in illegal revenues from the UN-managed program.[22] And according to the GAO, the UN's inspectors checked only 7 to 10 percent of the deliveries Iraqis received under the program.[23] Clearly, oil-for-food was full of holes and was not reliable. UN overseers claimed that they had not been aware of this skimming, which would mean that Saddam's regime could have used the billions not simply for personal aggrandizement but also to covertly build up Iraq's weapons programs. Since the doubling of the oil-for-food program occurred just as Iraq was barring UNSCOM inspectors from Iraqi sites, the UN could not monitor whatever illicit programs Iraq was running.

And after the 2003 Iraq War, it became apparent that the corruption in the oil-for-food program ran far deeper. In January 2004 the Iraqi newspaper *al-Mada* published a spreadsheet (in Arabic) that reportedly had been recovered from the Iraqi Oil Ministry. It gave details about how Saddam Hussein had exploited the multibillion-dollar UN program. Specifically, the document indicated that Saddam had given key allies around the world massive kickbacks in the form of vouchers for purchasing Iraqi oil; apparently the vouchers entitled the recipients to buy oil at below-market prices and then profit mightily when a middleman sold the oil to refineries. According to the list published in *al-Mada,* French entities received a total of 150.8 million barrels of crude oil, and the Syrians got 116.9 million barrels, while Russian recipients got more than a billion barrels. France and Russia were key allies of Saddam Hussein on the UN Security Council, so their special status on the list was not surprising. Another name on the list was that of a UN assistant secretary-general, Benon V. Sevan, who was in charge of the oil-for-food program.[24] It is possible, then, that the UN was profiting from this corrupt scheme, although in mid-2004 these allegations were still under investigation. In short, the evidence indicates that by doubling the oil-for-food program, Secretary-General Annan only doubled the amount of kickbacks going to Iraq's friends.

What did not require much further investigation was the fact that Iraq could use this illegal income to rebuild its military capability and thereby undercut UN resolutions. Charles Duelfer, the former UNSCOM deputy executive-director, would replace David Kay in 2004 as head of the CIA's Iraq Survey Group, which sought to find what happened to Iraq's weapons of mass destruction. Duelfer gave congressional testimony on March 30, 2004, in which he disclosed the military impact of the oil-for-food scandals: "Iraq derived several billion dollars between 1999 and 2003 from oil smuggling and kickbacks. . . . This was revenue outside UN control and provided resources the regime could spend without restriction. It channeled much of the illicitly gathered funds to rebuild Iraq's military capabilities through the Military Industrialization Commission, the MIC. The budget of MIC increased nearly 100-fold from 1996 to 2003, with the budget totaling $500 million in 2003. Most of this money came from illicit oil contracts. Iraq imported banned military weapons and dual-use technology through oil-for-food contracts."[25]

Kofi Annan probably did not understand the full implications of what he was doing back in 1998. But it seems clear that the consequences of the oil-for-food program were devastating. Not least, it apparently allowed Saddam Hussein to exploit the UN in order to buy diplomatic protection for himself and prohibited weapons for the Iraqi Army.

After ramping up the oil-for-food program, Annan personally delved into inspecting Iraq's weapons of mass destruction. In February 1998, the secretary-general led a UN mission to Baghdad to meet Saddam Hussein. Iraq had refused to give an accounting of its weaponry, but Annan and the UN did not focus on this flouting of UN resolutions. Instead, Annan made a priority of treating the Iraqi regime with respect and sensitivity. Before the trip, Annan told the BBC how important it was "not to insist on humiliating Saddam Hussein."[26] He had fallen for Iraqi arguments that the UN needed to respect the "dignity" of Iraq. According to this view, UNSCOM inspectors had not been sensitive enough to the needs of Saddam's regime. Significantly, Richard Butler was excluded from the trip. Annan had also succumbed to pressure from two of Iraq's powerful friends: The Russians had pushed the idea of the trip to Baghdad, and French president Jacques Chirac even supplied Annan with his own presidential jet for the mission.[27]

On February 23, 1998, Annan reached a Memorandum of Understanding with the Iraqis. With this agreement, Annan tried to alleviate Iraq's concerns about UNSCOM's inspections. Baghdad had been lobbying to exempt presidential sites—huge areas covering seventy square kilometers and more than a thousand buildings—from the most vigorous UNSCOM inspections. Recognizing that the Iraqis could easily hide illegal weaponry at these sites, Butler had opposed the Iraqi request that diplomats accompany UNSCOM inspectors to these sites, because making this concession would rob UNSCOM of one of its most important advantages: unannounced inspections. The IAEA had failed before the Gulf War in large part because it could not perform inspections without giving prior notice. Nevertheless, Annan acceded to the Iraqis' request and agreed that diplomats would have to accompany weapons inspectors to the presidential sites. Tipped off by friendly diplomats, Iraq would be able to cleanse a site before UNSCOM arrived. Indeed, when UNSCOM and the diplomats reached their first presidential site, all they found were empty buildings that the Iraqis had already sanitized.

Annan's Memorandum of Understanding earned him a hero's welcome when he returned to UN headquarters in New York, with hundreds of staffers applauding him in the lobby. He headed to the UN Security Council to report on what he had achieved. At a press conference he described Saddam Hussein as a man "I can do business with." His criticism was largely reserved for UNSCOM. His senior staff had described the UN weapons inspectors as a bunch of out-of-control "cowboys" who had ignored Iraq's national sensitivities.[28]

Annan and his staff may not have been working against Butler alone. While the U.S. ambassador to the UN, Bill Richardson, had opposed the Annan mission, reports indicated that other parts of the Clinton administration had actually promoted it. The *New York Times* carried a front-page investigative report on February 25, 1998, claiming that the "fingerprints" of Secretary of State Madeleine Albright were all over Annan's accord with Saddam Hussein.[29] Albright had apparently worked out its terms in a secret visit to Annan's Manhattan home on February 15. According to the report, Albright indicated that the United States might launch air strikes against Iraq if Saddam's regime did not honor the agreement—a strike that Annan was trying to forestall.

Despite the excitement at the UN over Annan's Memorandum of Understanding with Iraq, it later became clear that the Iraqis had not conceded much. Annan maintained that the arrangement would govern repeated visits and long-term monitoring of presidential sites, but the Iraqis claimed that Saddam Hussein had granted permission only for a one-shot visit to these sensitive facilities. Annan's diplomatic venture to Baghdad was far from a triumph; he had come back empty-handed. All he had done was to undercut the authority of his own weapons-inspection team.

Kofi Annan's campaign against UNSCOM continued. His personal envoys to Baghdad, led by Lakhdar Brahimi, a former Algerian foreign minister, seemed to be circumventing UNSCOM and undermining its mission. Brahimi was transparently antagonistic to UNSCOM, impatient with the specifics on disarmament with which it dealt, and sympathetic to Saddam Hussein's Iraq.[30] Annan then began appointing his own people to new positions that overlapped with UNSCOM. In making one appointment, Annan wrote to the Security Council about "the need for improved lines of communication"—language that implied criticism of UNSCOM. These new Annan appointees, the most senior of which came from Third

World countries, were hostile to Butler and UNSCOM. For example, Prakash Shah of India, who became Annan's special envoy to Baghdad, appeared before the Security Council in June 1998 and praised Annan's Memorandum of Understanding as a "new chapter" in Iraqi-UN relations that would get beyond "the past historical baggage of suspicion and mistrust" between the UN and Saddam Hussein's Iraq. Shah was firing a broadside at UNSCOM, blaming the inspectors for Iraq's hostility to the UN. He also spoke about the need to "avoid at all costs" any conflict that might "involve the use of military force in the region."[31] Richard Butler would attack Shah's characterizations as nothing less than "moral equivalency." The envoy to Baghdad was elevating the legitimacy of Iraq's claims against UNSCOM while denying the UN's right to enforce its own resolution with military force, in accordance with Chapter VII of the UN Charter.

Even when it became clear that Annan's Memorandum of Understanding had utterly failed, the secretary-general persisted in his efforts to absolve Iraq of responsibility for the deteriorating relations between the UN and Baghdad. For example, on August 5, 1998, Saddam Hussein's regime suspended UNSCOM's disarmament work in Iraq. Here was a clear-cut violation of Resolution 687, the cease-fire resolution that had brought an end to the Gulf War more than seven years earlier. But instead of pressuring Baghdad, Annan's office called on the Security Council to conduct a "comprehensive review" of whether Iraq was complying with its disarmament commitments. In other words, Annan shifted the responsibility for assessing Iraq's weapons of mass destruction from the professionals at UNSCOM to the members of the Security Council, whose judgments were clouded by their economic and strategic interests in Iraq.

It was not surprising that when Annan's detailed proposal for a "comprehensive review" was released, it looked very much like a well-known Russian document that Moscow's diplomats in New York had prepared.[32] Whatever the origin of the proposal, the secretary-general had kowtowed to an Iraqi regime that had repeatedly defied the UN. In a blistering attack on Annan's initiatives in Iraq, A. M.

Rosenthal wrote in his column in the *New York Times*, "No other Secretary General did so much to diminish the moral difference between a killer dictator and the countries that oppose him."[33]

## THE EVIDENCE MOUNTS, AND THE UN DOES NOTHING

Was there a real basis for UNSCOM's continuing pursuit of Saddam's weapons of mass destruction? Yes. In fact, the UN had very good reasons to insist on getting Iraq to account for its biological weapons. For example, in its final report to the UN Security Council, UNSCOM determined that Iraq had not accounted for 520 kilograms of yeast extract growth medium that was specifically intended for anthrax production. This was enough growth medium to produce 26,000 liters of anthrax spores—more than three times the amount that Iraq had declared before the UN in 1995. According to Terence Taylor, a former British UNSCOM commissioner, a missile delivering just 30 kilograms of anthrax spores over an urban area could kill 80,000 to 100,000 people, making it as lethal as the Hiroshima atomic bomb.[34]

Iraq had completely denied the existence of this weaponry until 1995, when Saddam Hussein's son-in-law Hussein Kamel sought asylum in Jordan and disclosed to Western security agencies the secrets of Iraq's offensive biological weapons program. Moreover, UNSCOM subsequently learned that Iraq had weaponized that anthrax in the past; the inspectors found anthrax spores in seven Iraqi warheads. Clearly, from the data that UNSCOM had accumulated, the scale of the Iraqi biological weapons program was far greater than anything that Saddam's regime had officially disclosed. But there was a special problem with Iraq's biological weapons: UNSCOM could not verify Iraq's claim that the weapons had been destroyed. In contrast, UNSCOM had witnessed and recorded the destruction of Iraq's chemical weapons. In the case of these biological weapons, however, the UN could do nothing to test the validity of Saddam Hussein's advisers' contentions.

UNSCOM had a solid basis for believing that Saddam Hussein's regime could use its biological weapons. In a frank private meeting with Butler, the Iraqi deputy prime minister, Tariq Aziz, admitted that chemical weapons and missiles had saved Iraq "from the Persians" during the Iraq-Iran War. Butler was struck that Aziz was using the ethnic name, "Persian," and not the nationality, "Iranian." To Butler, using this term in the context of a discussion about weapons of mass destruction hinted at a desire to use this weaponry against specific racial groups. In similar fashion, Aziz stated that Iraq reserved its biological weapons for "the Zionists."[35]

One of Iraq's highest officials was using genocidal language indicating that whole ethnic groups could become the targets of attacks. And it became apparent that Iraq might well possess the missiles necessary to deliver these weapons to targets hundreds of kilometers away. Under Resolution 687, the UN had permitted Iraq to hold on to its artillery missiles with a range of 150 kilometers or less. These were considered battlefield weapons. But UNSCOM soon discovered that Iraq had 500 tons of rocket fuels that could be used only for longer-range missiles.[36] Why did Iraq need the long-range fuels if it possessed only short-range weapons? Did Iraq have a clandestine missile program? Tariq Aziz would actually admit in 2000, "If anyone can produce a missile of 150-kilometer range, they can produce one with a 1,000-kilometer range."[37] In short, there were strong reasons for believing that Iraq had both the means and the political will to employ biological weapons against its enemies.

UNSCOM recognized these realities, even if Kofi Annan didn't. And that is why the Iraqis so opposed the weapons inspectors. In a revealing conversation between Annan and Tariq Aziz, the Iraqi deputy prime minister asserted that UNSCOM had played a negative role in the disarmament process and not "a UN role."[38] Aziz's admission implied that UNSCOM didn't play by the rules of others in the UN. The Iraqis had hoped for an ineffectual UN organ that would "understand" Iraq's repeated claims to respect its sovereign sensitivities. They wanted the UN of the 1970s and 1980s, which had ignored Saddam Hussein's aggression into Iran and had done nothing to help the Kurds. Baghdad needed an organization dripping in moral equivalence that would criticize every "affront" to Iraqi sovereignty with the same vigor with which it would pursue the question of Iraq's missing weapons. But instead it got an organization that was determined to aggressively uncover illicit weapons of mass destruction and long-range delivery systems. UNSCOM represented a new, more robust, and more determined UN.

Yet Kofi Annan was willing to roll back this advance. First, he undermined UNSCOM, and ultimately, in 2000, he replaced it with a new organization, the United Nations Monitoring, Verification, and Inspection Commission (UNMOVIC). The man put in charge of UNMOVIC was Hans Blix, who had given Iraq a clean bill of health in the 1980s, when it was developing nuclear technology without IAEA knowledge.

But even UNMOVIC would complain about Iraq's lack of forthrightness. In March 2003 it revealed a long list of "unresolved disarmament issues." For instance, UNMOVIC noted that "based on the available evidence, the strong presumption is that about 10,000 litres of anthrax was not destroyed and may still exist."[39] It also noted that Iraq had obtained "bulk quantities" of specialized growth medium that were "particularly suitable" for highly contagious diseases. According to the UNMOVIC report, it was known that Iraq had imported smallpox virus for research in the 1970s and had set up three new genetic engineering facilities from 1998 to 2003.[40] Unlike anthrax, which kills only those who come directly into contact with its spores, smallpox virus is highly contagious and could decimate large unvaccinated populations.

Also of note was Iraq's continuing interest in ricin toxin, for which there is no known antidote. UNMOVIC determined that the Iraqis had reconstructed a plant capable of producing ricin that had been destroyed in December 1998; the plant did not cease production until mid-2001.[41] The head of an al-Qaeda affiliate network, Abu Mussab al-Zarqawi, was trained in the use of ricin in Afghanistan before he relocated to Iraq in 2002. It was an ideal biological weapon for terrorists. An al-Qaeda suspect arrested in Italy prior to the Iraq War told his interrogators that members of the al-Zarqawi network had purchased toxins from Iraq.[42] And according to Secretary of State Colin Powell's February 2003 testimony before the UN Security Council, the al-Zarqawi network had a training center in northeastern Iraq, where its operatives were taught how to use ricin. (Significantly, although the Senate's Select Committee on Intelligence later criticized aspects of Powell's UN presentation on prewar intelligence, it did *not* find fault with the terrorism portions of his speech.)

In a post-9/11 environment, Iraqi stonewalling at the UN was particularly dangerous because Iraq's banned biological weapons could possibly have ended up in the hands of terrorists. According to the initial findings of the staff of the 9/11 Commission published in June 2004, "al-Qaeda had an ambitious biological weapons program and was making advances in its ability to produce anthrax prior to September 11." The report cited CIA director George Tenet, who had concluded that "al-Qaeda's ability to conduct an anthrax attack is one of the most immediate threats the United States is likely to face."[43] British intelligence reported in October 2002 that "Al Qaida has shown interest in gaining chemical and biological expertise from Iraq," an assessment that was not disputed in the July 2004 "Review of Intelligence" issued by Lord Butler's special bipartisan British committee. The Butler report also disclosed intelligence that by March 2003 al-Zarqawi had erected a network of sleeper cells in Baghdad for a postwar insurgency; British intelligence raised the possibility that these cells had received chemical and biological weapons from al-Qaeda in northeastern Iraq. After the Iraq War, David Kay, who led the U.S. team seeking Iraq's missing weapons of mass destruction, disclosed, "We know there were terrorist groups in state [Iraq] still seeking WMD capability. Iraq, although I found no weapons, had tremendous capabilities in this area. A marketplace phenomena was about to occur, if it did not occur; sellers meeting buyers. And I think that would have been dangerous if the war had not intervened."[44] But the majority of states sitting on the UN Security Council back in 2003 did not recognize the urgency of the situation.

UNMOVIC could not come up with an adequate explanation for why the Iraqis invested considerably in a program to produce the biological agent aflatoxin, which did not kill instantly but caused lung and liver cancer over a period of time.[45] In 2003, Iraq officially declared that it was still conducting research on aflatoxin. UNMOVIC did not make much of the fact that Iraq had already used weapons of mass destruction against the Kurds, including, reportedly, aflatoxin. The Iraqi leadership could have chosen to use the biological agent against hostile minority populations like the Kurds or even the Shiites. Since aflatoxin could be mixed with chemical agents to mask its detection, it was an ideal biological agent for a regime bent on committing genocide but at the same time concerned about covering its tracks.

Thus, even the UN's own reports, if carefully analyzed, showed reasons to be concerned about Iraq's systematic violations of its commitments to destroy its weapons of mass destruction. After the Iraq War, there was considerable debate over the true extent of Iraq's WMD programs. Much of this controversy focused on Saddam Hussein's nuclear and chemical programs. There was little debate, however, about the Iraqi biological weapons program or its potential lethality. Moreover, UNMOVIC was aware that the Iraqis were actively developing the delivery systems for its weapons of mass destruction. Iraq was aggressively restoring its long-range missile program and even negotiated with North Korea, between 1999 and 2002, to obtain No Dong missile technology.[46]

Clearly, Iraq had preserved a biological weapons program that it could easily bring to full production and had invested in acquiring delivery systems for its weapons of mass destruction. But the UN had little political will to do anything about Iraq. Its capacity to reveal what happened to Iraq's weapons was equally limited when Baghdad was determined to block the inspection system. In January 2004, David Kay was asked during Senate hearings if the UN inspection process had been given a chance, maybe it would have revealed Iraq's suspected weaponry. After all, the UNMOVIC inspectors of Hans Blix were inserted into Iraq on November 27, 2002. They were the first UN monitors on the ground since UNSCOM was removed in 1998. Kay was certain that the UN would *not* have gotten very far: "We have had a number of Iraqis who have come forward and said,

'We did not tell the UN about what we were hiding, nor would we have told the UN because we would have run the risk of our own'— I think we have learned things that no UN inspector would have ever learned given the terror regime of Saddam and the tremendous personal consequences that scientists had to run by speaking the truth." The UN was not going to solve the Iraq problem.[47] It would fall to the United States and President George W. Bush to act in its stead.

## THE UN'S FALSE REVIVAL

The 1991 Gulf War victory had created the mistaken impression of a revived UN that could insert itself in the problems of the post–Cold War world and resolve conflicts effectively. By accepting this notion so readily, the world community suffered through a number of international crises that never should have escalated. The situation in Iraq in the years leading up to the 2003 Iraq War showed the devastating consequence of the UN's moral equivalence and appeasement policies.

As noted, much has been made of the difficulty that U.S. forces had coming up with the weapons of mass destruction that had provided one of the main justifications for the American war effort in 2003. David Kay disclosed in early 2004, "We know from some of the interrogations of former Iraqi officials that a lot of material went to Syria before the war, including some components of Saddam's WMD program." And in early June 2004, UNMOVIC reported to the UN Security Council that equipment and material for producing weapons of mass destruction in Iraq had been removed and shipped abroad; missile parts turned up in the Netherlands and in Jordan.[48] But regardless of what happened to the banned Iraqi arsenal, what is generally forgotten is that the UN did not have a shadow of a doubt that Iraq possessed weapons of mass destruction back in 1991; UN Security Council Resolution 687, adopted on April 3, 1991, gave Iraq *fifteen days* to declare the locations, amounts, and types of its prohibited biological, chemical, missile, and nuclear weapons systems. The UN clearly put the burden on Iraq to come up with the weapons—not on UNSCOM, the United States, or anyone else. And Saddam Hussein made a commitment to honor those terms, which were unequivocal (the resolution said that Iraq must "unconditionally accept" the eradication of its weapons of mass destruction). Yet *twelve years* went by, and still Iraq had not fulfilled its obligations. Over the years the UN Security Council adopted fully sixteen legally binding resolutions designed to ensure that Iraq did not threaten international peace and security, almost all of which explicitly called on the Iraqi regime to cooperate fully with UN weapons inspectors.

Because of Iraqi intransigence, however, neither UNSCOM nor UNMOVIC could verify that Iraq had fulfilled its original obligation to turn over all of its most deadly weapons. In fact, in 1998, Baghdad forced UN monitors out of Iraq altogether, openly defying UN resolutions. Without any inspectors present, Saddam Hussein's regime had more than four years to rebuild its nonconventional capabilities. Iraq was given a last chance by the UN Security Council in 2002 with the adoption of Resolution 1441, which decided that Iraq was in "material breach" of its UN obligations. But Baghdad still did not provide a complete disclosure of its weapons programs.

And still the UN did not stand up to the Iraqi threat. Saddam Hussein repeatedly ignored the UN's most severe resolutions. David Kay, who reported that his Iraq Survey Group had not yet found Iraqi weapons of mass destruction, nonetheless told the Senate Armed Services Committee in January 2004, "In my judgment, based on the work that has been done to this point of the Iraq Survey Group, and in fact, that I reported to you in October, Iraq was in clear violation of the terms of Resolution 1441. Resolution 1441 required that Iraq report all of its activities: one last chance to come clean about what it had. We have discovered hundreds of cases, based on both documents, physical evidence, and the testimony of Iraqis, of activities that were prohibited under the initial U.N. Resolution 687 and that should have been reported under 1441, with Iraqi testimony that not only did they not tell the U.N. about this, they were instructed not to do it and they hid material."[49] The Iraqi dictator made a mockery of the UN as a guarantor of international security. The fact that the president of the Security Council issued at least thirty statements acknowledging Saddam's repeated violations of UN resolutions only underscored the UN's impotence: Even when it acknowledged the problem, the UN did not take decisive action in order to safeguard international peace and security.

As troubling as the Iraq situation was, it was not the only time the UN failed to deal with international crises that it should have prevented. In fact, the UN had operational responsibility on the ground during some of the worst massacres that the world had witnessed since the Holocaust. The ineffectual UN response to the Kurds and the Shiites was only a prologue to the disasters of the 1990s in which the UN had a direct role.

# CHAPTER 6

# Impartial to Genocide

### *The UN in Rwanda*

There is perhaps no more damning indictment of the UN than its failure to prevent genocide in Africa in the 1990s.

It was the post–Cold War era, and the fulfilling of the UN's raison d'être—dealing with aggression—should have become easier. In fact, the 1990s should have been the greatest decade for UN peacekeeping in the organization's history. Just as President George H. W. Bush laid out a vision of a post–Cold War world in which the UN played a central role, Bill Clinton's administration came into office in 1993 calling for "assertive multilateralism." And the end of the superpower rivalry meant that the UN Security Council could become far more active in dozens of regional conflicts around the globe. Thus, whereas in 1988 the UN had only 11,000 peacekeepers deployed worldwide, by December 1994 it had 78,000.[1] It seemed likely that the UN would assume a new, more prominent role in global affairs.

Yet it repeatedly ignored or excused aggression because of the competing interests of its member states. Consider, for example, how major powers in the UN Security Council that had an interest in protecting Iraq—in particular, France, Russia, and China—enabled Saddam Hussein to wiggle out of the inspection system that the UN had created at the end of the 1991 Gulf War. The UN's neutrality in the face of aggression was a moral flaw that nullified its ability to protect international security.

**RWANDA AND ITS NEIGHBORS**

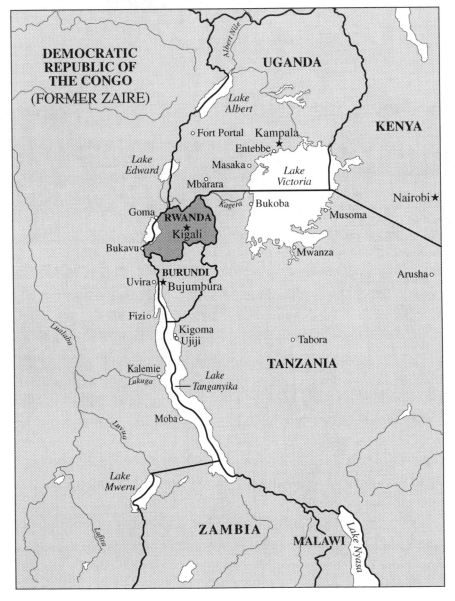

This amorality also affected the UN's ability to make judgments about the *victims* of aggression. In the 1990s the UN was witness to the worst massacres perpetrated against innocent civilians since the Second World War. But it was more than a witness to these slaughters. By doing nothing even when its own peacekeeping forces were supposedly in control of the situation, the UN shared responsibility for the deaths of hundreds of thousands of innocent people. Quite simply, the UN's peacekeeping forces could not or did not keep the peace. When the UN was confronted with a true crisis in the African country of Rwanda, its peacekeeping mission went horribly wrong.

## "AN INSTITUTIONAL IDEOLOGY OF IMPARTIALITY"

The UN became involved in Rwanda in late 1993. The landlocked Central African country had gained its independence from Belgium in 1962, after a period of intertribal violence. Even while a Belgian protectorate, Rwanda (then called Ruanda) had been ruled by a king from the Tutsi tribe, despite the fact that the Tutsis made up only about 10 to 15 percent of the Rwandan population. Resenting the Tutsi tribe's dominance of the political system, in 1959 the Hutu tribesmen began attacks, killing thousands of Tutsis and forcing many others to flee the country. Over the next two decades, the Hutu systematically purged the Tutsis from government and universities.[2] In 1986, exiled Tutsis and moderate Hutus in neighboring Uganda formed the Rwandese Patriotic Front (RPF), which invaded Rwanda four years later. The Hutu regime of President Juvenal Habyarimana pushed back the invasion with the help of paratroopers that France's president, François Mitterrand, had dispatched to the French-speaking African country. The RPF resumed its offensive in February 1993 and was stopped only by another intervention of French troops. In August, the Rwandan government and the RPF reached a peace agreement in Arusha, Tanzania, which established new power-sharing arrangements between the parties and also called for the deployment of international peacekeepers.

Between October and December 1993, the UN Security Council deployed 2,500 peacekeepers as part of the UN Assistance Mission for Rwanda (UNAMIR), which was responsible for monitoring the implementation of the Arusha Accords. The international force had a Canadian commander, Major General Romeo Dallaire, and troops from Belgium (the former colonial power), Bangladesh, and Ghana. Its mission was to demobilize the combating forces and help create a new, unified national army. Dallaire believed that he really needed 5,000 troops to do the job properly. The UN force was basically intended for supporting the fragile peace process.

Hovering over Dallaire's mission in Rwanda was the recent UN debacle in Somalia. That disastrous peacekeeping effort produced two infamous setbacks: First, in June 1993, twenty-five UN peacekeepers from Pakistan were ambushed and killed, and several months later, Somalis downed two Black Hawk helicopters and killed eighteen American soldiers, later dragging some of the mutilated corpses through the streets of Mogadishu. The UN would reach the conclusion that its peacekeepers had come under fire because it had taken sides in a humanitarian relief operation and thus had lost its neutrality. But the real problem in Somalia was that there were no sides with which the UN could become aligned; it was an anarchical situation involving numerous rival Somali clans and warlords. This unique, multisided civil war doomed the UN's Somali mission. Still, after the Somalia fiasco, the UN became rigid about staying away from the "Mogadishu Line"—the point at which UN forces would lose their neutrality and the consent of the parties for their deployment. This inflexible new policy ignored the fact that Rwanda was a completely different situation from Somalia.

On January 11, 1994, General Dallaire sent a coded cable from Rwanda to the Department of Peacekeeping Operations at UN headquarters in New York, alerting his home office to alarming new intelligence he had received from a Hutu informant. To emphasize the reliability of the information he was about to report, Dallaire began by saying that a "very very important government politician" had put him in contact with the informant. He then explained what his Hutu contact had revealed: The extremist Hutu Interhamwe militia had been training in official Rwanda army camps, and it apparently had a new mission apart from its traditional role of protecting Kigali, the Rwandan capital, from the RPF. The informant said that his superiors had ordered him to register all Tutsis in Kigali—"for their extermination," the informant suspected. The Hutu militia, he argued, could kill a thousand Tutsis in twenty minutes. Explaining that he was opposed to the extermination of innocent Tutsis, the informant said that he was prepared to provide UN peacekeepers with the location of major weapons caches that the Hutu militia planned to use.[3]

Armed with this intelligence, Dallaire informed New York of his intention to seize the Hutu militia's weapons caches and thereby try to thwart its extermination plan.

Upon receiving the Dallaire cable, the Department of Peacekeeping Operations—which was headed by Kofi Annan, who would become UN secretary-general within three years—convened a meeting. Led by Annan's assistant, Iqbal Riza, the department ordered Dallaire *not* to take the action he was proposing. Instead, it instructed him to pass along the information he had received to the U.S., French, and Belgian embassies, as well as to the Hutu president of Rwanda. No suggestion was made to share this information with the RPF. In its response, Annan's department argued that the operation Dallaire contemplated "goes beyond the mandate entrusted to UNAMIR."

It was an odd argument, since the UN Security Council resolution creating UNAMIR specifically said that the force was supposed to help make the Rwandan capital "a weapons-secure area." Iqbal Riza would later argue that UNAMIR's mission was merely to assist the Rwandan parties in establishing their "weapons-secure area" and not to go after illegal weapons by itself.[4] The cable that the Department of Peacekeeping Operations sent to Dallaire reflected such an overly cautious approach, for, it explained, "The overriding consideration is the need to avoid entering into a course of action that might lead to the use of force and unanticipated consequences."[5]

What was the purpose of UN peacekeepers if they were to avoid the use of force almost at any cost? The UN's passivity was directly leading to greater escalation; its men on the ground in Rwanda were reporting in February 1994 more assassination attempts, as well as political and ethnic killing.[6]

Dallaire recalled in his memoirs his reaction to the UN reply to his cable: "The code cable from Kofi Annan, signed by Riza, came to me and the SRSG [Special Representative of the Secretary-General]; its contents caught me completely off guard. It took me to task for even thinking about raiding the weapons caches and ordered me to suspend the operation immediately . . . I was absolutely beside myself with frustration."[7]

Years later, Iqbal Riza attempted to explain why the UN's peacekeeping department had turned down Dallaire despite his warnings of impending massacres. First, he downplayed the message, saying, "There are a number of cables that we get of this nature." Elsewhere he argued that there was "hyperbole in many reports."[8] He also said that he had asked the UN mission in Rwanda to "find out how reliable this source was." In other words, Riza claimed that the UN Department of Peacekeeping Operations had good reasons for taking its time and for not even considering that an act of genocide was imminent, despite the fact that Dallaire's informant had used the word "extermination."

Riza was putting forward flimsy arguments, however. The peacekeeping department had had key evidence indicating that Dallaire's Hutu informant was a reliable source. In fact, the UN secretary-general's personal representative in Rwanda, Jacques-Roger Booh-Booh, cabled Riza that he had met with the prime minister designate of Rwanda, who said that he had "total, repeat total confidence in the veracity and true ambitions of the informant."[9] This cable should have been particularly striking, because, as will be seen, Booh-Booh was suspected of being close to the Hutu leadership.

Moreover, Dallaire's message was not an isolated report. The UN had already received reports in 1993 that at least 10,000 Tutsis had been detained and 2,000 murdered since the RPF's 1990 invasion of Rwanda.[10] Also in 1993, the UN Human Rights Commission had visited Rwanda and published a report pointing out the risk of genocide, but key UN decision-makers ignored the findings of this study.[11] Some warnings came out of Rwanda itself. Senior Rwandan officers wrote to Dallaire in December 1993 disclosing a Hutu plan to massacre large numbers of Tutsis.[12] A Hutu radio station was inciting the Hutu population against the Tutsis, whom it delegitimized. Warning signs of impending massacres were everywhere. Clearly Dallaire's analysis of the situation was based on more than a single report of one informer. But somehow the message did not set off alarm bells at the UN.

Given the intelligence it was receiving, Kofi Annan's team at the Department of Peacekeeping Operations should have consulted with the UN Security Council for instructions rather than dismiss Dallaire's alert so easily. Security Council members, such as the Czech ambassador to the UN, later complained that the UN Secretariat and its peacekeeping department were not supplying them with the full story of what was going on in Rwanda.

Why didn't Dallaire's message set off alarm bells? Here is where the specter of Somalia haunted the UN. Top UN officials did not want to rush to judgment about which side was at fault; they did not want to get into the question of blame. Riza later told an interviewer, "Look, since the 1960s, there have been cycles of violence—Tutsis against Hutus, Hutus against Tutsis. I'm sorry to put it so cynically."[13] This was probably the most bald confession of moral equivalence in the Rwanda genocide. To the UN, there were no victims or murderers, just a "cycle of violence" that had no cause.

Annan's team at the Department of Peacekeeping Operations clung to its position through February 1994, even as further cable traffic came in from Rwanda predicting "catastrophic consequences" if the UN force on the ground did nothing.[14] Dallaire wanted to initiate "deterrent operations." He still wanted to seize the Hutu militia's weapons caches. Annan merely emphasized that the opposing parties in Rwanda—and not UN peacekeepers—were responsible for establishing the "weapons-secure area" that Resolution 792 called for.[15] The UN was not to take sides.

This tendency to see the parties in a conflict in strictly symmetrical terms was endemic to the UN system. The UN bureaucracy made it doctrine that the UN would maintain neutrality in conflicts where its peacekeepers were deployed. Indeed, Kofi Annan would later admit that the UN had "an institutional ideology of impartiality even when confronted with attempted genocide."[16] Annan himself betrayed this misguided impartiality with regard to Rwanda. According to Dallaire, Annan cabled him at one point to say that his proposed raid on the Hutu weapons caches "would only be viewed as hostile by the Rwandan government."[17] And that, to Annan and the other UN bureaucrats, was enough to rule out the mission. It was important not to alienate a government even if it was allowing an extremist militia to use its military bases in planning massacres.

Unfortunately, no international powers pressured the UN to revise this policy orientation. Even the Clinton administration's diplomats, in the words of one observer, "did not want to do anything to disrupt the peace process."[18] Thus the UN continued to operate with blinders on. It focused on its "first priority," which according to Riza was to "reestablish the cease-fire" and save the Arusha Accords.[19]

But soon there would be nothing to save.


## GENOCIDE


On April 6, 1994, President Habyarimana, the Hutu president of Rwanda who had signed the Arusha Accords, was killed when his plane was shot down near Kigali. (Burundi's president also died in the crash.) This began the genocide. The Rwandan army and the extremist Hutu militia immediately began mass killings of Tutsis and even some moderate Hutus. Thousands were butchered the first day. On April 7, Rwandan troops surrounded a Belgian peacekeeping contingent of ten soldiers that was protecting the Rwandan prime minister and her five children. The Rwandan soldiers demanded that the Belgians surrender their weapons, and on orders from their commanding officer at headquarters, the Belgian soldiers disarmed. The Rwandans then took the Belgians to their military base and tortured, killed, and mutilated them.[20] Meanwhile, the Rwandan troops caught the prime minister trying to escape her home and murdered her. By April 10, the International Red Cross would estimate that tens of thousands of Rwandans had already been murdered.

The situation had almost instantly escalated out of control. Still, the UN did not change its position. The Belgian government, which as the former colonial power had an intimate understanding of Rwanda's internal dynamics, had been pushing the UN for months to stop its policy of passivity toward the Hutu militias. Now that its soldiers had been massacred, the Belgian cabinet decided that it would withdraw its peacekeeping contingent—the strongest in the UN force—unless the UN reinforced UNAMIR and broadened the force's mandate to take offensive action.[21] Separately, Dallaire pushed for a similar change in policy; he wanted UN headquarters to expand UNAMIR to 5,000 soldiers and give it a more forceful mandate. But in response, Kofi Annan's Department of Peacekeeping Operations instructed Dallaire, "You should make every effort not to compromise your *impartiality* or to act beyond your mandate [emphasis added]."[22] Thousands upon thousands of Rwandans were being slaughtered, but the UN was focusing only on "impartiality."

The problem was not that troops were unavailable; it was a failure of political will. In testimony before the Belgian Senate inquiry on Rwanda, Belgium's foreign minister, Willie Claes, would argue that his government had considered military intervention but that "Paris said a firm no." Little help came from Washington either. According to Dallaire, if the UN had galvanized the Western powers to join a military intervention to stop the genocide, enough troops would have been available. Although he had requested 5,000 troops, he said that UNAMIR, combined with the 900 elite Belgian and French troops who eventually joined a special "evacuation force," along with the 300 U.S. Marines who were in neighboring Burundi, would have constituted a strong army that "could have easily stopped the massacres."[23]

The Western powers did consider creating an "evacuation force," however. This force would focus exclusively on evacuating foreign refugees from Rwanda.

Instead the UN told Dallaire simply to focus on evacuating foreigners from Rwanda. Dallaire told officers that he had received orders from UN headquarters in New York that no Rwandans were to be rescued: "Orders from New York: no locals." A few brave UNAMIR officers ignored this UN directive. According to Human Rights Watch interviews, UNAMIR officers, as well as their superiors at UN headquarters, feared that giving shelter to members of the threatened Tutsi tribe could threaten UN "neutrality." One person connected with UNAMIR concluded, "If you wanted to do some good, you just had to do it and not ask New York."[24]

If doing the morally right thing in Rwanda meant ignoring the UN, what did this say about the organization?

The UN ordered the Belgian peacekeepers to regroup in order to assist in the evacuation effort. One of the first signs that the Belgians were changing their mission came on April 11, when ninety Belgian soldiers withdrew from a technical school, known as École Technique Officielle des Pères Salésians de Don Bosco, where they had been protecting 2,000 Rwandan refugees, including some 400 children. The Belgians pulled out of the school despite the fact that the Hutu militia waited outside, drinking beer and chanting "Hutu Power," and despite the cries of refugees who shouted, "Do not abandon us."[25] As the Belgian peacekeepers left the school, they fired warning shots over the heads of the refugees. The Hutu militiamen went in after the withdrawal from the school was completed, firing machine guns and throwing grenades. Most of the Rwandan refugees were immediately killed.

The Belgian government had a strong case for insisting that the manpower and mandate of UNAMIR be expanded. But for Belgian forces to knowingly abandon refugees to certain death raises serious questions about their responsibility for the massacre that followed, even if they were only complying with the new mission they were given by the UN of evacuating only foreign nationals.

Within four days of the incident at the technical school, the Belgians had completely withdrawn their peacekeeping contingent, leaving the Rwandan Tutsis at the mercy of the Hutu militia's extermination campaign. With the main contingent of UNAMIR gone, the UN Security Council voted to cut its Rwandan peacekeeping force from 2,500 troops to a mere 270. The UN effectively deserted Rwanda. When UNEF withdrew from the Sinai Peninsula in 1967, it triggered a war; when UNAMIR left Rwanda, it enabled genocide to occur.

In some cases, UN forces actually colluded with those engaging in mass murder, further disgracing the UN's record. A UNAMIR detachment from Ghana that was supposed to protect Rwandan chief justice Joseph Kovaruganda simply turned over the Rwandan judge to a Hutu death squad. Worse, the UN soldiers then stood laughing and drinking with his killers as they assaulted his wife and daughters. The UN itself confirmed the details of this incident in its official inquiry into the UN role in the Rwanda genocide.[26]

By the end of April, an estimated 100,000 people had been murdered in Rwanda. Desperate to end the savagery, the RPF's representative in New York appealed to the president of the UN Security Council, New Zealand ambassador Colin Keating. According to the RPF's letter, Rwanda was witnessing nothing less than a carefully planned campaign to exterminate the Tutsi ethnic group. Calling on the international community to act, the letter invoked the 1948 Genocide Convention and reminded the Security Council of the UN's very purpose: "When the institution of the UN was created after the Second World War, one of its fundamental objectives was to see to it that what happened to the Jews in Nazi Germany would never happen again."[27] The RPF's letter seemed to influence Keating, for he moved to formally characterize what was going on in Rwanda as genocide. He had to act quickly, however, because his monthlong term as president of the Security Council would be over at the end of April. Moreover, he faced a substantial obstacle: The United States and Britain, key members of the Security Council, did not want to use the word "genocide" to characterize the events in Rwanda.

The reason the Americans and the British hoped to avoid using the term "genocide" was that such a designation would bind the international community to intervene under the Genocide Convention. According to Article 9 of the convention, signatories are expected to call on the UN to take specific actions to prevent or suppress acts of genocide; a Security Council determination of any sort that genocide had occurred would trigger the treaty. Clearly neither Washington nor London wanted to get dragged into Rwanda after the UN's debacle in Somalia a year earlier. Keating did not even propose a Security Council resolution on the Rwanda situation; he called simply for a "presidential statement," which provides a sense of the Security Council's viewpoint but is not a legally binding act. Nor did Keating's presidential statement define the Rwandan massacre directly as "genocide"—the reference to genocide was oblique: it merely reminded the international community that "the systematic killing of any ethnic group, with intent to destroy it in whole or in part, constitutes an act of genocide." The other members of the UN Security Council had blocked any more forceful action, like explicitly charging that genocide had occurred. The United States and Great Britain successfully blocked Keating's initiative to ratchet up UN involvement. Thus, the UN remained silent, content to sit on the sidelines.

The most absurd aspect of the UN's handling of the massacres was that throughout the crisis, the representative of Rwanda's Hutu-dominated government sat on the UN Security Council. Rwanda had become one of the Security Council's ten nonpermanent members on January 1994, and it remained on the Council even after the Council had deployed peacekeepers to the Central African country. This ambassador received his instructions from a regime that had collaborated with the militia in planning and executing the genocide that was in progress. Thus, as UN members sought accurate information about the extent of the killings in Rwanda, the ambassador repeatedly denied that any genocide was under way.

Even with these repeated Rwandan denials in New York, the international community could not ignore the mounting evidence of the Rwandan massacres. For example, in May, a *New York Times* reporter described how the Hutu militia had butchered thousands of Tutsis and dumped the bodies into the Kagera River, where they floated downstream to Lake Victoria.[28] The article directly contradicted the Rwandan representative's earlier unsubstantiated denial that large number of bodies were flowing down the same river—a denial that appeared in an official UN document (S/1994/1115).

## "WELCOME FRENCH HUTUS"

Eventually the UN would take a more active role in Rwanda, but not on the side of the victims of genocide. France, a permanent member of the Security Council, drove the UN to do more—but not more to protect the Tutsis. Paris had twice previously dispatched paratroopers to protect Rwanda's Hutu-dominated government, and remarkably the bloodbath in Rwanda did not change France's pro-Hutu orientation. On April 27, in the midst of the massacres, French president François Mitterrand hosted two Hutu militants who belonged to extremist organizations.[29] They had meetings with the entire French leadership, from Prime Minister Edouard Balladur to Foreign Minister Alain Juppe. According to a French political scientist advising the French Ministry of Defense, Gerard Prunier, the French government was secretly delivering arms and supplies to the Rwandan army in order to save its Hutu allies.[30] Additional reports indicated that in mid-June 1994, the French helped the Rwandans smuggle arms supplies in from Zaire. The French officially denied all these charges.

The French government then urged the UN to authorize a French "humanitarian" military intervention in Rwanda. The UN Security Council bought into the idea. On June 22, it endorsed the deployment of French forces and gave them a broader mandate to use force than it had given the UNAMIR peacekeeping forces. Indeed, by empowering the French to lead an intervention rather than expanding the authority of UNAMIR, the UN totally undermined its own peacekeeping force. The French deployment raised an important question, as well: Given France's close ties with the Hutu leaders and its past efforts to block an RPF takeover of Rwanda, how could the UN maintain its strict doctrine of impartiality after deploying a French-led force to the region? The question seemed even more pressing when the Hutu militia warmly greeted the French with slogans like "Welcome French Hutus."

Within a week of its arrival in Rwanda, the French military had occupied a quarter of the country. Did the French-UN intervention save lives? Some argue that France's Operation Turquoise saved 10,000 Tutsis in western Rwanda. At the same time, however, reports indicate that thousands of Tutsis were killed inside the French-occupied zone. And the French forces did not take measures against those Hutu who had engaged in genocide.[31] The French press cried foul. *Libération* carried a report that French instructors had trained Hutu death squads; it based the charges on an interview with one of the death squad members.[32] The president of the French charity Survie wrote that French intelligence was running Rwanda in league with the Rwandan army.[33] The UN had deputized a strange partner.

The UN-authorized French force did little if anything to cope with the slaughters in Rwanda. In large part the problem in dealing with the genocide was the UN's slow decision-making process; while diplomats had haggled in New York, Hutu militants had continued to murder Tutsi tribesmen. By the time the French force arrived in Rwanda in late June, most of the genocide was already over. Over the course of a hundred-day killing campaign that ended in mid-July, Hutu militants had slaughtered an estimated 800,000 Rwandans, mostly of the Tutsi tribe.

If the hidden purpose of the French campaign was to save Rwanda from the RPF, then the French failed here as well. The RPF captured the Rwandan capital of Kigali on July 18; the ousted Hutu government fled to Zaire. The French withdrew from Rwanda after sixty days.

## THE UN ABDICATES ITS RESPONSIBILITY

Who was responsible for the UN's behavior in Rwanda in failing to stop the genocide of 1994? The UN secretary-general at the time, Boutros Boutros-Ghali, has pleaded ignorance of many of the events in Rwanda. In memoirs that he published years later, Boutros-Ghali wrote, "Throughout most of January 1994 I was away from UN headquarters in New York and not in touch with the Rwanda situation." He claimed, for instance, that it wasn't until three years later that he heard of Dallaire's famous January 11, 1994, cable warning of the impending massacres.[34]

Travel is a weak excuse for a chief executive. Boutros-Ghali should have known more. He handpicked his own personal representative, Jacques-Roger Booh-Booh, the former foreign minister of Cameroon and his personal friend, to oversee UN affairs on the ground in Rwanda and to report back to New York along with Dallaire. Sometimes Dallaire and Booh-Booh reported back jointly. But on other occasions, as Human Rights Watch observed, Booh-Booh minimized the extent and organized nature of the massacres in Rwanda, undermining Dallaire's reports. If the UN needed reports to justify its own passivity, then Booh-Booh supplied the goods.[35] Besides his overly optimistic reporting, Booh-Booh was a curious choice for a UN representative in Rwanda because he reportedly enjoyed good connections with the Hutu militant elite. The RPF claimed to have intelligence intercepts of suspicious, unscheduled meetings between Booh-Booh and army officers of the Hutu-led government.[36] One wonders whether Boutros-Ghali knew more than he has claimed.

What about Kofi Annan, who served as undersecretary-general for peacekeeping operations during the genocide? As noted, it was Annan's deputy, Iqbal Riza, who convened the staff of the

Department of Peacekeeping Operations and signed its weak response to Dallaire's January 11 cable warning that the Hutus were planning an extermination campaign. That his deputy signed the cable does not absolve Annan, who kept Riza as his right-hand man when he was promoted to secretary-general in 1997. In any case, Annan's real problem was his rigid doctrine of impartiality that he imposed on the UN's peacekeeping department worldwide, even in cases when the UN faced pure evil. Strictly following this mandate in Rwanda, Annan's department stressed that the peacekeepers' role was to help the Hutu-led government and the RPF preserve the Arusha Accords "peace process."

The official UN inquiry into the UN's own actions in the Rwanda genocide stressed this point. The report found "disturbing" the record of meetings between the UN Secretariat and the Hutu-led government, which showed "a continued emphasis on a cease-fire." Similarly, Madeleine Albright, who served as the U.S. ambassador to the UN at the time, later wrote that most talk at the early stage of the genocide was "how to get the peace process back on track." She added that in talks with UN officials, "we tried to stay neutral and condemned the violence *on all sides* [emphasis added]."[37] Insisting on this stance of moral neutrality, the UN did not express outrage even when genocide was under way.

What could Kofi Annan have done? The UN inquiry pointed out that UN Security Council representatives complained about the poor quality of the information they received from the UN. In other words, member states were kept in the dark about the situation in Rwanda. One problem, of course, was that the Rwandan government had the perfect platform from which to prosecute its disinformation campaign: the UN Security Council. But the problems went beyond that. Boutros-Ghali rarely appeared before the Security Council on the issue of Rwanda and sent a personal representative instead. Didn't Annan's department have any intelligence beyond Dallaire's cable that massacres on a massive scale were imminent? Yes, it did.

In fact, as noted, the UN had plenty of warning signs that something on the scale of genocide was possible—from the UN's own internal reports. Furthermore, in December 1997, when the Belgian Senate issued the results of its inquiry on the Rwanda genocide, one of its most explosive revelations was a cable that the Belgian ambassador to Rwanda sent on March 27, 1992, which stated, "A secret command exists which is planning *the total extermination of the Tutsis* in order to resolve, once and for all, the ethnic problem and to destroy the Hutu opposition to this plan [emphasis added]."[38] It is not known whether the UN was aware of this intelligence but ignored it, or the Belgians simply refused to share it with Annan's staff. Either case would represent a serious dereliction of duty.

Certainly the Department of Peacekeeping Operations, which sent officials like Iqbal Riza to the Security Council, could have shared with the rest of the UN the warning signs of genocide that were accumulating. And even if the Clinton administration, not wanting to get drawn into another murky African peacekeeping operation after Somalia, was initially reluctant to characterize the slaughter of the Tutsis as genocide, Kofi Annan had a responsibility, with the information his department had received, to personally go to the Security Council and even pound his fist on the table in order to arouse world public opinion.

The official UN inquiry on Rwanda concluded that Annan's peacekeeping department should have consulted the Security Council regarding Dallaire's cable. According to the inquiry, even if the peacekeeping department disagreed with Dallaire, and believed that using UN peacekeepers to go after the Hutu arms caches was not within the UN Security Council mandate under which the general operated, the peacekeeping department should not have assumed that member states would concur with its cautious impartiality. After all, there was mounting evidence that a campaign of extermination was about to begin. But because Annan's group did not consult with the Security Council, the Hutu arms caches were not raided and the Hutu plot to murder the Tutsis was not deterred.

As the UN inquiry on Rwanda pointed out, Dallaire had anticipated the moral dilemmas he would face in Rwanda months before he sent his famous cable of January 11, 1994. Back in November

1993, he had sent the Department of Peacekeeping Operations a draft document outlining the sort of detailed "Rules of Engagement" that he felt his UN peacekeeping force would need but that the UN Security Council's mandate had not provided. Dallaire wrote, "There may also be ethnically or politically motivated criminal acts committed during this mandate which will morally or legally require UNAMIR to use all available means to halt them." According to the UN inquiry, Annan's department "never responded formally" to Dallaire's request.[39] The problem was not that Annan's team had said "no" to Dallaire; rather, it was that the peacekeeping department hadn't even bothered to get back to its commander in the field.

Clearly the UN suffered from serious internal deficiencies in dealing with the Rwanda genocide. The Belgian Senate's Parliamentary Commission of Inquiry specifically criticized the "deficient performance of the United Nations Secretariat and Department of Peacekeeping Operations."[40] It concluded that both Secretary-General Boutros Boutros-Ghali and Undersecretary-General Kofi Annan bore responsibility for the UN's "lapses."[41] This is a critical point, for one cannot blame the UN's failure in Rwanda simply on the members of the UN Security Council who lacked the political will to intervene. After all, UN members act according to their national interests, and few states, with the exception of France, with its unique status in Francophone Africa, had vital interests in Rwanda. The UN's role is to defend the interests of world order, including adherence to the Genocide Convention, and recruit the international community to protect the principles for which it stands, even if few national interests of the member states are affected. For top UN officials to abdicate this responsibility is a terrible failure to fulfill the organization's duty.

If there is a hero in the Rwanda disaster it is General Dallaire, the Canadian commander of UN forces in Rwanda, who warned UN headquarters in New York of the impending extermination of the Tutsis but was nonetheless ignored. Dallaire also stood out for defying the instructions he received from Kofi Annan's Department of

*"United" or "Allied"?:* To be a founding member of the UN, in 1945, a state had to have declared war on the Axis Powers. In fact, Winston Churchill—shown here with Roosevelt and Stalin—wanted to call the organization the "Allied Nations." FDR saw the UN chiefly as "four policemen"—the United States, Britain, China, and the USSR—that would nip aggression in the bud and thus prevent another world war.

*Early doubts:* President Harry Truman was a UN enthusiast and attended the organization's founding conference in San Francisco, where he shook hands with the conference's secretary-general, Alger Hiss. But Truman quickly became disillusioned with the UN. His secretary of state, Dean Acheson, called the UN Charter "impracticable" and bypassed the UN Security Council when seeking authorization for the U.S. invasion of North Korea.

*Bettmann/CORBIS*

*The UN as diplomatic theater (part I):* The UN had almost nothing to do with resolving the Cuban Missile Crisis. The United States relied on a "recommendation" from the Organization of American States (OAS) to justify its naval blockade. Here, UN ambassador Adlai Stevenson displays America's evidence to the UN Security Council. But, by this point, the U.S. Navy had already begun to implement the blockade.

*Associated Press*

*The UN sparks a war:* UN secretary-general U Thant, left, ignited 1967's Six-Day War by badly miscalculating in his dealings with Egyptian president Gamal Abdel Nasser, right, and refusing to take a forceful stand against an Egyptian act of war. Recognizing the UN's limitations, President Lyndon Johnson remarked at the time, "I've never relied on [the UN] to save me when I'm going down for the third time."

Kathy Willens, Associated Press

Elise Amendola, Associated Press

*The UN as diplomatic theater (part II):* By February 2003, Iraq had violated sixteen different UN Security Council resolutions. Was another resolution necessary to authorize the use of force? In the Stevenson tradition, Secretary of State Colin Powell went before the deadlocked Security Council to present U.S. intelligence data on Iraq. Powell, holding a vial that could contain anthrax, makes his presentation to French foreign minister Dominique de Villepin (front row, left) and UN secretary-general Kofi Annan (front row, center), among others.

*Impartial to genocide:* The 1990s were supposed to be the UN's great opportunity to create a new world order. But, as UN peacekeeping missions multiplied, the UN failed to prevent some of the worst mass murders since the Second World War. In 1994, UN peacekeepers who had been ordered to remain "impartial" stood by as more than 800,000 Rwandan Tutsis were slaughtered. This churchyard was the site of only one of countless massacres.

*Moral equivalence and mass murder:* Just a year after Rwanda, UN peacekeepers failed again in Srebrenica, Bosnia, where more than 7,000 Bosnian Muslims were slaughtered in a UN "safe area." As in other areas, UN officials confused the aggressor with the victim, frequently blaming the Muslims instead of the invading Serbs.

*Morality rejected:* The UN commander in Rwanda, Major General Romeo Dallaire, actually warned UN headquarters in New York of an impending "extermination" campaign by the extremist Hutu militia against the Tutsis. But, according to Dallaire, the UN "took him to task" for even proposing to try to seize the Hutu militia's weapons caches.

*Protest of the betrayed:* Rwandans felt that the UN and the rest of the world had let them down. When Secretary-General Boutros Boutros-Ghali visited Rwanda in July 1994, protestors poured into the street; one demonstrator held up a placard that read, "Where Was the UN before the Genocide?" At the first anniversary of the massacres, shown here, similar sentiments were voiced.

Mahmoud Tawil, Associated Press

*Shaking hands with terror:* UN secretary-general Kofi Annan shakes hands with Hezbollah leader Sheikh Hasan Nasrallah on June 20, 2000. In September 2002, Undersecretary of State Richard Armitage remarked that Hezbollah is actually the "A-team" of international terrorism; al-Qaeda, he said, might only be the "B-team."

IDF spokesperson/Government Press Office, State of Israel

*The UN and suicide bombing:* Palestinian terrorist organizations have deeply penetrated the UN Relief and Works Agency (UNRWA), which is supposed to provide humanitarian aid. The extent of their penetration of this UN organ was revealed during Israel's Operation Defensive Shield in the West Bank city Jenin. Here, actual UN uniforms and an official UN poster ("UNRWA EMERGENCY SERVICES: MAKING THE DIFFERENCE") are found alongside posters extolling suicide bombers against Israel.

*A people unprotected:* An international refugee crisis exploded after the 1991 Gulf War when 1.5 million Kurds tried to flee Iraq, desperate to escape Saddam Hussein's ethnic cleansing campaign. Many went to Turkey, including this man, shown carrying his daughter across the border. But thousands of refugees could not get out of Iraq. It was the United States and Great Britain that offered the refugees international protection—the UN only followed.

*Abandoned to Saddam:* Not only the Kurds feared for their lives after the 1991 Gulf War. Here, Shiite women in Safwan, Iraq, demonstrate outside a U.S. refugee camp, asking the UN to guarantee their safety after U.S. forces leave. The UN ignored their pleas. Saddam Hussein's army exterminated thousands of Shiites.

*Finding Saddam's weapons:* According to UN Security Council Resolution 687 from April 1991, Iraq had *fifteen days* to declare the locations of its prohibited weapons of mass destruction. Twelve years later, Saddam Hussein still had not made a full disclosure. In the meantime, the UN Special Commission (UNSCOM) found evidence of illegal weapons and destroyed many, but UNSCOM had reason to believe that Iraqi weapons of mass destruction were still hidden.

*Undermining the UN's own success:* Richard Butler (left) headed UNSCOM in 1997 and 1998, but Secretary-General Kofi Annan systematically undermined his efforts. The UN then established a new and less robust monitoring agency, UNMOVIC, headed by Hans Blix (right). Blix felt his inspections should have been given more of a chance in 2003, but after Saddam's ouster, Iraqi scientists told the United States that they never would have disclosed anything to the UN.

Peacekeeping Operations by trying to protect Rwandan civilians, who otherwise might have been slaughtered. According to the report of the Organization of African Unity on the Rwanda genocide, Dallaire and his soldiers might have saved between 20,000 and 25,000 Rwandans.[42] But Dallaire's actions had nothing to do with the moral compass of the UN and its top diplomats in the Secretariat; rather, the men in the field acted despite the silence coming from UN headquarters.

Dallaire would remain haunted by the genocide of Rwanda. In February 1998, he appeared before the UN Criminal Tribunal investigating Rwanda. While barred under an agreement with UN lawyers from disclosing his 1994 secret communications with UN headquarters in New York, he was still able to drop a bombshell in public. Asked if a well-equipped peacekeeping force could have stopped the genocide, he unhesitatingly replied, "Absolutely."[43] He went further and explained that the UN Security Council could have easily created such a force in April 1994. He told the tribunal that they "cannot even imagine" his sense of regret. Dallaire quietly resigned from the Canadian military. In contrast, Kofi Annan was promoted to UN secretary-general in 1997 and much of his staff, including Iqbal Riza, rose with him.[44] The promotion only further illustrates the lack of accountability in the UN system. Unlike demo-cratic leaders, UN bureaucrats do not have to face an electorate who can judge their level of responsibility when military fiascos occur.

Let there be no doubt: the UN bears significant responsibility for the genocide in Rwanda. To be sure, the extremist Hutu militia were the ones who slaughtered hundreds of thousands of Rwandans. But by failing to take a stand against the rising tide of Hutu militancy, the UN signaled that it would stand by and do nothing even if massacres broke out—as indeed they did. General Dallaire had implored the UN to act against the Hutu militia because, he believed, the peacekeeping forces needed to *deter* those planning the massacres against the Tutsis. The UN's inaction ensured that the Hutu forces were not deterred.

## GLOBAL CHAOS

The UN is supposed to be a force for international security. Instead it has allowed crises to explode. And the UN's failure in one conflict only creates other crises, as the aftermath of the Rwandan genocide reveals.

Chaos spread over Central Africa. More than a million Rwandan Hutus fled from the victorious RFP forces in July 1994, settling in Zaire. The Hutu refugees, many of whom who had engaged in the genocide, received international aid, including aid from the UN. Hutu militias exploited these refugee camps to launch raids against the new regime in Rwanda. They also attacked the Tutsis of Zaire. As a result, both Rwanda and neighboring Uganda backed the effort that overthrew the pro-Hutu regime of Joseph Mobutu in Zaire, which in turn set off civil war. Zaire's internal wars spread across the borders of neighboring states. In 1998, five African states invaded Zaire, which by then had changed its name to the Democratic Republic of Congo. The conflict pitted the forces of Rwanda and Uganda against those of Zimbabwe, Namibia, and Angola.

By refusing to address the crisis in Rwanda when it had the opportunity, the UN set off a devastating chain of events. Instead of protecting peace, the UN had fueled chaos on the continent of Africa.

Even before these other crises had erupted, it was clear to some that the UN had ignored its duties and allowed some 800,000 people to be massacred. These people did not have to wait for a long UN inquiry to be completed to know who was to blame. On July 14, 1994, Secretary-General Boutros Boutros-Ghali visited Rwanda. Four white UN helicopters landed at a Catholic missionary compound in Nyarbuye, which had become a memorial for the Rwanda genocide. Barefoot villagers streamed toward the landing site to demonstrate before the UN's highest official. One demonstrator's placard read, WHERE WAS THE U.N. BEFORE THE GENOCIDE? Boutros-Ghali walked past the protestors with his head bent down.[45] Little more needs to be said.

# CHAPTER 7

# "Scenes from Hell"

*The UN and the Srebrenica Massacre*

These are truly scenes from hell, written on the darkest pages of human history."[1]

Those words easily could have been uttered to describe the mass killings that the UN allowed to occur in Rwanda. But they were not. Instead, this graphic language, offered by a judge from the International War Crimes Tribunal for the Former Yugoslavia, referred to still another atrocity that the UN failed to prevent. This massacre was, in fact, Europe's worst slaughter of civilians since the Second World War. And it occurred just a year after the Rwandan genocide.

As horrifying as the slaughters in Rwanda were, it is perhaps even more shocking that the UN could so easily and so soon repeat the same mistakes. But the UN's abdication of responsibility in Rwanda was not an aberration, as the 1995 Bosnian crisis made clear only one year later. In Rwanda, the UN insisted on being impartial when one party tried to exterminate the other; in Bosnia, the UN repeatedly sided with the aggressor against the victim. In both cases, the results of this defective moral compass were catastrophic. The organization that many people around the world insist is the source of "international legitimacy" betrayed, once again, the fact that it is singularly unequipped to cope with the tasks for which it was designed.

## THE BOSNIAN CONFLICT IN THE FORMER YUGOSLAVIA

## "UP TO THEIR KNEES IN BLOOD"

The Balkan wars began in 1991 with the breakup of the Federal Republic of Yugoslavia, after Croatia and Slovenia declared their independence. The fighting shifted southward in April 1992, soon after the Republic of Bosnia and Herzegovina declared independence. Like the other breakaway Yugoslav republics, Bosnia was not ethnically homogeneous. The two largest groups were Muslims, who constituted 44 percent of the Bosnian population, and Serbs, who represented 31 percent.[2] Though Serbs were the smaller of the two major groups, they enjoyed a distinct military advantage over the Muslims; they formed the Bosnian Serb army as an offshoot of the well-armed Yugoslav People's army.[3]

In March 1993, Serb forces drove more than 60,000 frightened Bosnian Muslims into the town of Srebrenica and the surrounding area. At that point, the UN commander in Bosnia, General Philippe Morillon of France, ventured to the enclave to declare his support for the Muslims. "You are now under the protection of the United Nations," he announced. "I will never abandon you."[4] The UN flag was raised over the city, and a month later the UN Security Council adopted Resolution 819, which declared the entire 30-square-mile enclave a UN "safe area." (It would be the first of several UN "safe areas" in Bosnia.) Muslim refugees flooded Srebrenica. The UN then deployed peacekeepers to the enclave to prevent further conflict between the Serbs and the Muslims.

The UN peacekeeping force was undermanned, however. By mid-1995, only 429 Dutch peacekeepers—half of whom were support troops—were overseeing Srebrenica.[5] The Dutch commanders assumed that if they ever did face a tangible threat, they could make up for their inadequate numbers by receiving air support from NATO fighter bombers based in Italy. After all, the UN had authorized the UN Protection Force in Bosnia (UNPROFOR) to call in NATO air strikes in order to compel the parties to comply with Security Council resolutions.

Yet when the Bosnian Serbs renewed their offensive against the Serbs, on July 6, 1995, the Dutch officers learned that their assumption had been mistaken. The Serbs assaulted UN peacekeeping positions and broke the Muslims' defense. Still, when the Dutch commander on the ground, Lieutenant Colonel Ton Karremans, made repeated requests for massive air strikes, the commander of all UN forces in the former Yugoslavia, General Bernard Janvier of France, refused the requests.

The Serb commander, General Ratko Mladic, encountered no resistance and captured Srebrenica within days, on July 11. That evening his troops began separating the Muslim men and boys from the women and children, and over the next week, Mladic's forces slaughtered more than 7,000 Bosnian Muslims and deported nearly 40,000 to other parts of Bosnia. These were the "scenes from hell" that the judge from the International War Crimes Tribunal for the Former Yugoslavia would later describe. When Mladic was indicted in absentia for war crimes, the judge summarized the evidence against the Bosnian Serb general: "After Srebrenica fell to the besieging Serb forces in July 1995, a truly terrible massacre of the Muslim population appears to have taken place. The evidence tendered by Prosecutor describes scenes of unimaginable savagery: thousands of men executed and buried in mass graves, hundreds of men buried alive, men and women mutilated and slaughtered, children killed before their mothers' eyes, a grandfather forced to eat the liver of his own grandson."[6]

How could the UN allow these atrocities to occur within its own self-declared safe areas? The problem was not simply that General Janvier did not call for NATO air support. The Dutch commanders on the ground decided to abandon Srebrenica and retreated northward with a two-mile-long column of refugees.[7] In 2001 the French parliament concluded an investigation of the Srebrenica massacre that sharply criticized the Dutch battalion for failing to put up any resistance to the Serb onslaught and for essentially turning over the Bosnian Muslims to their executioners. The Netherlands press also slammed the Dutch soldiers, suggesting that some even assisted the

Serbs with the deportation.[8] According to one Dutch newspaper, the Dutch peacekeepers crassly celebrated their evacuation from Srebrenica to Zagreb, the Croatian capital, even while the massacre persisted. The paper described how the soldiers, given a heroes' welcome in Zagreb on July 22 by Crown Prince Willem Alexander of the Netherlands, partied with Dutch ministers: "While the Bosnians were standing up to their knees in blood, the Dutch soldiers in Zagreb were standing up to their ankles in beer."[9] The drunken Dutch soldiers were reportedly dancing in a chorus line to a forty-two-piece band that played old Glenn Miller songs.[10]

At that point, however, the Dutch had not reported the slaughter that was occurring in Srebrenica. The deputy to Dutch commander Karremans, Major R. A. Franken, had signed a declaration as late as July 17 that the Bosnian Serbs had treated the Muslim refugees well according to international humanitarian law.[11] But the soldiers began to leak their first reports of the massacre the day after their revelry in Zagreb. The real story came out slowly.

Karremans himself was implicated in allowing the atrocity to occur. A Dutch historian later described Karremans as pro-Serbian and an admirer of General Mladic, the Serb commander. True, the Dutch commander ordered air strikes against the Serbs that the UN would not ultimately authorize, keeping to the procedures he believed he was instructed to follow. Nonetheless, he displayed an affinity for the Serbs. After the Serbs entered Srebrenica, Karremans went to a meeting with General Mladic, where he toasted the Serb leader with champagne and accepted a gift for his wife—a point noted and criticized in a Dutch newspaper editorial. He also praised Mladic as a "brilliant strategist" and called the Serb attack an excellently planned military operation."[12] He made these comments not with Serb guns pointing at him in Srebrenica but rather within the safety of Zagreb.

When the Netherlands Institute for War Documentation, under instructions from the Dutch ministers of defense and foreign affairs (and with parliamentary backing), came out with its own report on Srebrenica in April 2002, it blamed the Dutch government for failing to prevent the massacre. The report's publication forced the entire cabinet of Prime Minister Wim Kok, who had been in office back in 1995, to resign. The exhaustive report also blamed the UN, but notably there were no resignations in the blue-green tower on First Avenue in New York.

## DUTCH, FRENCH, OR UN RESPONSIBILITY?

As the 2002 report from the Netherlands made clear, the Dutch peacekeepers were not solely responsible for the Srebrenica massacre. Other reports confirmed that the failings were much more extensive, going to high levels of the UN. The highest civilian UN official on the ground in Bosnia from 1993 through 1995 was the secretary-general's special representative, Yasushi Akashi. Frederick H. Fleitz, Jr., a former CIA analyst who worked with the Clinton administration on UN issues, described Akashi as a "notoriously inept Japanese UN official."[13] According to Fleitz, the UN had promoted Akashi to the top civilian position in Bosnia after incorrectly crediting him with the organization's successes in Cambodia, failing to recognize that behind the scenes an Australian general had done the actual work in that peacekeeping operation. In reality, Akashi's term in Cambodia and Bosnia was "an unmitigated disaster," said former Australian foreign minister Gareth Evans.[14]

Akashi was well accustomed to the UN bureaucracy's amoral ethos. In Cambodia, he had been part of the UN effort to make Pol Pot's murderous Khmer Rouge, which had slaughtered 2 million of its countrymen, part of the internal "peace process." He rarely took a tough stand on Khmer Rouge violations of UN-brokered understandings. Now, in the Balkans, Akashi sat in a pivotal position. As part of the arrangement to authorize UNPROFOR to call for NATO air strikes, the UN and NATO had devised a "dual-key" process for approving the use of air power: NATO and the UN each had to "turn its own key" to put NATO fighter bombers in the air and attack Serb positions. Akashi held the UN key.[15]

Of course, the UN commander in the former Yugoslavia, General Janvier, had opposed NATO air strikes. Authoritative newspaper investigations later indicated why: According to these investigations, General Janvier had cut a deal with the Serb commander, General Mladic, during a secret meeting on June 4, 1995, a month before the Srebrenica offensive. The deal was simple: The UN would hold back further air strikes, and the Serbs would leave UN peacekeepers alone.[16] A Dutch television documentary concluded that Janvier had been working on instructions from the highest authorities in France. President Jacques Chirac, according to this report, reached a "gentleman's agreement" with General Mladic to hold back NATO air strikes in exchange for the release of up to 400 (mostly French) UN peacekeepers whom the Bosnian Serbs had held hostage since May.[17] What is definitely known is that Akashi met Serbian president Slobodan Milosevic in Belgrade on June 17, 1995; in that meeting, Milosevic revealed that Chirac had claimed he had received assurances from President Clinton that there would be no more NATO bombing without French approval.[18] France apparently had veto power over UN/NATO air operations.

Reports of this deal raised troubling questions about the UN's involvement in the Srebrenica massacre. Had the UN been involved in reaching this agreement with Serbs? Had the UN backed the aggressor in the Bosnian War because it was the only party capable of posing a real threat to UN personnel?

Other evidence indicated that Janvier's decision to oppose air strikes against the Serbs was not his alone or even simply a French decision. Dutch peacekeepers seem to have been as much in the loop on the decision to refrain from using airpower as were the French. Karremans had initially appealed not to Janvier but to a fellow Dutch officer, Brigadier General Cees Nicolai, the chief of staff of UN forces in Bosnia, who reported to General Janvier. Nicolai turned down the request, telling Karremans that a NATO air attack would disrupt a pending European Union peace initiative.[19] In other words, a high-ranking officer in the UN peacekeeping force expressed concern that taking sides would undermine the "peace process." That same logic had held back the UN Department of Peacekeeping Operations in Rwanda, when the UN had been afraid to side against the Hutu militia because it might undermine the Arusha peace process. In Srebrenica, the UN was so concerned about taking sides that it instructed its forces to withdraw from observation posts coming under Serb attack instead of defending them.

If senior UN staff, military and civilian, opposed any bombing campaign, not everyone dealing with the Bosnian crisis shared that view. The eventual architect of the 1995 Dayton Accords that ended the Bosnian War, U.S. ambassador Richard Holbrooke, completely opposed this passive military approach. Holbrooke has written, "For a week I called on our ambassador in the Netherlands, Terry Dornbush, instructing him to press the Dutch to allow air strikes, but to no avail."[20] The Dutch government apparently refused to allow air strikes unless all its soldiers were out of Bosnia. Thus, although Dutch officers had originally counted on airpower to make up for their quantitative inferiority, the Netherlands became more concerned about the vulnerability of its troops to becoming hostages of the Serbs.[21] There were clearly contradictory interests at play, and UN peacekeepers had to make the best of the impossible situation into which they were placed. Because the UN did not share Holbrooke's sense that using force would accelerate diplomacy, it did not deter the Serbs' aggression.

## ESCALATION OR APPEASEMENT?

Some UN commanders on the ground had pushed for more forceful action in the lead-up to the July 1995 Srebrenica massacre. Lieutenant General Rupert Smith of Britain, who had replaced General Morillon as commander of UN forces in Bosnia, recognized that the UN safe areas created an untenable situation for his troops. In the safe areas, the UN had become a shield for the Bosnian Muslim army, which allowed the Muslims to rearm; at the same time, the UN troops could easily become hostages of the Bosnian Serbs. The UN Secretariat had requested 34,000 troops to defend all the safe areas, but the UN Security Council had supplied only 7,600 troops for this mission.[22] Undermanned, UNPROFOR really had only two choices: escalate, or appease the Serbs.

In May, the conflict began to escalate. Early in the month, after a Bosnian Serb mortar attack near Sarajevo, another UN safe area, Smith asked Akashi and Janvier to expand the target list for NATO air strikes, but they refused the request. The Serbs had deployed their heavy weaponry within NATO's "exclusion zone" around the perimeter of Sarajevo, and they also began removing heavy weapons from a UN weapons-collection point. Smith gave the Bosnian Serbs a twenty-four-hour ultimatum. After they refused to comply with his demands, he ordered an air strike on two bunkers in the Bosnian Serb capital of Pale. Given the blatant violation of the exclusion zone by the Serbs, Akashi was hard-pressed to block Smith. Janvier was not present and could not turn Smith down.[23]

The Bosnian Serbs retaliated, shelling all of the safe areas. This shelling led to another NATO air strike. It was then that the Serbs seized 350 Dutch peacekeepers as hostages. Smith still felt that if NATO escalated further, the Serbs would back down. But General Janvier warned in early June "against any action which might degenerate into confrontation."[24] Of course, by being so concerned about doing anything that could "degenerate into confrontation," UN officials enabled the Bosnian Serbs to slaughter thousands of Muslims in Srebrenica.

The 2001 French parliamentary inquiry exposed critical UN documents that shed light on the appeasement strategy that key UN officials urged in the weeks leading up to the July massacre. In early June, representing Secretary-General Boutros Boutros-Ghali, Akashi complained to General Smith about the policy of stopping all negotiations with the Serbs until UN hostages were released: "Zagreb [meaning Janvier] and New York believe that some discussions should take place." Janvier concurred with Akashi, insisting that the UN had to recognize that UNPROFOR was a peacekeeping force between warring parties and that at this point it was essential "to allow for political progress to begin." Under such conditions, he said, the UN forces "cannot go toward confrontation." He added that the Serbs "want to modify their behavior, be good interlocutors." Meanwhile, Akashi told Smith that he needed to refine his military strategy: "You need to bring new elements into the peacekeeping context, which means consent, impartiality, use of force for self-defense, and freedom of movement." According to Akashi, "The hostages' release will become harder unless the [Bosnian] Serbs get assurances of no further air strikes." He added—perhaps for the written record—that such assurances were "impossible" to grant.

But had the UN already granted those assurances? Janvier and Akashi were offering these instructions to Smith days *after* the UNPROFOR commander's secret June 4 meeting with General Mladic. In a report Janvier later gave to the UN, he did not explicitly acknowledge that he had guaranteed that NATO air strikes would be halted. He did note, however, that Mladic had prepared a written memo laying out three parts of an understanding that he wanted the UN commander to confirm with UN headquarters in Zagreb:

1. The Bosnian Serb Army will no longer use force to threaten the life of and safety of UNPROFOR.
2. UNPROFOR commits to no longer make use of any force which leads to the use of air strikes against targets and territory of the Bosnian Serb Republic.
3. With the signing of the agreement, all "prisoners of war" would be freed.[25]

A signed document from the June 4 meeting has not been produced, but certain evidence indicates that the two parties did reach an agreement. An aide to Janvier subsequently confirmed that the French general had struck a deal with the Serbs, but the aide later retracted his story. Just as suspicious was the way Akashi handled reports of the Mladic-Janvier discussions. Akashi relayed a report of the meeting to UN headquarters in New York only on June 15, eleven days after the meeting took place, and only after UN head-quarters had specifically asked for it with the question, "Perhaps its transmission to New York was inadvertently overlooked?" And the report he did transmit was only four and a half pages long, which seemed excessively brief considering that the meeting had lasted five hours.

Akashi's timing on the report was significant, for General Smith was in the dark about the meeting when Janvier and Akashi were ordering him not to take a "combative approach" to the Bosnian Serbs. Still, UN records indicate that other parts of the UN were aware that the French general had reached an agreement with the Serbs, even if Akashi had submitted no formal report and even if no one made Smith aware of the deal. Kofi Annan, who still headed the Department of Peacekeeping Operations, knew about the Mladic-Janvier meeting just one day after it took place, for he informed troop-contributing countries about it.[26]

Subsequent events lent further credence to the idea that the UN and the Bosnian Serbs had struck a deal whereby NATO airpower would be held back and, in exchange, the Bosnian Serb army would release UN hostages. Just two days after the meeting, on June 6, the French secretly sent a military envoy from Paris to the Bosnian Serb capital of Pale; 111 UN hostages were released the next day. Perhaps the French envoy agreed to Mladic's terms outside of the UN chain of command. On June 13, another 28 hostages were let out, and the Bosnian Serbs' foreign minister announced, "We understand the international community will keep their promise to President Milosevic that there will not be any more bombing." The UN still denied that any deal had been struck. The remaining UN hostages were soon released.[27]

## A FAMILIAR PATTERN

Unaware of any deal that might have been reached with the Bosnian Serbs, Lieutenant General Rupert Smith challenged the instructions he received from Yasushi Akashi and Bernard Janvier in early June. Akashi told him to treat the Serbs and the Muslims evenhandedly, claiming that if the UN forces in Bosnia lost the consent of one of the parties, they would cross "the Mogadishu line"—the point at which UN forces would lose their neutrality. If Akashi was trying to avoid the disaster that had befallen UN forces in Somalia, Smith argued, the approach was misguided. "We are already over the Mogadishu line," the British general retorted. "The Serbs do not view us as peacekeepers." In his view, the Bosnian Serb army regarded UNPROFOR as the enemy. The UN and the Serbs had reached the point of confrontation, Smith said.

Despite General Smith's forceful rejoinder, UN officials did not share his clear sense of the organization's duty. Once again they fell back on the doctrine of impartiality. In this case, some UN officials considered the Bosnian Muslims even more culpable than the invading Serbs.[28] The Dutch peacekeepers in Srebrenica had notoriously poor relations with the local Muslim leaders, whom they regarded as gangsters and war profiteers.[29] Phillip Corwin of Britain, who served as the chief UN political officer in Bosnia in 1995, has disclosed that he received a death threat from a Bosnian Muslim government minister. Corwin argues vociferously that the UN compromised its doctrine of impartiality by arranging for NATO to launch supporting air strikes: "I was deeply distressed by NATO's massive military intervention against the Bosnian Serbs, an intervention not very well camouflaged under UN cover." Corwin captures the ideology of UN peacekeeping. Rather than focusing on the issue of aggression, he asserts, it is more important "to redress reasonable grievances." Achieving a durable peace is his highest moral calling, but he does not realize that morally distinguishing the aggressor from the victim and acting accordingly is the way to achieve it, rather than continually "redressing" the "grievances" of both sides.[30]

Corwin was not alone. Addressing the UN Security Council on May 24, 1995, more than a month before the Srebrenica massacre, General Janvier urged the UN to withdraw its peacekeeping forces from the Bosnian safe areas. He argued that the Bosnians were strong enough to defend themselves. Janvier reserved his harshest criticism for the Bosnian government, which he said was abusing the safe areas in order to launch raids into Serb territory.[31] All of this may have been true, but the net effect was that the supreme UN commander was expressing more sympathy for the forces that were threatening his troops than for the people whom he was supposed to protect. Akashi acted much the same way. Even six days into the Bosnian Serbs' invasion of Srebrenica, Akashi was still blaming the Bosnian Muslims for provoking the Serbs.[32]

This attitude could have informed the UN's slow response to the Bosnian Serbs' attack on Srebrenica. In his memoirs, former Secretary-General Boutros Boutros-Ghali portrays the UN as acting swiftly and decisively in response to the attack. He writes that General Janvier sent Akashi a request for close air support on July 11, 1995, at 12:25 P.M., and that Akashi approved the request immediately. The air attacks began right away, according to Boutros-Ghali.

But in reality, the situation unfolded much differently. Janvier had approved the strikes, in principle, during the night of July 10, but then inexplicably put them off until morning. Lieutenant Colonel Karremans, the commander of the UN Dutch peacekeepers, had assured the townspeople of Srebrenica that fifty NATO planes would bomb the Serbs at 6 o'clock on the morning of July 11. More delays occurred that morning, however, when Karremans was told that he had submitted his request for close air support on the wrong form. As he redid and refiled the necessary paperwork, the NATO attack was delayed another hour and half. In the meantime, most of the NATO aircraft that had been in the skies of Bosnia since early morning had run out of fuel and returned to their bases in Italy. Thus, the attack that was finally carried out was of severely reduced strength. The great NATO air campaign against the Serbs involved two Dutch F-16 fighters that dropped a total of two bombs on Serb positions.

Boutros-Ghali doesn't supply all these details. Instead he blames the Dutch defense minister, Joris Voorhoeve, for pressing Akashi to stop the attacks after only two hours because Dutch peacekeepers were too close to the Serbs. Whether the air attacks were ineffectual because of the Dutch, the UN, or Janvier's repeated delaying tactics is really a moot point: the attack was a case of too little, too late. Srebrenica fell to the Bosnian Serb army that same afternoon, July 11.

The real issue, that Boutros-Ghali does not address, is why the UN waited so long to call for air support in the first place. The Serb assault on Srebrenica actually began on July 6, five days before the first air strike. The UN Security Council was receiving incorrect briefings about the situation on the ground as late as July 10.[33] Airpower at an earlier stage might have deterred the Bosnian Serb army, protected the UN safe area, and prevented the murder of thousands of innocent civilians.

The fact of the matter was that on July 6 and again on July 8, Lieutenant Colonel Karremans requested air support, but Janvier turned him down.[34] By the time Karremans made the second request, Dutch peacekeepers had abandoned three observation posts and urged the UN "to find a means of preventing a total massacre."[35] Janvier refused Karremans's third request for air support as well. On July 9, the Bosnian ambassador to the UN, Mohamed Sacirbey, wrote a letter reminding the UN Security Council of the terms of the agreement that the Bosnian government had reached with the UN on May 8, 1993: The Bosnian Muslims disarmed their defense units protecting the population of Srebrenica, and in exchange, the UN and NATO assumed responsibility for defending the enclave. Implicit in the letter was a strong rebuke: The UN command was reneging on its commitments to the Bosnian Muslims when it vetoed NATO air strikes.

The UN had blocked an alternative to airpower that might have deterred Serb aggression. The British and French governments had been contemplating establishing a "rapid reaction force" to reinforce the beleaguered UN troops. Yet on June 19, less than two weeks before the Srebrenica attack, Akashi wrote to the Bosnian Serb leader, Radovan Karadzic, "I wish to assure you that these theatre reserve forces will operate under the existing United Nations peacekeeping rules of engagement and will not in any way change the essential peacekeeping nature of the UNPROFOR mission." He emphasized that the rapid reaction force would be "an impartial force." The United States protested both the substance and the timing of Akashi's letter, for good reason: the UN had essentially assured the Serbs that nothing would stand in their way.[36]

The UN cannot plead ignorance of the Bosnian Serbs' intentions. Chief political officer Phillip Corwin wrote in his diary on July 12, 1995, that well before the assault on Srebrenica, he had no illusions about what would happen if the Serbs took over Srebrenica: "Not a single one of us believes that the Moslem population of Srebrenica will be safe. The pattern is all too familiar, and it is a pattern used by Croats as well. The draft-age men will be separated from their families, then tortured, imprisoned, executed. Women will be raped. Mass graves will be hurriedly dug to hide the evidence."[37] Dutch government ministers were aware of the risks to the Muslims as well, although for years they refused to admit it. Finally, in 2002, in testimony before the commission that produced the Netherlands Institute for War Documentation report, former minister Jan Pronk acknowledged, "We all knew that the Serbs would consider all boys and men above fifteen years as soldiers and might murder them."[38]

That is precisely what the Serbs did. Muslim men were shot or knifed to death. Most were forced to dig their own graves in surrounding fields and woods. The slaughters were swift and merciless. According to a UN report, by July 13 one town had no males above the age of twelve and below the age of sixty.

At the UN compound in Srebrenica, Dutch peacekeepers released 239 Bosnian Muslim refugees to the Serbs even after the Serb forces had begun executing Muslim men. According to a 1999 UN report on Srebrenica, the Muslim men in the compound pleaded not to be abandoned to the Serb forces, but UN officials ignored their pleas. The compound was filled with UN observers, aid workers from Médecins Sans Frontières (Doctors Without Borders), and the UN High Commissioner for Refugees, but amazingly they deferred to the Dutch commanding officer's decision to release the Muslims. In one case, Hasan Nuhanovic, a Bosnian Muslim who had worked as a UN interpreter for two years, begged the UN Dutch peacekeepers to spare his family by letting them remain in the compound, but the peacekeepers provided only him personally with asylum. Nuhanovic never saw his family again.[39]

The incident was eerily reminiscent of what UN peacekeepers had done in a Kigali technical school during the Rwanda genocide, abandoning Tutsi refugees to Hutu death squads.

The UN peacekeepers had no justification for their action. The deputy Dutch UN commander, Major Franken, could manage only to claim that he had believed the Serbs would not dare to kill Muslims whose names appeared on a UN list. Once again, the UN failed to recognize, and respond appropriately to, pure evil.

## COVER-UP?

The reports of the Srebrenica massacre did not reach the UN quickly. Refugees who escaped the enclave did not reach Muslim-controlled territory until July 16. As the Dutch peacekeepers made their full retreat to Zagreb, Dutch military spokesmen in Zagreb maintained that nothing pointed to large-scale murders. The commander in chief of the Dutch army, General Hans Couzy, who was visiting his forces in the Balkans, said there was no "hard evidence of mass killings."[40] He also praised the Bosnian Serb commander, General Mladic: "As a military man I admire the manner in which he deals with things. The basic rules of combat are always: surprise the enemy and attack him where he is weakest. Well those starting points he applies daily with great insight."[41] Meanwhile, Couzy told his troops not to speak to the media. Some reports indicated that his peacekeepers had videotaped Serb abuses of the Muslims during the fall of Srebrenica but that he had ordered the tape destroyed.[42] The Dutch later denied this claim, but the various measures they took during this time raised questions about whether a cover-up was in progress.

Even if Dutch officials hadn't wanted reports of the Srebrenica massacre to get out, some Dutch soldiers began talking to the press in Zagreb. Agence France-Presse picked up the story on July 17.

Though eyewitness testimony of mass murder was emerging, Akashi, the most senior UN official on the ground in the former Yugoslavia, still had reported nothing of the atrocities.[43] Thus, when peacekeeping department head Kofi Annan opened his morning newspaper on July 17 in New York, he was surprised to read, "A hunting season [is] in full swing. . . . It is not only men supposedly belonging to the Bosnian government who are targeted. . . . Women, including pregnant ones, children and old people aren't spared. Some are shot and wounded, others have had their ears cut off and some women have been raped." The AFP wire report was all over international and local newspapers. Annan wrote to Akashi on July 18 asking for a detailed report.[44] Akashi responded by saying that the debriefings of Dutch soldiers "did not reveal any first-hand accounts of human rights violations."[45]

There was a clear discrepancy between what the UN was reporting and what Western media outlets were beginning to disclose. But the press reports were making an impression on some senior UN staff in New York. For example, in July, UN undersecretary-general Shashi Tharoor told a U.S. official, "I think we're facing a humanitarian disaster of historic proportions. There are reports of mass killings in Srebrenica."[46]

Still the UN did not stop the mass murders. As late as July 23, the head of the UN Center for Human Rights in the former Yugoslavia, Peruvian diplomat H. Wieland, would claim, "We have not found anyone who saw with their own eyes an atrocity taking place."[47] In contrast, the UN special rapporteur for human rights for the former Yugoslavia, former Polish prime minister Tadeusz Mazowiecki, had condemned the Srebrenica attacks as "barbaric" and was warning that the UN needed to protect another UN safe area, Zepa, from a Serb offensive. Sickened by the UN's refusal to defend the Bosnian Muslims against the Serb aggressors, Mazowiecki resigned from the UN on July 27, saying that he "cannot continue to participate in the pretense of the protection of human rights."[48]

Just as in the Rwanda genocide, no one at the UN paid a price for the massacre. Some UN member states were relieved when Yasushi Akashi left Bosnia in October 1995. "Good riddance," U.S. officials told the press when they heard of Akashi's departure; they blamed him for the UN's policy of "appeasement" toward the Serbs.[49] Bosnian Muslim diplomats were even harsher in their appraisal of the role of the UN's chief diplomat on the ground. One described Akashi's "negotiating approach" as follows: "accommodate the stronger party (i.e. the Serbs) and squeeze everything from the weaker party (i.e. the Bosnians)."[50] He charged that these very tactics were in part responsible for bringing about the Srebrenica massacre.[51] But the UN did not discipline Akashi for his poor judgments and counterproductive tactics in Bosnia. Far from it. Less than a year after the Srebrenica atrocities, he was promoted to undersecretary-general for humanitarian affairs.[52] His promotion only highlighted the lack of accountability in the UN system. It is little wonder that Akashi expressed no remorse about his actions in Bosnia, insisting in an interview that he made no major mistakes during the fall of the Srebrenica enclave.

How can we ever expect the UN to correct itself when it not only ignores its most shocking failures but actually rewards them?

## THE MYTH OF IMPARTIALITY

David Rieff captured the growing disgust with the UN's behavior among a limited community of journalists who covered the Bosnian War up close: "What continued to shock and anger many in the press was the UN's lack of ability to see how morally wrong it was to choose always to mediate between killers and rapists and those who were suffering at their hands, not only at first but long after it had become clear for all to see that the murderers and rapists planned to go on murdering and raping no matter what promises they might make."[53] This was the heart of what went wrong at Srebrenica. The UN would not take sides. Coming back from Srebrenica, Lieutenant Colonel Karremans, the UN Dutch commander, told the press, "We learned that the parties in Bosnia cannot be divided into 'the good guys' and 'the bad guys.' "[54]

When the UN completed its own investigation of Srebrenica, its report concluded, "The Serbs repeatedly exaggerated the extent of the [Muslim] raids out of Srebrenica as a pretext for the prosecution of a central war aim: to create a geographically contiguous and ethnically pure territory along the Drina [River], while freeing their troops to fight in other parts of the country. *The extent to which this pretext was accepted at face value by international actors and observers reflected the prism of 'moral equivalency' through which the conflict in Bosnia was viewed by too many for too long* [emphasis added]."[55] Evenhandedness in the face of outright aggression put the UN on the side of the aggressor—the very opposite of what the UN was supposed to do.

It was true that the Bosnian Muslims themselves engaged in war crimes against the Serbs. The Croats had evicted tens of thousands of Serbs as well, so that everyone in the former Yugoslavia engaged in "ethnic cleansing" of one sort or another. It was also true that the Bosnian Muslims looked for help wherever they could get it, whether from Iran or even from Osama bin Laden's mujahideen, who left Afghanistan and joined the war against the "Christian Serbs" in the Balkans. But those facts had little bearing on the immediate danger: thousands of civilians faced torture, rape, and massacre—citizens whom the UN commander in Bosnia had dramatically declared to be "under the protection of the United Nations." The UN and its peacekeepers, fully aware of the imminent carnage, could have taken steps to prevent it, even without judging which side in the war was ultimately more evil. This was the moral call that the UN needed to make.

The tragedy in Srebrenica exposed the UN's declared policies of "neutrality" and "impartiality" for what they so often are: excuses for not performing its duty. A truly impartial force would protect both sides in a conflict from genocidal violence. In the case of Srebrenica, however, the UN turned the notion of impartiality on its head, putting itself on the side of aggression and against the defense of human rights. The UN actually refused protection to those facing imminent extermination. The families pleading not to be abandoned, the women and children separated from their husbands and fathers, the hundreds of refugees fleeing into the UN's (allegedly) safe areas—all deserved protection regardless of the general record of their side in the conflict. While the UN debated with itself about how to respond to a clear case of aggression, thousands perished in the woods and fields of eastern Bosnia.

The UN's failure in Srebrenica spread chaos in the former Yugoslavia. The other UN safe areas came under assault. On August 28, 1995, Serb artillery shelled Sarajevo; one mortar attack killed thirty-seven civilians in the Sarajevo market. Ethnic cleansing became even more prevalent, as Croatia attacked Krajina Serbs and an undeterred Slobodan Milosevic applied his doctrine of ethnic cleansing to Kosovo.

The Bosnian crisis would finally be contained in the fall of 1995 with the Dayton Peace Accords. The peace process was set in motion in late August 1995, when Kofi Annan, as head of the Department of Peacekeeping Operations, informed U.S. ambassador to the UN Madeleine Albright of a significant change in UN military policy: He had instructed UN military commanders and civilian officials to temporarily relinquish their authority to veto NATO air strikes.[56] In the "dual-key" arrangement governing the use of airpower, the UN had turned its key over to NATO. And because NATO finally did take sides in the fall of 1995, the aggression of the Bosnian Serb army finally stopped. Only with the aggression halted could the diplomacy begin. That diplomacy produced the Dayton Accords.

In short, the conflict was resolved only after the UN stepped aside and let someone else take over.

# CHAPTER 8

# Institutionalized Moral Equivalence

## *The International Criminal Court*

The atrocities in Rwanda and Bosnia created a new urgency for a UN response to crimes against humanity. The Security Council had established ad hoc international tribunals to deal with those specific situations, but the UN was under pressure to do more. Secretary-General Kofi Annan addressed why the time had come to create a new international legal mechanism against war crimes: "Many thought that the horrors of the Second World War—the camps, the cruelty, the exterminations, the Holocaust—could never happen again. And yet they have." He mentioned Cambodia, Bosnia, and Rwanda. Annan reiterated how the decade of the 1990s "has shown us that man's capacity for evil knows no limits."[1] The time for the UN to take action against its own inertia had come. It needed to come up with a permanent system for bringing to justice those behind the worst atrocities against mankind.

The idea of an international court to prosecute crimes against humanity had first been proposed in the earliest days of the UN, soon after the end of the Second World War. The 1948 Genocide Convention envisioned that persons charged with genocide be tried by an "international penal tribunal" (Article VI). The UN General Assembly's International Law Commission did some initial work on establishing an international criminal court to try those charged with genocide "or other crimes of similar gravity," but as the Cold War intensified, the efforts halted, partly as a result of the East-West struggle.

Now the UN moved swiftly to make such a court a reality. As British human rights lawyer Geoffrey Robertson noted, the UN "worked at breakneck speed" to draft a treaty establishing the court. Starting in 1996, its Preparatory Committee took only twenty-seven months to produce a draft text.[2] Then, at the recommendation of the UN General Assembly, in the summer of 1998, the UN opened a conference in Rome to finalize the details of the International Criminal Court (ICC) and sign the treaty. The UN pressured the delegates to finish off the negotiations quickly. As Hans Correll, the UN legal adviser and personal representative of Kofi Annan, told one of the main caucuses in Rome at the opening of the Conference, "Time is running short."[3] The delegates had from June 15 to July 17 to hammer out a consensus.

The conference was the culmination of what the *New York Times* called "one of the most ambitious efforts ever undertaken to extend the rule of international law."[4] But no matter how ambitious the effort, and no matter how noble the goal of bringing war criminals and tyrants to justice, the majority of delegates recognized that the most important consideration was passing *something,* anything. Representatives from more than a hundred nongovernmental organizations (NGOs)—including groups like Amnesty International, Human Rights Watch, and the World Federalist Movement—arrived in Rome to push negotiators to hammer out a consensus at all costs. Pro-ICC NGOs held demonstrations in Rome, including one that accused President Bill Clinton of "genocide" because of his economic embargo of Iraq. In the last week of the conference, Human Rights Watch put out a press release condemning "a threat by the United States to sabotage the establishment of an independent and effective Court."[5] Recognizing the pressure to approve the ICC, the delegates were feverishly making compromises. They had little time to argue over language that might damage the vital interests of some states; the conference sought simply to reach a document that reflected, in Robertson's words, the "least common denominator."[6]

Despite the readiness to compromise, a great deal was at stake in Rome. The ICC would be very different from any previous international court. Whereas the International Court of Justice in The

Hague ruled in disputes between states, the ICC would indict and judge individuals. Moreover, disputants had to agree to accept the International Court of Justice's decisions before it had jurisdiction, but the ICC would not always require a state's prior consent to proceed. Instead, what would determine its jurisdiction was the sort of crime a suspect was alleged to have committed. The ICC would deal with three "core crimes"—the crime of genocide, crimes against humanity, and war crimes. Here, however, is where the pressure to reach an agreement by the fast-approaching deadline undercut the UN's efforts at establishing an effective system for dealing with the problems it faced. Although the delegates agreed ultimately to put the crime of aggression under the ICC's jurisdiction, the Rome conference could not agree on a definition of the term. In other words, the UN put off defining "aggression" until a later date; the earliest a conference would take up the issue again would be 2009. Just as important, although many parties pushed to include terrorism as one the ICC's "core crimes," the Rome conference decided not to do so. As in the case of aggression, the conference left the subject of terrorism to a future review conference.

Finally, on July 17, 1998, just five weeks after the Rome conference's opening, the statute creating the ICC was approved by a vote of 120–7, with 21 states abstaining. Despite the overwhelming vote, there remained significant questions about the new international court—not least because the world's sole superpower, the United States, had been one of the seven states to vote against the Rome Statute. As one Dutch delegate put it at the time of the vote on the Rome Statute, "You cannot have a court of universal jurisdiction without the world's major military power on board."[7]

From the beginning, then, the ICC's credibility was in question.

## MORALITY TURNED ON ITS HEAD

When the Clinton administration ordered its delegation to vote against the Rome Statute, it was not because the U.S. government opposed efforts to bring war criminals to justice. In fact, the Clinton administration had strongly supported international war-crimes tribunals for the former Yugoslavia and Rwanda. But the United States had significant concerns about the unprecedented authority the Rome Statute gave the ICC.

With its claim to universal jurisdiction, the new UN body could reach into any UN member state and lodge claims against its citizens. It could, for example, pull American citizens outside of the protective umbrella of the U.S. Constitution, whether the U.S. government agreed or not. As such, it was the first UN body whose powers actually superseded the sovereignty of its member states. One American critic noted, "Were the United States to become a State party to the Rome Statute, it would, for the first time since July 4, 1776, acknowledge the superior authority of an institution neither elected by the American people, nor accountable to them for its actions."[8]

The fear of politicization was at the heart of American concerns about the ICC. The question was, would the ICC root out evil in the world, or would it become a blunt instrument used actually to harm those defending freedom? One of the causes of concern was that the same institution selected both the ICC's prosecutor and its judges, meaning that the system lacked the checks and balances on a prosecutor that are found in the American legal system.[9] The body that elected (or removed) the prosecutor and judges was known as the Assembly of State Parties, which had representatives from every state that voted for the Rome Statute. Among the member states charged with deciding how the ICC would deal with crimes against humanity were such paragons of human rights as Iran, Syria, and Zimbabwe.

Ambassador David J. Scheffer, who led the U.S. delegation to Rome, told the Senate Foreign Relations Committee in July 1998 that the United States was concerned about the broad authority granted to the Office of the Prosecutor. Scheffer called attention to the fact that the Rome Statute empowered the prosecutor to initiate investigations by himself (he needed the consent of two judges to proceed beyond an initial stage), without any state party turning to the ICC or without the recommendation of the UN Security

Council. And any state could provide the ICC prosecutor with the evidence he might need to pursue such an independent investigation. This provision enabled states to make politically motivated allegations to the ICC about "war crimes" supposedly committed by their adversaries.

The Rome Statute also specified that evidence for such prosecutions could come from NGOs or "other reliable sources." While some NGOs had conducted important investigative work of past war crimes, they nonetheless were not accountable to anyone except their boards of directors and their contributors. For the United States, this provision raised a particular problem, because the UN body that recognizes NGOs, the Economic and Social Council in Geneva, mostly approves those that would have serious reservations about any assertion of American power.

UN organs other than the Security Council could also push the ICC prosecutor to consider unwarranted prosecutions. The UN gave an indication of what kind of influence its bodies might have over the ICC when on December 3, 2003, an Emergency Special Session of the UN General Assembly sought a nonbinding "advisory opinion" from the International Court of Justice in The Hague concerning the legality of Israel's security fence in the West Bank. Normally, the International Court of Justice hears only "contentious" disputes between states that have agreed to seek its arbitration and accept its ruling. For example, if Qatar and Bahrain are arguing over who has sovereignty over a coral island between them, they can both turn to the International Court of Justice in order to obtain its decision. So by seeking an "advisory opinion" on a security fence, the UN did an end run around the court's rules of jurisdiction.

Such an end run could happen with the International Criminal Court as well. If the experience with the International Court of Justice is any guide, most governments are reluctant to give an international panel of judges automatic veto power over what they regard as their vital national interests. In 1984, for instance, the United States withdrew the automatic jurisdiction that it had given the International Court of Justice back in 1946, after Nicaragua went to the court to get the U.S. government to stop backing the Contras; the French did the same in 1974, when Australia and New Zealand tried to get the International Court of Justice to halt France's nuclear testing in the South Pacific.[10]

In this case, Israel argued that the security fence was vital to its national security, stating that the wave of suicide bombings by Palestinian terrorist organizations had forced it to build the barrier. Given that the Palestinians themselves were not effectively policing these terrorist groups, a Hamas suicide bomber could walk unobstructed across a field from a Palestinian city to any Israeli town and attack a shopping mall or school. The fence would prevent that. But the International Court of Justice ignored the Israelis' objections to what they considered a politically motivated effort on the part of the UN's Arab bloc; the court agreed to the General Assembly's request to hear the case.

The court forged ahead even after more than thirty countries, including the United States and the members of the European Union, submitted letters opposing the court's taking the case on. And the International Court of Justice hardly came off as an independent arbitrator in a dispute between two parties. The General Assembly's resolution calling on the court to offer an advisory opinion attacked Israel's security fence but did not address the Palestinian terrorism; indeed, the word "terrorism" did not even appear in the resolution. And the UN Secretariat, under Secretary-General Kofi Annan, added fuel to the fire by supplying the judges at the International Court of Justice with eighty-eight "supporting documents," none of which dealt with the waves of suicide bombings that Israel had endured.

On July 9, 2004, the International Court of Justice ruled against Israel (with the U.S. judge on the court dissenting). In its ruling, the court explained that it had at its disposal a "report" from the secretary-general, as well as "a voluminous dossier" that he had submitted. Given the limited terms of reference from which the court worked, it was no surprise that the ruling criticized Israel for building the fence and called for its removal. It completely downplayed the suicide terrorism attacks that Israel had endured for nearly four years. The court specifically refused to recognize Israel's right of self-defense under Article 51 of the UN Charter, because the threat the Israelis faced was terrorism from "within" and did not result from an external armed attack. It was as though the International Court of Justice, under UN direction, had illegalized the shield protecting Israeli civilians while taking no tangible measure against the sword of terrorism that was still drawn against them. An Emergency Special Session of the UN General Assembly was then convened on July 20 to demand that Israel comply with the court's nonbinding "advisory opinion."

The court's ruling had enormous global implications, for it set a dangerous precedent concerning the rights of states to defend themselves against terrorism. The entire episode demonstrated how international courts could be manipulated by those at the UN with a political agenda to subvert the war on terrorism and make Western democracies more vulnerable.

All this happened, of course, with a court that has a much narrower mandate than the ICC. If a UN body could compel the International Court of Justice to take up a case despite the fact that one of the disputants did not agree to accept the court's decision and despite the strenuous objections of the United States and its allies, what happens when the ICC does not even have to consider a state's prior consent before proceeding with a case?

Another of the U.S. government's objections to the Rome Statute was that it granted the ICC jurisdiction even over states that didn't sign it. The statute held that the ICC could get involved if either the state where the war crime was committed or the state that perpetrated the alleged crime was party to the Rome Statute. Since any government, NGO, or UN body like the General Assembly could turn to the ICC, the potential for spurious prosecutions was high. For instance, even if the United States did not sign the Rome Statute, U.S. troops, as well as their military commanders and civilian leaders, could come before the ICC if they were sent as peacekeeping forces to a country that had signed the treaty and they were alleged to have been involved in what the ICC defined as a war crime. Moreover, the statute held that the UN Security Council could halt an ICC prosecution only through an affirmative vote; the permanent five members could not block the ICC individually with their veto power. So, for example, if the United States wanted to stop the ICC prosecutor from pursuing an anti-American initiative, it would need the support of Russia, France, and China; any of those states could veto Security Council interference in the ICC's work. In effect, the Rome Statute gave the ICC primacy in sensitive areas of international peace and security over the Security Council, defying the UN Charter. It also served the agenda of many UN members that wanted to curtail the powers of the permanent five Security Council members, especially those of the United States, and give more authority to wider international bodies like the Assembly of State Parties of the ICC.

Strangely, though, the Rome Statute was drafted in such a way as to make it difficult to achieve its real goal: going after war criminals. While U.S. troops and leaders could be prosecuted for war crimes before the ICC, some tyrants and war criminals could commit their atrocities without ever having to answer to the UN's international court. For example, if in the future a leader like Slobodan Milosevic of Yugoslavia didn't sign the Rome Statute and his forces engaged in mass murder of a minority that he was seeking to expel, the ICC would have no jurisdiction in this case because the war crime in question occurred on the tyrant's territory against his own nationals.

It was classic UN diplomacy: Many aggressors could continue their activity with impunity, while leaders of states defending international peace and security faced potential criminal prosecution. Morality was again being turned on its head.

Critics also felt that the ICC lacked the deterrent capability its supporters hoped it would have. But the advocates of the ICC, who came mostly from the legal profession or the human rights community, did not factor in strategic considerations. For example, with the ICC in place, it is extremely unlikely that a future Saddam Hussein would agree to step down from power peacefully and go into exile, since he could not be sure that he would not face an ICC prosecution. He would have all the incentive to cling to power at any cost, even if that meant he would face military action by a UN coalition; rather than accept defeat, such a leader, trapped with no choices, might consider "going down" after using weapons of mass destruction.

Earlier war tribunals have not deterred war criminals from committing atrocities. The UN had created the International Tribunal for Yugoslavia back in May 1993, but the Bosnian Serbs massacred some 7,000 Bosnian Muslims in Srebrenica more than two years later; clearly the existence of the tribunal did not deter them from committing atrocities. The UN tribunal did indict General Ratko Mladic, but the Bosnian Serb commander remained at large a full nine years after the Srebrenica massacre, as did most of the other Bosnian Serb leaders. Even if dictators do not cling to power at all costs, they plan escape routes and count on not being caught. Mladic used this tactic to thwart the international war-crimes tribunal for years, and it was the tactic that Saddam Hussein tried to use in Iraq. It is naïve to expect to the ICC to deter tyrants from committing crimes against humanity, and in fact the existence of the international court might even lead dictators to commit further atrocities in a desperate attempt to hold on to power.

## "ONE MORE POLITICAL TOOL"

The U.S. government was not alone in objecting to the ICC because of its potential for politicization. Joining the United States in voting against the Rome Statute were six other states, including Israel.

Probably no one else attending the Rome conference had more of a personal stake in the prosecution of war criminals than Judge Eli Nathan, a Holocaust survivor who headed the Israeli delegation at the end of the UN meeting. It fell upon Judge Nathan to explain to the delegates present why Israel, a state that had been born in the ashes of the worst war crimes in world history and that had called for an international criminal court nearly fifty years earlier, was forced to vote against the Rome Statute. "Mr. President," Nathan said, "it causes me considerable pain, both personally as a victim of the Nazi persecution of the Jewish people, and on behalf of the Israeli delegation which I proudly head, to have to explain the negative vote which Israel has been unwillingly obliged to cast today."

Judge Nathan referred to the "leading Jewish legal minds and statesmen" who had originally made the call for a means of bringing war criminals to justice. He didn't name those leaders, but it was clear that he was talking about several key founders of the human rights movement: Raphael Lemkin, who fathered the Genocide Convention; René Cassin, who worked with Eleanor Roosevelt on the Universal Declaration of Human Rights; and Shabtai Rosenne, who drafted the first UN statute for the international criminal court in the 1950s. Nathan simply concluded, "This was, Mr. President, inter alia, our idea!"

The reason Israel had to vote against the Rome Statute, Judge Nathan explained, was that it was seriously flawed. Like the United States, the Israeli government believed that the states could exploit the ICC to wage political warfare against their adversaries, regardless of the legal merits of their cases. Nathan agreed with the ICC's purpose contained in the Rome Statute's preamble: to address "unimaginable atrocities" and "grave crimes which deeply shock the conscience of the whole international community." Yet he noted that when the Rome Statute defined the "most heinous and grievous war crimes," suddenly it delved into the issue of Israeli settlement activity. The rush toward completing the Rome Statute had led to rigid rules that did not allow individual states to register their reservations about any single provision in the treaty, including the effort by the Arab states to define settlement activity as a war crime. This set off alarm bells in the Israeli delegation, and for Judge Nathan it had the effect of "sullying the entire statute."

What happened in Rome was the continuation of long-term debate between Israel and the Arab states over the applicability of the 1949 Fourth Geneva Convention to Israeli settlements in the West

Bank and Gaza Strip—a debate that had begun in the halls of the UN General Assembly. The Geneva Convention dealt with the protection of civilians in time of war. Article 49 specifically prohibited "individual or mass forcible transfers" from occupied territory to the territory of the occupying power or to other countries. It added that the occupying power was not supposed to deport or transfer its own population into the territory under occupation. The Rome Statute reversed this order, however, first listing the issue of the occupying power moving its own population into an occupied territory and only afterward addressing the forcible transfer of the civilians out of an occupied territory.

But regardless of the order, the question remained, did any of this legal language apply to Israel's situation? Certainly U.S. administrations did not think so. Though the United States voiced *political* objections to Israeli settlements, calling them "an obstacle to peace," it did not say that they were *illegal*. Indeed, back in February 1990, the U.S. ambassador to the UN in Geneva, Morris Abram—who had served on the U.S. staff at the Nuremberg trials and thus was, in his own words, familiar with the "legislative intent behind the Fourth Geneva Convention"—explained Washington's view that the convention "was not designed to cover situations like Israeli settlements in the occupied territories, but rather the forcible transfer, deportation, or resettlement of large numbers of people."

With the Rome Statute, however, the UN was including Israel's settlements among the "most heinous and grievous war crimes." In other words, it was comparing Israel's policies to those of the Nazis in Poland and the Ukraine. The comparison with Nazi Germany outraged Judge Nathan and the Israeli delegation, but his response was nonetheless controlled: "Without entering here into the question of the substantive status of any particular alleged violation of the Fourth Geneva Convention, which clearly Israel does not accept, can it really be held that such an action as that listed in Article 8 [of the Rome Statute] above really ranks among the most heinous and serious war crimes, especially as compared to the other, genuinely heinous ones listed in Article 8?" In the Israeli view, a group of states had abused the Rome Statute to legitimize its political attack on an enemy. Judge Nathan warned that the ICC was in danger of becoming compromised at its birth as "one more political tool in the Middle East conflict."

## JUDICIAL OVERREACH

On December 31, 2000, as one of his final acts as president, President Clinton suddenly ordered the signing of the 1998 Rome Statute. It was a surprising move, for nothing had materially changed since 1998, when the United States voted against the Rome Statute. Even more surprising was the decision by the Israeli government, under Prime Minister Ehud Barak, to follow suit at the same time as Clinton. It was clear, however, that neither government's legislative branch would ratify the statute. Clinton publicly acknowledged that the treaty still had "significant flaws," and thus he recommended to President-elect Bush that the treaty not be submitted to the Senate for consideration "until our fundamental concerns are satisfied."[11]

On May 6, 2002, the Bush administration notified the UN that the United States would not approve the Rome Statute. Undersecretary of State for Arms Control and International Security John Bolton wrote to Secretary-General Kofi Annan with the news: "This is to inform you, in connection with the Rome Statute of the International Criminal Court adopted on July 17, 1998, that the United States does not intend to become a party to the treaty." Bolton carefully informed Annan that the United States had no legal obligations arising from the Clinton administration's signature.[12]

Bolton had been a vociferous critic of the ICC back in 1998. An experienced UN veteran who had served as the assistant secretary of state for international organizations under George H. W. Bush, Bolton had at the time of the Rome conference pointed to serious defects in the statute creating the ICC. He was particularly critical of how the Rome Statute defined the kind of "war crimes" over which the ICC claimed jurisdiction.[13] No one could argue with its language targeting those who were "intentionally directing attacks against civilian objects, that is, objects which are not military objectives" (Article 8, 2, b, ii). But what about a situation in which a U.S. military commander seeks to destroy a terrorist command center in Afghanistan, located near a civilian area, where a new attack is being planned? In order to minimize collateral damage to civilians, American forces use precision-guided munitions with a reduced explosive charge. Can the Pentagon be absolutely certain that no civilian will be affected by the use of American force? No. Nevertheless, the Rome Statute includes this kind of scenario, by calling a "war crime" the act of "intentionally launching an attack in the knowledge that such attack will cause incidental loss of life or injury to civilians or damage to civilian objects" (Article 8, 2, b, iv).

The Rome Statute also described "widespread, long-term, and severe damage to the natural environment" as a war crime. Hurting someone's feelings could even be a war crime, according to the statute's Article 8, which specifically defined "committing outrages upon personal dignity, in particular humiliating and degrading treatment" as a war crime (Article 8, 2, b, xxi). In many situations, the ICC, armed with an activist prosecutor, could stretch its jurisdiction and make politicized indictments. The Rome Statute promised the safeguard of "complementarity"—that is, the ICC would obtain jurisdiction only when a state failed to prosecute war crimes by itself. But that safeguard didn't mitigate American concerns about unfair prosecutions, for it is doubtful that the United States and its allies would actually initiate legal actions against their own soldiers in these circumstances.

The Bush administration was right to fear what could happen with a politicized prosecutor in the ICC. Other cases show that a court granted universal jurisdiction over nationals of any country can abuse its powers. In 1993, Belgium adopted a universal jurisdiction law that allowed Belgian courts to try a suspect for war crimes and genocide even if the individual in question and the events he was charged with causing had absolutely nothing to do with Belgium or its citizens.[14] And in 2003, just a year after John Bolton informed the UN that the United States would not be a party to the Rome Statute, the Belgian courts took up cases against alleged war criminals from the U.S. government. In March 2003, seven Iraqis filed a complaint against former president George H. W. Bush, Vice President Richard Cheney, and Secretary of State Colin Powell for their roles in the 1991 bombing of a Baghdad bomb shelter that killed 403 Iraqi civilians. Two months later a far-left Belgian politician filed an action in the Belgian courts against General Tommy Franks, the commander of coalition forces in the 2003 Iraq War, charging him with war crimes. The Belgian legal authorities should have thrown these complaints out, but instead they pursued them. The Belgians did not change their tune until Secretary of Defense Donald Rumsfeld warned Belgium that if U.S. officers faced war-crimes trials, then it would be too dangerous for them to visit NATO headquarters in Brussels. The implication was clear: If Belgians tried American officers in cases of this sort by claiming universal jurisdiction in war crimes, NATO would move its headquarters out of Belgium.

The Belgians folded and changed their law. To some major backers of the ICC, Belgium's decision to amend its law and drop its commitment to universal jurisdiction for war crimes was a major setback. Human Rights Watch, which had lobbied extensively for the ICC, actually criticized the Belgian government, writing, "It is regrettable that Belgium has now forgotten the victims to whom it gave a hope of justice."[15] Despite Human Rights Watch's dedication to an international court no matter the costs, the entire episode with the war-crimes cases against American civilian and military leaders demonstrated how a court with universal jurisdiction to try war-crimes charges can be completely misused. And in fact, the cases against the Americans were only one example of how politically motivated groups could exploit the court. The Belgian law, it must be remembered, had been on the books for a full decade before the government succumbed to U.S. pressure and changed it.

Even before the claims against U.S. officials, a Belgian court had agreed to hear war-crimes complaints against Israeli prime minister

Ariel Sharon. An international ad hoc committee and, later, twenty-eight Palestinians filed complaints charging Sharon with war crimes for his alleged responsibility for the Lebanese Christian Phalangist militia's 1982 attacks against the Sabra and Shatila refugee camps outside Beirut, where, according to the International Red Cross, 328 Palestinians were massacred (Israeli military estimates put the number higher, at around 800). A Belgian court ruled in early 2003 that Sharon could be tried in Belgium, even if he was not present, but it said that the Israeli prime minister still had immunity until he left office.[16] NGOs like Human Rights Watch hailed the ruling as a "huge victory."[17]

At the time of the Phalangist militia's attacks, Sharon was Israel's defense minister, and as a result of the Lebanon War, the Israeli army had operational responsibility for the refugee camps. An Israeli commission of inquiry, the Kahane Commission, determined in 1983 that while Israel had no direct responsibility for the massacre of the Palestinians, Sharon could be charged with "indirect responsibility." He should have anticipated the attacks, the commission concluded, even though he did not receive any intelligence warning—from the Mossad or Israeli military intelligence—that such atrocities might occur if the Phalangists were allowed to enter the refugee camps. Sharon was forced to resign as defense minister.

There was an enormous irony in the fact that the Belgians were judging Israel in this case. After all, in 1994 Belgian forces serving as UN peacekeepers in Rwanda had abandoned their operational responsibility in the capital of Kigali just before the genocide of 800,000 Tutsi tribesmen. While the UN and the Belgians had definite prior intelligence of a plot to exterminate the Tutsis, they did nothing to stop it. Sharon had no such intelligence. The Phalangist massacre of the Palestinians lasted less than two days. In fact, by the time he learned of the Sabra and Shatila massacres, they were already over. In contrast, the Rwandan genocide lasted a hundred days; a rapid intervention force could have brought the murders to a halt.

The Belgian courts pursued the case against Sharon despite the fact that information indicating that the Lebanese commander of the raid had been completely responsible for the atrocities was in the public domain. In 1999, Robert Hatem, who was the security chief for Elie Hobeika, the commander of the Lebanese Christian militia in Sabra and Shatila, wrote an unauthorized biography of Hobeika that detailed his account of what happened at the refugee camps (the book was banned in Lebanon). According to Hatem, Hobeika gave the orders to his men to wipe out the Palestinian camps; his words were "total extermination." Moreover, Hatem reported that Hobeika was seeking "to tarnish Israel's reputation worldwide." At the same time, Hatem wrote, the Lebanese commander had been secretly working for the Syrians and had even met with the Syrian vice president in 1982. Still, the Belgian courts took no initiatives against Lebanese or Syrian politicians.

The Sharon case could have created a dangerous precedent. By the same logic, if local forces allied to the United States, like the Northern Alliance in Afghanistan, committed atrocities, the U.S. government could be held accountable for war crimes. The same would be true of British and French forces backing a beleaguered government in Africa that attacked African civilians.

## ANTI-AMERICANISM

Whatever the U.S. government's objections to the ICC, the concerns are no longer merely theoretical. The Rome Statute came into force on July 1, 2002, after sixty states had ratified the treaty—and just two months after the Bush administration had told the UN that the United States would not be a party to the agreement. The new political axis in the Assembly of State Parties that was the driving force behind the Rome Statute should be a concern to the United States, because that axis will in all likelihood remain a central force in the assembly that elects judges to the ICC. Will judges be selected based on legal professionalism or to serve some political goal?

The axis that pushed through the Rome Statute, formally known as the Committee of the Whole, was made up of states from the

Third World, South America, and the European Union and was under the chairmanship of Canada. Many of these states resent the leadership of the United States, as was seen in the lead-up to the 2003 Iraq War; whether these judges can divorce themselves from this resentment is a large question that will loom over the future of the ICC.

The potential problems that could arise from political predispositions are considerable: In 2003, the *Wall Street Journal* investigated the attitudes and opinions of those ICC judges who had been selected; after looking at the judges' writings on twenty separate subjects, the newspaper concluded, "From these it may be readily ascertained that the composition of the ICC reflects the rainbow of so-called left-wing opinion."[18] Of course, the judges' views on domestic political questions like privatization, social welfare programs, or even illegal immigration is not a major concern, though it would be better to have a court that reflected a range of ideological perspectives. But if the judges harbor deep anti-American sentiments, oppose the continuation of NATO, oppose counterterrorist policies against those harboring al-Qaeda or Hizballah, or question the legitimacy of Israel, these opinions could have a significant influence on their rulings.

These attitudes are not uncommon in many of the states from which the ICC judges have been chosen. Even in its short history, anti-American advocacy groups have tried to use the ICC to punish the United States and its allies for supposed war crimes. In April 2003, a coalition of legal experts and human rights organizations announced that it was preparing to go to the ICC to prosecute the United States for alleged war crimes during the Iraq War. Because the U.S. government had not ratified the Rome Statute, the group said it would bring its case against America's ally Great Britain, which had signed the treaty. In January 2004, the president of one organization pushing to prosecute the case against Britain, the New York–based Center for Constitutional Rights, made the group's anti-American agenda clear: "The U.K. is like the Achilles' heel of getting at the United States."[19]

In some cases, the attacks came from the international legal community, only underscoring the point that the ICC must be careful in its selection of judges. In November 2003, a panel of senior international legal experts in Great Britain, including law professors from Oxford University and the London School of Economics, said it planned to issue a formal complaint at the ICC against British prime minister Tony Blair for his alleged involvement in war crimes.[20] Belgian and Greek lawyers issued similar complaints to the ICC, but the court, to its credit, rejected their petitions.

Almost from the beginning, then, politically motivated groups were looking to extend the jurisdiction of the international court as far as possible to continue their campaign against the United States and the war on terror. Hoover Institution research fellow Arnold Beichman argued that these cases were examples of the naked anti-Americanism that infects so many in the international community. He pointed out how bizarre it was for "so-called human-rights organizations" to try to charge the United States for war crimes "in a world inhabited by the likes of Fidel Castro, Kim [Jong] Il, Robert Mugabe—and only yesterday by Saddam Hussein." Beichman rightly observed that the complaints flooding into the ICC actually reflected the skewed moral outlook that had come to plague the UN. It was fitting, Beichman said, that on the same day the coalition of lawyers and human rights organizations first announced its plans to press a war crimes case against the United States and Britain, the UN nominated the following countries for membership on its Human Rights Commission: Cuba, North Korea, Iran, the Democratic Republic of Congo, Egypt, Nigeria, Russia, and Saudi Arabia. That was the same "Human Rights Commission" that in 2003 had been chaired by Libya—"yes, Qaddafi's Libya," Beichman wrote.[21]

With an international organization that turned a blind eye to tyrants' human rights abuses and that unblinkingly elevated rogue dictatorships and state sponsors of terrorism to its so-called Human Rights Commission, how could an observer reasonably expect its judicial arm to deal justly with those who have committed crimes against humanity?

The calls to indict the United States for alleged war crimes in Iraq raised the question of just whose standards the ICC will use to determine innocence or guilt. In 1977, most European states signed on to, but the United States rejected, Protocol I of the 1949 Geneva Conventions, which established that guerrilla or irregular fighters can be attacked only when they themselves are attacking. At other times, these guerrillas are to be treated as part of the civilian population and hence deserve the protection granted by the Fourth Geneva Convention.[22] From a military perspective, Protocol I limits terrorists' exposure to military attack; they can execute their operations swiftly and then melt into the civilian population to reclaim legal immunity as a noncombatant. This change provides a huge advantage to terrorist organizations. Universal adoption of Protocol I would have, for instance, made it illegal for the United States to launch military operations on the ground in Afghanistan to try to take out Osama bin Laden prior to al-Qaeda's September 11, 2001, attacks. All of this relates to the question of whether the right of self-defense, under Article 51 of the UN Charter, kicks in only when a state's territory has been actually invaded by a regular army. Even over this essential question there is no global consensus.[23]

Perhaps the single most important concern for the United States is how an international court will interpret the war on terrorism. Many European countries see the war on terrorism as a law enforcement issue, but to the United States, terrorists are combatants in a new kind of war, on a new kind of battlefield.[24] And international laws of war are completely different from a government's internal rules of law enforcement. In November 2002 the United States launched missiles against al Qaeda targets riding in a civilian vehicle on the Saudi-Yemeni border. From the European legal perspective, actions of this sort are like the police gunning down an alleged criminal without putting him on trial. But if terrorists are understood as combatants, then they are no more entitled to "judicial" process than any other individual soldier on the battlefield. Does anyone seriously suggest that each enemy soldier in a war be tried before the U.S. Army can open fire? European officials were similarly exercised in March 2003 when Israel killed the head of Hamas, Sheikh Ahmed Yassin. An Irish official condemned the attacks on Yassin and his entourage as "extrajudicial killings outside the law," and even the British foreign secretary, Jack Straw, called Israel's attack illegal.[25] With the ICC in place, the United States now has to worry about the legal criteria that an international court is using to judge American military actions.

The United States can easily become a target of those who disagree with its anti-terrorist policy. Moral equivalence is common among America's critics; some even suggest that American soldiers are no better than those they are fighting. Of course, Western military forces, at war, can be far from perfect and their actions may come under the scrutiny of the legal community. The Abu Ghraib prison scandal is a case in point: At this writing, suspicions have been raised about whether U.S. servicemen violated the Geneva Conventions with respect to the treatment of Iraqi prisoners. But there is clearly a world of difference between how the United States deals with prisoners and how the terrorist groups fighting the United States in Iraq treat their captives—consider the decapitation of American civilian Nicholas Berg as just one example. The key point is that the U.S. Army is investigating Abu Ghraib and prosecuting those who violated U.S. regulations and international law. The problem with the ICC arises if it goes beyond the requirements of U.S. law and interprets the fight against terrorists differently from how the U.S. government does—for such actions are likely to be politically motivated.

Whether the ICC proves to be a serious body that goes after real war criminals or becomes just another international body for political posturing now depends on the integrity and quality of its prosecutor and judges.[26] The court's architects made a major mistake in not establishing the checks and balances necessary to deal with prosecutors and judges who might be politically motivated or who otherwise lack integrity. Recognizing that anti-American and anti-counterterrorism forces could hijack the ICC, the U.S. government has wisely chosen not to depend on the good intentions of the ICC.

By early 2004, Washington had secured bilateral understandings from eighty-two countries that they would not cooperate with the ICC should it initiate legal proceedings against American citizens.

## UNACCOUNTABLE—AND UNNECESSARY?

One of the most basic questions about the ICC is whether it is even necessary. The UN continually calls for new global institutions when in many cases they are not needed. There is no dispute over the imperative of holding war criminals accountable for their actions. But why set up a sitting international court that has universal jurisdiction at all times? Why not have the UN Security Council establish an ad hoc tribunal if an atrocity occurs, just as it did with the special international tribunals for the former Yugoslavia and Rwanda? The ICC website argues that this would create "selective justice," implying that everyone in the international community should be treated the same.[27] Yet no one made this argument in 1945 when the Nuremberg trials were held; those trials dealt with Axis war criminals only.

The UN began to erode the Nuremberg model with the Yugoslavia tribunal, to which it granted jurisdiction over *all* war crimes in the former Yugoslavia, including those that might have been committed by NATO. In 1999 the tribunal's prosecutor began investigating NATO's bombing campaign over Kosovo, cross-examining NATO officials about whether they had committed war crimes.[28] If these rules, which the ICC extended to a global scale, had been applied to the Nuremberg and Tokyo War Crimes trials, their prosecutors would have been looking into indicting U.S. officials from President Truman right on down for bombing Germany and Japan. This, in fact, was one of the objections to the Rome Statute that John Bolton expressed in 1998; according to the provisions of the ICC, he said, the United States probably would have been guilty of a war crime for dropping atomic bombs on Hiroshima and Nagasaki.

Nuremberg was rightly set up to go after the Nazis, not the Allies. But with more recent criminal tribunals, the UN has bunched aggressors together with those who have sought to resist aggression. The ICC demonstrates, probably better than any other UN institution, how the UN has lost the moral clarity that separated good from evil in 1945.

CHAPTER 9

# The UN Backs Terrorism

By the beginning of the twenty-first century, the world faced very different threats from those that the UN had confronted in the wake of the Second World War. The single biggest threat to international security today is, of course, global terrorism. Even before the attacks of September 11, 2001, brought terrorism to American soil, it was clear that radical groups had embarked on a worldwide campaign of terror. Among many other attacks there were the June 1996 bombing of the al-Khobar Towers complex in Saudi Arabia that killed 19 U.S. Air Force servicemen, the August 1998 bombings of the U.S. embassies in Kenya and Tanzania that claimed 263 lives, and the October 2000 bombing of the USS *Cole* that killed 17.

If the UN were to live up to the mission laid out in the UN Charter to "maintain international peace and security," it would have to stand up to the terrorist threat.

In the late 1990s and especially after the September 11 attacks, the UN began to adopt Security Council resolutions against terrorism with greater frequency. But more important than what was written on the books in the New York headquarters was how the UN performed on the ground in the Middle East, the breeding ground for the world's worst terrorist organizations. Unfortunately, the UN did not stand up against terrorism. And to this day it still hasn't.

## "THIS IS A HUMANITARIAN ORGANIZATION?"

Those who know the inside world of global terrorism recognize that the Iranian-backed organization Hizballah (literally, "Party of God") is just as dangerous as al-Qaeda. In fact, many observers feel the Lebanon-based group is even more deadly than Osama bin Laden's terrorist network. In September 2002, a year *after* al-Qaeda's attacks on New York and Washington, Undersecretary of State Richard Armitage remarked that Hizballah "may be the A-team of terrorists" and that al-Qaeda "is actually the B-team."[1] Similarly, in early 2003 CIA Director George Tenet described Hizballah as "a far more capable organization" than al-Qaeda.[2]

Hizballah was conducting suicide bombings many years before al-Qaeda and its related groups were. More than a decade before al-Qaeda came onto the world stage, Hizballah was responsible for the suicide bombing of the U.S. Embassy in Beirut on April 18, 1983, which led to 63 deaths. Just months later, on October 23, it bombed the U.S. Marine barracks in Beirut, killing 241 American personnel. Hizballah attacked the U.S. Embassy in Kuwait twice—in 1983 and 1984. In 1984 it seized, tortured, and executed the CIA station chief in Beirut, William Buckley, and in 1988 it murdered another American officer, Lieutenant Colonel William Higgins, who was heading a UN peacekeeping force. In 1985 it hijacked a TWA aircraft bound for Athens from Rome. In 2001 a federal grand jury in Alexandria, Virginia, handed down a forty-six-count indictment that specifically identified the Saudi branch of Hizballah as responsible for the 1996 al-Khobar Towers bombing that housed U.S. Air Force personnel. Nineteen Americans were killed in the attack.[3]

Hizballah has attacked targets well beyond the Middle East. Like al-Qaeda, in fact, it has proven its global reach. Hizballah recruited Europeans into its ranks in the 1980s, and in 1986 its operatives set off a series of explosions in Paris, including in subway stations. When French and German authorities cracked Hizballah cells and imprisoned its operatives, they discovered secret arms depots on the

French-German border.[4] In 1984 Hizballah bombed a restaurant in Spain frequented by U.S. servicemen.[5] Hizballah struck at Israeli and Jewish targets in Argentina during the 1990s, proving it could reach into the Western Hemisphere. The organization has clearly articulated its global ambitions. In November 2002, the secretary-general of Hizballah, Sheikh Hasan Nasrallah, encouraged the Palestinian organizations that had adopted Hizballah's "martyrdom operations" to export their attacks: "I encourage the Palestinians to take suicide bombings worldwide."

Today, Hizballah receives financial backing from its funding networks in countries all over the world, including the United States. In July 2000, federal authorities arrested eighteen people in North Carolina suspected of raising money for Hizballah through cigarette smuggling; in June 2002, the ringleader, Mohamad Hammoud, was convicted of providing material support for a terrorist organization.[6] According to authorities, the North Carolina smuggling scheme was just a small piece of Hizballah's fundraising network in the United States. The terrorist organization also makes plenty of money from its global narcotics network based in Lebanon's Bekaa Valley; each year $1 billion worth of drugs (mostly heroin and hashish) are exported to Europe and the United States, and Hizballah's network controls the lion's share of that business.[7]

The Hizballah leadership is fiercely anti-American. Its founding charter states openly that "our determination to fight the U.S. is solid."[8] And in January 2003, Sheikh Nasrallah declared on Hizballah's Radio Nur, "The Arabs must understand that Israel is merely a battalion of the American army; and the United States is the principal enemy."[9] Given this deep hostility it was not surprising that a senior European diplomat stationed in Tehran reported during a lunchtime conversation in Washington that when Iranian president Mohammad Khatami saw on television the flames coming out of the World Trade Center on September 11, 2001, he feared that the attack had been conducted by a unit of Hizballah—not by al-Qaeda.

But for upwards of a decade, Hizballah was devoting most of its energies to its struggle with Israel. The UN was directly involved in this issue, having sent peacekeepers to the area along the Israeli-Lebanese

200 • TOWER OF BABBLE

border in the late 1970s. In March 1978, Israeli forces had moved into
southern Lebanon. In response, the UN Security Council passed Resolution 425, which called for Israel to withdraw and created the
United Nations Interim Force in Lebanon (UNIFIL) to serve as a
buffer between Israel and Lebanon. The Israelis withdrew, but they
continued to clash with the Palestine Liberation Organization (PLO),
which established a military presence in southern Lebanon and repeatedly tried to infiltrate northern Israel with heavily armed terrorist
units. Then, in June 1982, Israel invaded southern Lebanon, driving
out the PLO military presence. But Hizballah, which drew support
from southern Lebanon's Shiite Muslim population, for the most part
replaced the PLO. Iran and Syria gave the terrorist group significant
backing. Iranian cargo aircraft regularly landed at Damascus International Airport with fresh weaponry that was loaded on trucks and
shipped to Hizballah bases in the Bekaa Valley. Armed with hundreds
of Katyusha rockets, Hizballah pushed Israel to withdraw from the
southern Lebanon security zone.

The UN Security Council gave UNIFIL three specific objectives:
confirm the withdrawal of Israeli forces from Lebanese territory, restore international security along the Israeli-Lebanese border, and
assist the Lebanese government in restoring its authority in the
areas from which Israel withdrew. When Israel withdrew from
southern Lebanon on May 24, 2000, it seemed the UN could fulfill
these objectives and resolve the conflict. And just two months later,
on July 24, Secretary-General Kofi Annan certified that Israel had
fully complied with Resolution 425 by withdrawing to the "blue
line" that UNIFIL and UN cartographers had identified as the
Israeli-Lebanese border. He wrote a formal letter to the rotating
president of the Security Council stating that "the Israeli authorities
have removed all violations of the line of withdrawal."[10] Three days
later, the UN Security Council adopted Resolution 1310, calling on
"the parties to respect that line and cooperate fully with the United
Nations and with UNIFIL."

The UN had achieved the first of its three objectives, but the
Lebanese government refused to fully restore its own national au-

# THE UN, LEBANON, AND ISRAEL

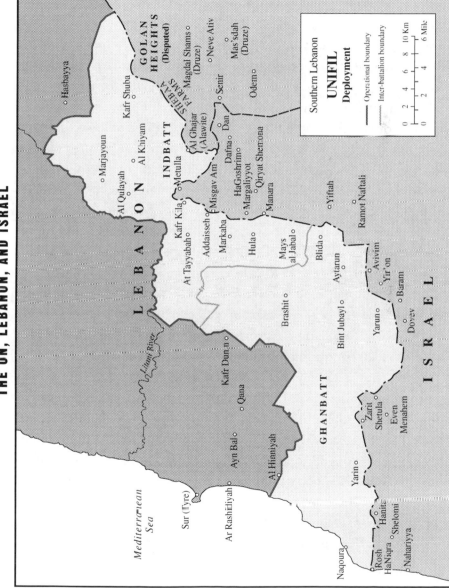

Southern Lebanon
**UNIFIL**
**Deployment**

— Operational boundary
‒ ‒ ‒ Inter-battalion boundary

0  2  4  6  8  10 Km
0    2    4    6 Mile

GOLAN
HEIGHTS
(Disputed)

Magdal Shams
(Druze)
Neve Ativ
Mas'dah
(Druze)

SHEBA'A
FARMS

Hashayya

Kafr Shuba
Senir
Odem

Marjayoun
Al Khiyam
Al Ghajar
(Alawite)
Dan
Dafna

INDBATT

Al Qulayah
Metulla
HaGoshrimo
Qiryat Shemona

Misgav Am
Margaliyyot
Manara

Kafr Kila
Addaisseh
Markaba
Hula
Mays
al Jabal
Blida
Yiftah
Ramot Naftali

At Tayyabah

Mediterranean
Sea

Litani River

Kafr Dunnn
Qana

Brashit
Bint Jubayl
Aytarun
Avivim
Yir'on
Baram

Ayn Bal
Yaruno
Dovev

Al Hinniyah

GHANBATT

Yarin
Zarit
Shetula
Even
Menahem

Sur (Tyre)

Ar Rashidiyah

Naqoura
Rosh
HaNiqra
Hanit
Shelomi
Nahariyya

LEBANON

ISRAEL

thority in southern Lebanon, as called for in Resolution 425. In January 2001, the Security Council adopted Resolution 1337, which called on "the Government of Lebanon to ensure the return of its effective authority and presence in the south, and in particular to increase the rate of deployment of the Lebanese armed forces."[11] It was clear that the primary military force in southern Lebanon after the Israeli pullout was supposed to be the Lebanese army, not Hizballah. Yet as early as June 20, 2000, less than a month after Israel pulled out of Lebanon, Annan showed he was willing to listen to the terrorist organization, meeting with Sheikh Nasrallah in Beirut and commending the Hizballah leader for showing restraint after Israel's withdrawal. Upon arriving in Israel the next day, Annan rejected criticism that he was legitimizing Hizballah. Using the UN's typically value-neutral language, he asserted, "In trying to calm the situation and create peace, the secretary-general—or any engaged and serious mediator—has to talk to all those who have an impact on the situation and can bring about peace." Annan added, "Hizballah is a player."[12] But he did not address the fact that the UN was supposed to be positioned between two sovereign states, Israel and Lebanon, not between Israel and a terrorist organization like Hizballah.

Hizballah continued its military campaign even after the UN had verified Israel's Lebanon pullout. Despite the fact that the UN Security Council had repeatedly called on "the parties" to respect the line of withdrawal, Hizballah continued to press its claim to an area called the Shebaa Farms. Hizballah spokesmen argued that the Shebaa Farms belonged to Lebanon, even though this area was located on the Golan Heights, which Israel had captured from Syria during the 1967 Six-Day War. UN maps marked the area as Golan territory. Lebanon had at one time controlled the Shebaa Farms, but the Lebanese government had transferred the land to Syria in the 1950s. The international community maintained that Israel and Syria would have to negotiate the final status of the Shebaa Farms, along with the rest of the Golan Heights; Lebanon was not a factor in this dispute. But for Hizballah, the Shebaa Farms provided a new *casus belli* against Israel.

The test case of how the UN would handle this situation came in October 2000, five months after Israel completed its withdrawal from Lebanese territory. In the early afternoon of October 7, three Israeli soldiers, Benny Avraham, Omar Swaid, and Adi Avitan—all experienced combat soldiers—were patrolling in an area of the Shebaa Farms along the Israeli-Lebanese fence near a border gate. The gate where they were patrolling could easily be seen from UNIFIL's observation post on a hill just four hundred yards away, particularly on that sunny afternoon, when visibility was excellent.

Suddenly, at 1:35, Hizballah began launching intense mortar and rocket fire on six Israeli positions. The jeep that had carried the three Israeli soldiers went up in flames. Two hours later, the Israel Defense Forces notified UNIFIL that they believed the three soldiers had been abducted by Hizballah. That evening, Sheikh Nasrallah of Hizballah publicly confirmed that his organization had captured the soldiers. Hizballah had conducted a daytime ambush, abducted the three soldiers, and smuggled them into Lebanon right under the noses of UNIFIL. Even after the kidnapping, UNIFIL took no special steps against Hizballah. UN peacekeepers could have put up roadblocks in their sector in order to intercept the vehicles carrying the Israelis. But nothing was done.

Just examining open-source material at the time revealed that UNIFIL saw the entire attack unfold. The *Daily Star* in Beirut carried a detailed story of the Hizballah operation on October 11, 2000, that was based on "interviews with UNIFIL troops *who witnessed the snatch* [emphasis added]." The story revealed that Hizballah had fired eight Sagger wire-guided missiles across the fence at the vehicle on the Israeli side. The newspaper account also detailed how Hizballah blew the padlock off the border gate in order to cross over and seize the wounded Israelis.[13]

More than eight months later, on June 28, 2001, the commander in chief of the Northern Command of the Israel Defense Forces, Major General Gabi Ashkenazi, confronted the UN special coordinator for the Middle East peace process, Terje Roed-Larsen, with his suspicion that UNIFIL actually possessed a videotape of the abduction. Moreover, Ashkenazi charged that the UNIFIL commander and UN headquarters in New York had known about the tape all along.[14] Roed-Larsen reportedly denied that the tape existed. He firmly rejected Ashkenazi's charges and demanded to know his source of information. The response did not surprise many Israelis, to whom the Norwegian was a controversial figure. Roed-Larsen had been a driving force behind the failed 1993 Oslo Accords between Israel and the PLO. Those accords collapsed in September 2000, when Yasser Arafat launched his armed intifada against Israel. Kofi Annan had hired Roed-Larsen as his personal envoy in late 1999, and by 2000, Israelis regarded Roed-Larsen as pro-Palestinian.

Protecting his sources, Ashkenazi stood by his charges against the UN without telling the UN officials how he could make these statements with such absolute certainty. It turned out that the charges were right. Not only did videotape of the events surrounding the abduction exist, but also the UNIFIL commander, General Kofi Obeng of Ghana, had known of the tape for months before informing UN headquarters of its existence. Finally, around March 10, 2001, some six months after the abduction took place, Obeng told the Department of Peacekeeping Operations about the videotape. In mid-May, he turned over a copy of the videotape during a visit to UN headquarters, according to the UN's own internal investigation. But he was extremely reluctant to show the UNIFIL videotape to Israel, arguing that UNIFIL should not share material that might have intelligence value for any party to the conflict. In other words, according to Obeng, letting the Israelis see the videotape would compromise UNIFIL's impartiality. The Department of Peacekeeping Operations agreed with the general, as did Secretary-General Kofi Annan when he was informed of the existence of the UNIFIL tape on June 26, 2001. The UN was consistent in this view. Back in early May, UN officials had hinted to families of the abducted soldiers that they had not made "every last item" available. They reminded the Israeli families that "UNIFIL had to maintain a delicate balance and could not simply share sensitive information about one side with the other."

Once again, the UN clung to a notion of "impartiality" as its guiding principle. But the strict impartiality it was supposed to observe applied to Lebanon and Israel, not to a terrorist organization. And Hizballah was not, to use UNIFIL's bureaucratically sterile language, just a "party" in this dispute; it was the aggressor. It had crossed the fence along the Lebanese border in order to seize the three Israeli soldiers, in violation of repeated UN Security Council resolutions. Moreover, there was reason to believe that Hizballah had posed as UN peacekeepers to kidnap the soldiers. Near the area of the abduction, UNIFIL found two abandoned vehicles with suspicious contents. The first, a white Nissan Pathfinder that could easily look like a UN vehicle, contained imitation UNIFIL license plates, a UN flag, UNIFIL uniforms from the Irish battalion, and UN stickers. The other was a blue Range Rover, the rear of which was smeared with blood. Thus it appeared that one of the world's worst terrorist organizations had tricked the Israeli soldiers by pretending to be UN officials and had violated UN resolutions by crossing the blue line in violation of UN resolutions.

Despite all this, the UN defended Hizballah. It even elevated the terrorist group's diplomatic status by making Hizballah a recognized party in the conflict. And as the official UN inquiry later revealed, the nature of the videotape itself indicated a surprising degree of cooperation between Hizballah and UNIFIL. Apparently, when UNIFIL recovered the abandoned vehicles with UN insignia and bloodstains, it turned them over to Hizballah, and taped the entire event.

Ashkenazi's exchange with Roed-Larsen blew the videotape scandal wide open. At the end of June, the Department of Peacekeeping Operations finally admitted to Israeli representatives that a videotape existed. Roed-Larsen told Israel's defense minister about the tape on June 29, just a day after he had had an angry exchange with the Israeli about the videotape.[15] On July 5, the UN disclosed to the press that the tape existed but claimed that the video would not shed any light on the fate of the missing soldiers because it was recorded eighteen hours after the kidnapping. The organization also maintained its stance of neutrality. "We are in a war zone with the agreement of the two sides of war," said Kofi Annan's spokesman, Fred Eckhart. "Probably on a daily basis our peacekeepers see things that would have intelligence value to one side or the other. In this case the tape certainly falls into that category."[16]

Soon it became clear that the UN still had not revealed the whole truth. A second tape emerged that showed the attack on Israeli positions across the entire front the day of the kidnapping. That video seemed to show a burning jeep. Clearly the UN had more than a tape that was recorded eighteen hours after the fact.

While the UN kept the videotapes from Israelis, UNIFIL might actually have given them to Hizballah. In response to Israeli requests to see the first videotape, the Department of Peacekeeping Affairs said it would show the families of the soldiers a copy but would obscure the faces of the Hizballah terrorists that appeared. On July 7, however, Secretary-General Kofi Annan's personal representative, Staffan di Mistura, reported to New York that Hizballah's chief of security had revealed to him that the Lebanese organization had known of the UNIFIL videotape's existence for the past three months. According to the official UN inquiry, Hizballah knew that the tape clearly showed the faces of its operatives. If that was the case, Hizballah had access to one of the most closely guarded items in UNIFIL's possession. Either its intelligence had penetrated UNIFIL or someone in UNIFIL had willingly shared the tape with Hizballah.

By a 411–4 majority, the U.S. House of Representatives adopted a resolution on July 30, 2001, calling on the UN to release the tape. Not until January 2002 did the UN show both videos to the families of the Israeli soldiers, and when it did play the tape for the families, it obscured the faces of the Hizballah operatives.[17] Although neither video showed the actual abduction, the tape of the Hizballah artillery assault showed the soldiers' jeep in flames. The families were stunned to hear on that tape that UNIFIL soldiers surrounding the cameraman were laughing as they watched the Hizballah operation. "They're screwing the Jews," one UN soldier was heard saying on the video. When the UN told the Israeli families that they would be allowed to see only twenty-one of the fifty-three items recovered from the two Hizballah vehicles, one parent lost all patience. The father of Benny Avraham shouted in anguish, "This is a humanitarian organization? This is an organization that should be ashamed that it even exists. They are forcibly trying to cover up information. This is a waste of time."[18]

## CHOOSING A TERRORIST SPONSOR TO FIGHT TERRORISM

The UN continued to cater to Hizballah after the Shebaa Farms abduction. Some UN officials betrayed sympathy for Hizballah. For example, in 2003, Timur Goskel, a senior political adviser to UNIFIL for more than twenty years, spoke of Hizballah as a force for stability, saying, "Today's calm in south Lebanon is due to the Lebanese Army, Lebanese intelligence, and Hizballah."[19] Others in UNIFIL were threatened by Hizballah. After all, Hizballah had kidnapped and murdered an American colonel serving with UNIFIL in the 1980s. The Lebanese terrorist group also accused UNIFIL of being a "tool for Israel."[20] In addition, Hizballah would intimidate UNIFIL peacekeepers by deploying its artillery within fifty meters of a UNIFIL position. Intimidation could get physical: In April 2002, Hizballah forces severely beat up four UNIFIL observers when they attempted to enter the Shebaa Farms area to monitor military activity there.[21] But whether it was sympathetic to or scared by Hizballah, the fact was that the UN did not stand up to one of the world's deadliest terrorist organizations.

The UN's strongest statement in support of Hizballah was its decision to accept Syria, one of Hizballah's two most important backers, as a member of the UN Security Council for a two-year term, from 2002 through 2004. According to the UN Charter, the nonpermanent members of the Security Council are elected by a two-thirds majority of the UN General Assembly, and Syria received far more than the necessary two-thirds. But the UN Charter also stipulates that in electing nonpermanent members, "due regard" should be given "in the first instance to the contribution of Members of the United Nations to the maintenance of international peace and security." This should have given the UN pause with Syria's candidacy. The 9/11 attacks had prompted the UN Security Council to adopt, on September 28, a tough antiterrorism resolution—Resolution 1373, which demanded that all states "refrain from providing any form of support, active or passive, to entities or persons involved in terrorist acts." The Security Council explicitly adopted the resolution under Chapter VII of the UN Charter, putting it in the most serious category of resolution that the UN could advance (just like the resolutions on Iraq). Now, not much more than a week later, the UN was empowering Syria to make sure that Resolution 1373 would be implemented.

This was an Orwellian moment for the UN. Syria had been on the U.S. State Department's list of states supporting terrorism since 1977—the year that the list was established. Syria provided sanctuary to thirteen Palestinian terrorist organizations in Damascus, and it had, of course, fully backed Hizballah's struggle in the Shebaa Farms, in defiance of repeated UN Security Council resolutions. Syria was also ignoring UN resolutions on Iraq; Damascus was violating UN sanctions by pumping Iraqi oil through its pipeline to the Mediterranean, outside of whatever controls existed in the UN's oil-for-food program. How was a state that so consistently undermined international peace and security, as defined by the UN itself, supposed to suddenly protect global security?

Some in the UN Secretariat hoped that Syria, knowing that it would soon become a member of the Security Council, would moderate its behavior, particularly with respect to Lebanon. But following the chronology of Hizballah's actions reveals that Syria did not moderate its behavior at all.[22] Syria's influence over Hizballah operations was extensive, which was not surprising given that Hizballah's bases in eastern Lebanon were relatively close to Syrian military encampments and that Iran's military supply lines to Hizballah came through Syria to Lebanon. In the summer of 2001, Hizballah's mortar barrages on Israeli positions in the Shebaa Farms halted almost immediately after Israeli fighter bombers retaliated by destroying a Syrian-manned radar station in eastern Lebanon. After the Syrian leadership absorbed the implications of the Israeli air strike, the entire front went quiet for nearly four months. Then, in October 2001, precisely when Syria was facing election to the UN Security Council, Hizballah resumed its shelling operations in the Shebaa Farms. Just five days before the vote in the General Assembly, Hizballah opened fire with mortar and antitank missiles. And once Syria was elected, Hizballah attacks just escalated; by April 2002, Hizballah was firing Katyusha rockets into Israel. It was as though the Lebanese organization felt it had a green light for more attacks through the UN's embrace of its Syrian sponsor.

By legitimizing Syria, the UN actually undermined another independent state. At the time Syria was elected to the UN Security Council, it was violating yet another Security Council resolution. The Syrian army had entered Lebanon in 1975, but in September 1982, the UN Security Council adopted Resolution 520, which took note of "the determination of Lebanon to ensure the withdrawal of all non-Lebanese forces from Lebanon" and called for "strict respect of the sovereignty, territorial integrity and independence of Lebanon under the exclusive authority of the Government of Lebanon." Syria did not loosen its military grip on Lebanon over the next twenty years, but the UN nevertheless invited it to join the Security Council. Ten years after uniting the nations of the world to liberate Kuwait from the Iraqi army in 1991, the UN was allowing Syria to keep its hold on Lebanon. As a result, Lebanon became host to more than a dozen pro-Syrian terrorist organizations as well as to forces from Syria's primary ally, Iran, which came in to reinforce Hizballah. The chances of restoring Lebanese sovereignty became more remote than ever.

Lebanon had been a founding member of the United Nations in 1945. Yet the norms that governed UN behavior in 2002 had veered so far away from the values of the organization's founders that Lebanon's very survival as an independent state had been compromised.

## THE UN RUSHES TO PROCLAIM A "MASSACRE"

On March 27, 2002, at 7:30 P.M., some 250 Israelis sat down in the Park Hotel in the coastal city of Netanya to celebrate the Passover Seder, a festive meal in which Jewish families commemorate the exodus of the Israelites from ancient Egypt and their liberation from slavery. A Palestinian suicide bomber entered the hotel dining room from the lobby and blew himself up, killing 21 Israelis and wounding more than 140. The Palestinian terrorist organization Hamas took credit for the attack on the Arabic al-Jazeera television network. Over the previous eighteen months, Yasser Arafat's Palestinian Authority had been waging a campaign of terrorist attacks against Israeli cities, in cooperation with terrorist groups, like Hamas and Islamic Jihad, that belonged to Arafat's fundamentalist opposition. His Fatah movement, which was the largest component of the PLO, even established joint military units with the Islamist groups. The attacks on Israel emanated from Palestinian cities on the West Bank that had been turned over to his Palestinian Authority in accordance with the 1993 Oslo Accords. While Oslo and its various implementation agreements had required Arafat to dismantle the "infrastructure" of terrorist groups like Hamas, he had steadfastly refused, and was harboring them instead. Indeed, for four years before the Passover massacre, the Palestinians had ignored Israel's repeated requests to arrest Abdul Basset Odeh, the suicide bomber who would enter the Park Hotel that evening in March 2002.

Hamas originally emerged in 1987 from the Gaza branch of the Muslim Brotherhood, the radical Egyptian Islamist organization of the late 1920s that had given rise to many of the militant Islamic movements that saw themselves as part of the global jihad. (Al-Qaeda itself was a hybrid of the Muslim Brotherhood and Saudi Wahhabism.) Hamas sent delegates to attend a radical Islamic summit meeting in Sudan in April 1991 called the Popular Arab and Islamic Conference; other attendees included Osama bin Laden, radical Afghan faction heads, and Yasser Arafat. Hamas also went to a follow-up conference in Sudan in 1995 that was attended by Algerian Islamist groups and even Hizballah. These international links paid off for Hamas, for it was able to recruit British Muslims of Pakistani origin and employ them in a 2003 suicide attack in Tel Aviv, at a bar near the U.S. Embassy called Mike's Place; the organization clearly had demonstrated its international capabilities.

Hamas shared a common anti-Western orientation with al-Qaeda and other jihadi movements, for Hamas leaders like Abdul Aziz Rantisi actually called for attacks on the United States.[23] Hamas, in fact, looked to many of the same Saudi clerics who legitimized al-Qaeda's own strategy of suicide bombing attacks.[24] But the organization had not actually launched military operations overseas. While al-Qaeda accepted some Hamas volunteers in its Afghan training camps, it let Hamas concentrate its effort on the war against Israel.

The Israeli military concluded that Yasser Arafat had been encouraged by Israel's unilateral pullout from Lebanon and wanted to push Israel out of the West Bank and the Gaza Strip. He hoped that in coordination with groups like Hamas he could cause enough casualties to achieve that goal without requiring a peace treaty, which he had refused to accept at the July 2000 Camp David Summit, under President Clinton. He also hoped that Israel would react to the wave of suicide bombings against its civilians by using excessive force, which would force the international community and the UN to intervene on his behalf.[25] To foil Arafat's strategy, Israel had followed a policy of restraint, even after it had lost hundreds of civilian lives. The Palestinian organizations tried to bait Prime Minister Ariel Sharon with more escalation. By the end of March, 420 Israelis had been killed—132 during March alone.

With the Passover massacre, Israeli restraint was finished; the Israelis launched Operation Defensive Shield to root out the infrastructure of terrorism in West Bank cities. For example, the Israel Defense Forces quickly took control of Ramallah and even seized government buildings in Yasser Arafat's compound. Israeli units went into Bethlehem, where two hundred of Arafat's Tanzim gunmen held Christian clergy as hostages in the Church of the Nativity, the birthplace of Jesus. One of the six cities Israeli forces entered was Jenin, the northernmost West Bank city, which had served as a springboard for so many suicide bombings that Arafat's Fatah movement called it "the capital of the suicide warriors" (*al-'asimat al-istashidin*) in an internal document captured by Israeli forces.[26] In one of the toughest battles of Operation Defensive Shield, Israeli forces went into the Jenin refugee camp, where the Palestinians engaged them in a tough eight-day battle.

The Palestinians also waged the battle for Jenin in the international media. Palestinian Authority negotiator Saeb Erekat went on CNN on April 10, 2002, to charge that Israel had killed "more than five hundred people." Two days later he was at it again on CNN, asserting that "a real massacre was committed in the Jenin refugee camp." He added that three hundred Palestinians were being buried in mass graves. On April 15, again on CNN, Erekat said, "I stand by the term 'massacres' " to refer to what the Israelis did in the refugee camps. He characterized the Israeli military operations in Jenin as "war crimes." There was little doubt that the Palestinian Authority hoped to elicit UN intervention on its behalf. Indeed, it had already called on the UN "to dispatch international monitors and to stop these Nazi massacres against our people."[27]

By April 12, UN secretary-general Kofi Annan was already calling for international forces to enter the West Bank to curb the violence. Speaking to reporters in Geneva, he said that UN humanitarian agencies were reporting "grave violations" by Israeli forces: "The situation is so dangerous and the humanitarian and human rights situation so appalling. The proposition that a force should be sent there . . . can no longer be deferred."[28] UN officials provided reports not very different from what the Palestinian spokesmen were saying on network television. For instance, Peter Hansen, the commissioner-general of the United Nations Relief and Works Agency (UNRWA), declared, "I had, first of all, hoped the horror stories coming out were exaggerations as you often hear in this part of the world, but they were all too true." The special coordinator for the Middle East peace process, Terje Roed-Larsen, told reporters, "What we are seeing here is horrifying, horrifying scenes of human suffering." He went on to say that the scene in Jenin was one of the worst disasters the UN staff had ever witnessed: "We have expert people here who have been in war zones and earthquakes and they say that they have never seen anything like it."[29] Finally he said, "After the military offensive in Jenin, the government of Israel has lost all moral ground in this conflict."[30]

As it turned out, however, the Palestinian spin that UN officials so readily accepted was far from accurate. At the end of April, after Israel's Operation Defensive Shield had ended, Palestinian officials dropped claims that hundreds had been massacred. The head of PLO's Fatah movement in the northern West Bank, Kadoura Mousa Kadoura, disclosed that Palestinian-appointed investigators had put the Palestinian death toll at 56—nowhere near the 500 that Erekat had repeatedly alleged.[31] The Israel Defense Forces came up with a similar number, finding 52 Palestinian bodies. A former Israeli military analyst's careful analysis of the names of these Palestinian fatalities indicated that 34 of them—or 65 percent—were well-known military operatives of Hamas, Islamic Jihad, or Fatah-Tanzim.[32] The Israeli military concluded that 38 were armed men and 14 were civilians.

On their websites, the Palestinian organizations involved in the battle admitted that they had intentionally employed Palestinian civilians as part of their defensive tactics. In contrast to initial reports, the Jenin camp was not leveled either, as some had asserted. Out of 1,896 buildings in the Jenin refugee camp, 130 buildings were destroyed—or less than 10 percent.[33] And many of these buildings collapsed because they had been booby-trapped with explosives by the Palestinians. The destruction that did occur was concentrated in an area the size of a football field, but television cameras repeatedly panned the area, giving the impression of vastly more widespread destruction.[34]

One reason that Palestinian losses were so light was that Israel took a different military approach from what the manuals of most

Western armies recommend for counterinsurgency operations in urban areas. Whereas, for instance, UN forces in Mogadishu, Somalia, had used helicopter gunships to fire sixteen rockets and two thousand shells on a building belonging to a Somali warlord on June 12, 1993,[35] Israel did not employ this kind of airpower. Nor did it use its artillery forces or order its troops to use flamethrowers in the battle for the Jenin refugee camp. Instead it sent experienced infantry soldiers in house-to-house operations, despite the risk from snipers on rooftops. These were reserve soldiers with families. Twenty-three Israeli soldiers died in the battle, but the tactic helped keep the collateral deaths of Palestinian noncombatants to a minimum.

It should be added that Israel itself contributed to the confusion of what was going on the Jenin refugee camp. While Israeli infantry was moving house to house, the Israeli army spokesman, Brigadier General Ron Kitrey, confused the term "casualties" with the term "fatalities." As a result, he was quoted as saying that there were "apparently hundreds dead." Within hours, however, his office issued a clarification saying that Kitrey's "comments made this morning regarding Jenin refer to casualties—those killed and wounded. There is no clear number of those killed," the statement said.[36] Civilian spokesmen like Foreign Minister Shimon Peres repeatedly played down the numbers of Palestinians killed in Jenin and never made Kitrey's error. For example, on April 20, Peres noted that seven Palestinian civilians had been killed.[37] Still, the error lent credibility to the repeated Palestinian charges.

Kofi Annan did not convince the UN to dispatch international forces to the West Bank as he had originally advocated, but he found ways of inserting the UN into the situation in a way he hadn't in either Rwanda or Srebrenica when reports of those atrocities began to emerge. His office convinced the Security Council to send a "fact-finding team" to the Jenin refugee camp. Resolution 1405, passed on April 19, 2002, expressed concern about the "unknown number of deaths" and the amount of destruction that had occurred in Jenin; the resolution also noted "the dire humanitarian situation of the Palestinian civilian population." Although these judgments were in a formal UN resolution, they were not based on firm standards of proof. They couldn't have been, because as it turned out, the proof didn't exist. Much had changed since 1962, when U.S. ambassador Adlai Stevenson appeared before the UN Security Council to present aerial photographs of Soviet medium-range missiles in Cuba; now the UN was working off the unsubstantiated claims of a Palestinian Authority spokesman, Saeb Erekat.

Resolution 1405 did not make a single reference to the Passover massacre or to Palestinian terrorism in general, which had murdered hundreds of Israeli civilians. Nor did the UN commit itself to investigating the scale of Palestinian terrorism in the Jenin refugee camp; its team of experts specialized in humanitarian relief and knew nothing about counterterrorism. This was not a balanced team. One member, Cornelio Sommaruga, a former president of the International Red Cross, had once refused to admit Israel's Red Cross, Magen David Adom, as part of the Red Cross federation by saying, "If we're going to have the Shield of David, why would we not have to accept the swastika?"[38] By focusing its investigation on Israel's military response, the UN was ignoring the original causes of that response.

## REFUSING TO PASS JUDGMENT

Keeping the subject of terrorism out of the fact-finding team's mandate might have served another UN interest: hiding the evidence that a UN organization had been penetrated by terrorist groups. Israel discovered substantial evidence that UNRWA, which was charged with providing humanitarian aid to Palestinians living in refugee camps, had allowed the camps to be used as sanctuaries for terrorism and as breeding grounds for incitement.[39] UNRWA employed nearly 20,000 Palestinians in the West Bank and the Gaza Strip, many of whom, it appeared, supported Hamas and other terrorist groups. When Israeli forces arrived in Jenin, they found UNRWA workers' homes plastered with posters praising suicide bombers. In the Gaza Strip, Israeli forces found one UNRWA worker, Nahad Rashid Ahmad Atallah, who used his UN-marked Fiat to transport Fatah operatives for terrorist attacks on Israel; he was in contact with the Popular Front for the Liberation of Palestine in Lebanon.[40] With UN diplomatic plates, a terrorist could get through an Israeli military roadblock without being inspected.

This pattern continued for years after, as well. The day before the world witnessed the brutal decapitation of the U.S. civilian Nicholas Berg in Iraq on May 12, 2004, Hamas paraded the body parts of Israeli soldiers they had killed in the Gaza Strip. Israeli defense minister Shaul Mofaz disclosed that the Palestinians "used UN ambulances and UNRWA to spirit away body parts from the site of the [original] attack." In other words, a terrorist organization carried out its barbaric acts apparently using UN vehicles.[41]

Although education was one of the fields in which UNRWA was supposed to provide aid, the agency did nothing to alter Palestinian educational texts that glorified violence and continuing war against Israel. UNRWA hid behind the argument that it must use the curriculum of the "host country."[42] It was true that UNRWA did not write the textbooks, but by acquiesing to distributing them, with their hate-filled content, the UN was unquestionably complicit in fostering the ethos of terrorism that grew in the refugee camps.

There were many ways in which that complicity was expressed. For instance, an UNRWA teachers' representative, Suheil al-Hindi, praised suicide bombers at the Jabalya refugee camp in the Gaza Strip. Rather than being thrown out of UNRWA, he was promoted by being elected to the clerks' union of UNRWA workers in June 2003.[43] Eight thousand UNRWA workers participated in that election; Hamas won twenty-three out of the twenty-seven available seats.[44] Hamas made a clean sweep in the "teachers' sector" of the UNRWA clerks' union, indicating to what extent UNRWA educational institutions were controlled by individuals committed to the Hamas ideology.[45] Israeli forces got some indication of how deeply the Hamas outlook had penetrated into UNRWA schools when they found in the Kalandia refugee camp a notebook laced with pictures of Palestinian "martyrs" (that is, suicide bombers). On the back cover of the notebook, an image of a masked gunman with a black hood was pasted above the word "UNRWA."[46]

UNRWA had even more links to terrorism. Another UNRWA worker, Mahmud Khawaja, took part in founding the Islamic Jihad; he was responsible for sending suicide bombers to their missions until he was killed in 1995. The director of UNRWA activities in Jordan argued in a June 2002 meeting of UNRWA teachers that the majority of those who committed suicide missions against Israel were in fact graduates of UNRWA schools. To his credit, he appeared to be disturbed by this trend. The Arabic newspaper *al-Bayan,* published in the United Arab Emirates, reported on the teachers' meeting and concluded that UNRWA schools were "greenhouses for suicide bombers."[47] Among the terrorist masterminds of the 1990s were prominent UNRWA graduates like Ibrahim Maqadama, who founded the military wing of the Muslim Brotherhood in 1983 and helped create the military structure of Hamas, and Salah Mustafa Shehada, another Hamas leader. At least forty-six terrorist operatives were students in UNRWA schools.

The UN was fully aware that refugee camps could become centers for terrorist training and recruitment, but it did nothing about the UNRWA problem. Tom Lantos, the ranking Democratic member on the Committee of International Relations of the U.S. House of Representatives, wrote to Kofi Annan on May 13, 2002, to express his concern about UNRWA's failure to prevent the refugee camps from becoming terrorist breeding grounds. Congressman Lantos pointed out that UN Security Council Resolution 1208 affirmed the "unacceptability of using refugee camps and other persons in refugee camps . . . to achieve military purposes" and that Resolution 1296 required the secretary-general to report to the Security Council situations in which "camps are vulnerable to infiltration by armed elements." Yet Annan had not issued any reports about terrorist infiltration into UNRWA camps. In fact, by that time he had disbanded the Jenin fact-finding team altogether.

Announcing that he was aborting the fact-finding mission on

May 2, 2002, the secretary-general argued that Israel had not cooperated with the investigation and had made it difficult for the team
to obtain an accurate account of "recent events." Indeed, Israel had
voiced objections to the fact-finding team's makeup. But a UN fact-
finding team with a mandate to report on terrorist activity in
UNRWA camps in the West Bank could have proven highly embarrassing for the UN. Not only would it have uncovered the extensive
links to terrorism in UNRWA camps, it also would have determined
what independent investigations revealed: that the charges of a
Jenin massacre that the UN had uncritically bought into had been
unfounded.

After Annan dropped the fact-finding mission to Jenin, the PLO
and the Arab bloc in the UN initiated an Emergency Special Session
of the UN General Assembly that called on him to issue a report.
The secretary-general's report, issued on July 30, 2002, noted that
the claim of a Palestinian Authority official that 500 had been killed
"has not been substantiated." That was minimalistic language in
light of the exceptional measures the UN had almost adopted to investigate Israeli actions. It could have come out and said that the reports about a massacre were baseless, as even Palestinian sources
had verified. The report did make reference to the fact that the hos-
pital in Jenin had confirmed 52 Palestinian deaths, but it did not
take a final position on the death toll, citing conflicting assessments.
To its credit, Annan's report acknowledged that "Palestinian militants in the camp, as elsewhere, adopted methods which constitute
breaches of international law that have been and continue to be
condemned by the United Nations."[48] It also noted that the Palestinian Authority was obligated to refrain from carrying out attacks
against civilians and to prevent groups within its territory from engaging in such attacks. Yet the report did not even touch on the harboring of terrorists in UNRWA facilities. Furthermore, it referred
only to "the ongoing cycle of violence," a value-free term that did
not require Annan to assign any blame, to label aggressor or
defender.

Why couldn't the UN issue a blanket condemnation of Hamas,

Hizballah, or the Fatah-Tanzim of Yasser Arafat? The reason, it seems, is that the organization could no longer set out clear standards banning terrorism and political violence, simply because powerful groups in the new UN opposed such standards. In April 2002, a bloc in the General Assembly, the Saudi-sponsored Organization of the Islamic Conference, met in Kuala Lumpur, Malaysia, and adopted a declaration on international terrorism that stated, "We reject any attempt to associate Islamic states or Palestinian and Lebanese resistance with terrorism." Even though Muslim states have been the targets of terrorism, according to the Organization of the Islamic Conference, "armed struggle against foreign occupation, aggression, colonialism, and hegemony" is not in the same category as terrorism.[49] Much of this language could, of course, be found in resolutions that the General Assembly had passed in the 1970s and 1980s, such as the 1982 resolution that reaffirmed the right of peoples to use "all available means, including armed struggle," against "colonial and foreign domination."

The UN has made as its lodestar the pursuit of impartiality and evenhandedness. But how can an organization dedicated to preserving international peace remain "impartial" in the face of the greatest threat to global security today? The UN, in both its main bodies and the office of the secretary-general, seems not to acknowledge that no cause or grievance could possibly justify sending an eighteen-year-old youth into a crowded hotel to murder innocent people, or sending men to hijack airplanes and drive them into skyscrapers.

The United States recognizes what the UN refuses to: The war on terrorism requires taking sides, it depends on moral clarity. But moral clarity is in short supply at the UN. Despite the lofty goals that its founders set out for it, the UN is ill equipped to deal with the single biggest threat to the world today. It has helped not to defeat terrorism but to perpetuate it.

In April 2004, the United States received a rude reminder of the damage the UN has done by perpetuating terrorism. A radical Iraqi Shiite cleric named Moqtada al-Sadr, who controlled a militia attacking U.S. troops who were trying to establish peace and stability in Iraq, commanded his followers to "terrorize your enemy"—that enemy being America, of course. As his forces attacked American soldiers with assault rifles and rocket-propelled grenade launchers, al-Sadr proclaimed, "I am the beating arm for Hezbollah and Hamas here in Iraq."[50]

This was not just rhetoric. Not long thereafter, U.S. intelligence sources revealed that Hizballah had been moving its men to Iraq to battle U.S. forces.[51] Even prior to the Iraq War, Saddam Hussein was apparently reaching out to a variety of terrorist groups, including Hizballah and Hamas, to lead an insurgency against U.S. forces—as the U.S. Senate's Select Committee on Intelligence confirmed in its July 2004 report on U.S. prewar intelligence.

Emboldened by their success and confident that the UN will not stand against those giving them sanctuary, Hizballah and other terrorist groups only expand their operations. The costs of the UN's failures could be devastating.

# From Moral Equivalence to World Order

The United Nations was founded on the bedrock of a great ideal: that the nations of the world could draw together and defend certain fundamental principles that were common to all of mankind, and in so doing, deter the outbreak of aggression as well as protect international peace. This was the essence of "collective security" as President Woodrow Wilson had first envisioned it for the League of Nations and as President Franklin Roosevelt adapted it at the end of the Second World War for the UN. It would be an alternative to raw power politics and spheres of influence.

But after more than fifty years, it has become clear that this noble vision just doesn't work. The British historian E. H. Carr noted that Wilson was once asked what if the League of Nations failed, to which he replied, "If it won't work, it must be made to work."[1] UN advocates similarly invoked, in the last decade, their aspirations for an effective United Nations without critically looking at how it has actually performed. In both cases, a wish cannot be a substitute for the adoption of policies that work.

The UN was exposed most obviously in the debate over Saddam Hussein's Iraq in the lead-up to the 2003 war. Saddam Hussein's regime challenged virtually everything for which the UN stood. Iraq had repeatedly and flagrantly violated basic human rights and had actually *used* weapons of mass destruction. That record was indisputable. The UN itself certainly did not dispute that record, as the

Security Council adopted from late 1990 onward some sixteen resolutions against Iraq—all of them Chapter VII resolutions, the most severe kind available. Iraq flouted these resolutions, and yet the UN did nothing to enforce them. The world organization failed, once again, to guarantee international peace and security. The UN had displayed its weakness for all the world to see. Many critics, especially in Europe, would focus on how the Bush administration explained its military campaign to topple the regime in Baghdad, but this criticism ignored the fundamental truth that the UN had failed to deal with the Iraqi threat even when it was clear that Saddam Hussein's regime would not cooperate.

Of course, the UN had a long list of earlier failures as well. The Iraq situation exposed how the UN could undercut its own authority by adopting resolutions that seemed to stand firmly for the protection of global security but then refusing to implement them. Another example of this came just after the terrorist attacks of September 11, 2001. The UN Security Council adopted Resolution 1373 as an unambiguous denunciation of international terrorism, as it expressly forbade states to harbor international terrorist organizations. Yet not much more than a week later, the UN General Assembly overwhelmingly elected Syria to sit on the UN Security Council, the very body responsible for implementing the antiterrorism resolution, despite the fact that Syria was a known sponsor of terrorism. (The U.S. State Department, as noted, had identified Syria as a state sponsor of terrorism every year for more than twenty years.) The UN thus completely undermined its claim to be a serious force in combating the greatest threat to the world in the twenty-first century.

The lack of enforcement is just one failure of the UN's collective security system. In many cases the UN has not even been able to establish clear resolutions in the first place, either in the Security Council or in the General Assembly. Many resolutions have undermined rather than upheld international peace and security, as they have contained loopholes and caveats. This became evident when the UN sought to define "aggression." Moreover, General Assembly resolutions in the 1970s and the 1980s handled the issue of terrorism by excusing the violence of armed groups to support "national liberation" movements. Such watered-down resolutions further undercut the UN's authority.

What was the impact on world order of such determinations of right and wrong? As E. H. Carr points out, there is such a thing as international morality; world order is based not on raw power calculations alone, but also on nations' adherence to certain principles.[2] In other words, world leaders sometimes formulate policies by trying to do the right thing as defined by the international community. The UN was supposed to help define that code of conduct for states, particularly through its nonbinding resolutions in its main bodies, the General Assembly and the Security Council. But what happened when those principles were eroded by the UN itself? It is here that the UN let the world down. Instead of providing the glue for world order, it supplied the fuel for chaos.

What is behind the UN's miserable performance? First, the UN lost the moral clarity of its original members in 1945, which had fashioned the UN Charter while the embers of the Second World War were still warm. Since a state had to have declared war on the Axis in order to be a founding member of the UN, the UN was as much an alliance as it was a universal organization. It was no accident that Winston Churchill wanted to call the organization the "Allied Nations." The early UN could define for itself who was the aggressor and who were the allies resisting aggression.

But right from the start, the UN lost its ability to make that distinction; the UN's early moral clarity was replaced with a corrosive moral equivalence. Its involvement in the first Arab-Israeli War planted the seeds for further rounds of the conflict, as the armistice system that it created failed to halt the repeated armed infiltrations and encroachments into Israel that eventually deteriorated into full-scale wars. In Kashmir, on the Indian subcontinent, the UN failed to identify the aggressor and as a result helped perpetuate the conflict between India and Pakistan. It was no surprise, then, that after 1972, Indian diplomats insisted on keeping the UN out of all future diplomacy on the Kashmir issue. Nor was it a surprise, as eminent Middle

East historian Bernard Lewis has noted, that India and Pakistan were able to reach some sort of accommodation on refugee matters without the help of the UN, while in the Arab-Israeli conflict, in which the UN has been intimately involved for decades, the refugee problem was not resolved, and in many respects has worsened.[3] Others went outside the UN as well. In 1979, for instance, Israelis and Egyptians established a distinctly non-UN peacekeeping force, the Multinational Force and Observers (MFO), to separate their armies in the Sinai Peninsula.

The 1990s was supposed to be the UN's great decade. The Cold War's end removed the automatic clash of wills between the superpowers at the Security Council, meaning that the paralysis in UN decision-making should have come to an end. But with the UN at the hub of the new world order that followed the 1991 Gulf War, greater global chaos emerged. Unable to judge aggression in the Balkans, the UN continued to insist on its doctrine of impartiality, even as those it was supposed to protect—the Bosnian Muslims—were massacred in the thousands. A year before that, in Rwanda, the moral equivalence of UN peacekeepers had had even more disastrous consequences; upwards of 800,000 Tutsis were slaughtered despite the fact that the UN had received clear warnings that genocide was imminent. In Afghanistan, domestic opponents of the Taliban must have felt that the UN betrayed them in 1995–1996, since UN-appointed mediators insisted on maintaining strict neutrality despite the Taliban's brutality and the enormous aid that dangerous regime received from outside parties like Pakistan.[4]

The UN's failures had broader repercussions. By not adequately dealing with the conflict in Bosnia, the UN fueled the Balkan crisis, which eventually spilled over into Kosovo and Macedonia. The failures in Rwanda fueled a massive central African war in which five nations invaded the Democratic Republic of the Congo, where approximately 2.5 million people died in the next four years. And as Iraq flagrantly violated UN resolutions on weapons of mass destruction, Libya, Iran, and North Korea ignored the UN's international control system on nuclear weapons. Since the UN spent about the same amount of time finding loopholes for resolute action against terrorism as it did combating the threat, UN member states harbored or financed international terrorist organizations with impunity until September 11, 2001—and in some cases even after 9/11. In large part because of the UN, the 1990s became the decade of new world *dis*order.

Despite those obvious and repeated failures, the UN is still held in high regard, viewed as the final authority in all international disputes—the "source of international legitimacy," as so many have put it both in the United States and abroad. This is utterly ridiculous, and shows how unaccountable the UN and its officials remain. Consider that Kofi Annan was promoted to the position of UN secretary-general *after* his Department of Peacekeeping Operations sat by as both the Rwanda and Srebrenica massacres occurred. (Outrageously, these patterns only seemed to continue, albeit on a lesser scale. Human Rights Watch detailed in a July 2004 report how UN international police and NATO "failed catastrophically" to protect Kosovo's ethnic minorities during rioting in March 2004. Peacekeepers looked on as hundreds of homes—and even entire villages— were burned to the ground. When they briefed the Security Council about what happened, UN officials voiced no self-criticism.)[5] As former Swedish deputy prime minister Per Ahlmark put it, "That is the culture of the UN: believe the best of barbarians, do nothing to provoke controversy among superiors, and let others be the butt of criticism afterwards. Even subsequent revelations about Annan's responsibility for the disasters in Rwanda and Bosnia did not affect his standing. On the contrary, he was unanimously re-elected and awarded the Nobel Peace Prize."[6]

So much for accountability.

## LEGITIMACY?

The UN's credibility took another hit—or should have taken a hit— when the Iraqi "oil-for-food" scandal was revealed in early 2004.

With this program, the UN allowed Iraq to sell a limited amount of oil in order to purchase food, medicine, and other humanitarian goods. But by 2004 it was clear that by instituting this program, the UN had allowed Saddam Hussein's regime to pocket billions of dollars—$10.1 billion, according to the U.S. General Accounting Office—through oil smuggling and other illicit oil proceeds from the supposed humanitarian program.[7] It appeared that the Iraqis had also exploited the UN program to give kickbacks to friends and accomplices around the world. An Iraqi newspaper published a list from the Iraq Oil Ministry showing that hundreds of foreign dignitaries and businesses had allegedly received vouchers to purchase Iraqi oil at well below market rates. On the list was UN assistant secretary-general Benon Sevan, the executive director of the oil-for-food program, who apparently received a voucher for 11.5 million barrels of oil, which would have been worth as much as $3.5 million. Sevan denied the allegation, but it was enough to raise questions about whether UN officials had actually profited off the scheme.

At the very least, there were legitimate questions as to how the UN could have enabled a dictator under stringent UN sanctions to get away with such rampant corruption. Some charged that the UN had knowingly propped up Saddam's regime by expanding the oil-for-food program in 2002, even after it should have been clear that Iraq was systematically exploiting the program.[8] Worse, many observers wondered whether the UN was actually obstructing investigations into the scandal in the spring of 2004. UN Resolution 1483, adopted in May 2003, had requested that the secretary-general turn over "all relevant documentation" on oil-for-food contracts, but nearly a year later, the UN Secretariat had turned over only about 20 percent of those documents. Moreover, congressional investigators turned up two letters that had gone out on Benon Sevan's UN stationery to key oil-for-food contractors. On *Meet the Press,* NBC's Tim Russert summed up one of the letters this way: "So Mr. Sevan, who's being investigated, is telling a company that's also being investigated, 'Don't cooperate with government authorities unless you clear it with me.' "[9] The other letter had much the same message, instructing the company that all documentation "shall be treated as confidential and shall be delivered only to the United Nations authorized officials."[10]

Despite all the revelations about the UN's oil-for-food program, Sweden's Per Ahlmark remarked, "The world is clamouring to entrust" Kofi Annan and the UN "with the future of more than 20 million Iraqis who survived Saddam Hussein's dictatorship."[11] Indeed, in 2004 many pundits clamored for throwing the whole issue of Iraq to the UN, which they expected would better oversee Iraq's reconstruction and development than the United States and its allies. It was as if they were completely unaware of the UN's recent record in the 1990s. As Ahlmark aptly observed, such calls for expanded UN authority in Iraq reflected that the UN had become "an institution in which no shortcoming, it seems, goes unrewarded."[12]

It should have come as no surprise that the man the UN picked to be its troubleshooter in Iraq during 2004 was Lakhdar Brahimi, a former Algerian foreign minister whom Richard Butler, as head of the UN weapons inspectors, suspected of being sympathetic to Saddam Hussein. Little wonder, then, that both Iraqi Kurds and Shiites greeted the appointment with considerable consternation and ultimately rejected his recommendations for a new Iraqi interim leadership.

Whatever illusions might persist about the UN's effectiveness and international authority, the U.S. government has recognized, at least since the late 1990s, that the UN's failures mean that in some situations the United States is compelled to protect world order by itself, or within more limited coalitions outside of the UN. Both Democratic and Republican administrations have reached this conclusion. In Kosovo, for example, the Clinton administration led a NATO coalition to counter ethnic cleansing, without any authorization whatsoever from the UN Security Council. Only after the war, in 1999, did the UN reinsert itself in Kosovo. Even then, it did little besides set up an interim administration mission to help rule the province; after five years it had not advanced Kosovo toward any diplomatic solution. In 1998, the Clinton administration again initiated military operations without a UN resolution, when it teamed with Great Britain to begin a limited bombing campaign against Saddam Hussein—Operation Desert Fox. Finally, President Bush was compelled to launch the 2003 Iraq War, teaming with the "coalition of the willing" and working outside the framework of the UN Security Council.

In each case, the United States was taking a firm position against threats to international security—filling the void that the UN left when it abdicated its responsibility. And while the UN's failure to deter aggression has fueled other conflicts, decisive U.S. action has actually contained and even rolled back disorder. The broader repercussions of the 2003 Iraq War are a prime example of the effectiveness—necessity, in fact—of a swift and decisive response to aggression. While the world complained when the United States did not quickly turn up Iraq's weapons of mass destruction, the Iraq War helped flush out illicit nuclear weapons programs around the world. Most notably, in late 2003, Libya disclosed its advanced nuclear weapons program and agreed to dismantle it under U.S. supervision. Just the implicit threat of Anglo-American intervention was enough to turn the Libyans around; had Muammar Qaddafi believed that the United States would need the approval of the UN Security Council before leading a strike, he might not have felt compelled to open up his illicit nuclear program. Even the clerical regime of Iran, whose continuing nuclear program has been a source of deepening concern, felt compelled to disclose more elements of its clandestine program to the International Atomic Energy Agency than ever before.

## FIGHTING RACIAL DISCRIMINATION?

If the UN serves as a temple of moral equivalence that frequently cannot separate aggressors from the victims of aggression, then why has it been so remarkably consistent in condemning one member state, Israel? Although the UN General Assembly has a hard time reaching conclusive moral judgments in so many cases, it adopts around twenty anti-Israel resolutions every year. There is no contradiction here, however. In the General Assembly, what generally emerges is an amalgamation of positions, with a least common denominator prevailing that can command the support of the widest group of states. The same can happen in the UN Security Council, as its members negotiate agreed language on a proposed resolution. What frequently emerges from this process of global consensus-building is moral slush, which makes it nearly impossible to adopt decisive measures against impending aggression or even genocide. And it can equally mistake the victims of violence for its perpetrators.

In this sense, the UN's treatment of Israel is a warning sign of a more general failure of the UN system. As a Western democracy, Israel is among the minority in the UN, vastly outnumbered by the authoritarian regimes and Third World nations that populate the UN. Israel is particularly vulnerable in this situation not simply because it is a target for a wide group of Arab and Islamic states that seek the automatic support of Africa as well, but also because it is not part of a general bloc of states like the European Union. If the UN went after the Netherlands, for example, the European Union would band together; if Togo or Benin were unfairly treated, the African Union would step in. While Israel has benefited from an American diplomatic umbrella in the form of a U.S. veto in the Security Council, it is exposed in all other UN bodies.

It is telling that the UN sponsored the infamous 2001 World Conference Against Racism in Durban, South Africa, and invited NGOs that turned the event into an outright attack on the right of a UN member state—Israel—to exist, as well as a festival for renewed anti-Semitism. According to Canadian minister of justice Irwin Cotler, a leading human rights advocate, by sponsoring the conference, the UN legitimized and gave protective cover for such actions.[13] In fact, the UN commissioner for human rights, Mary Robinson, had paved the way for the Durban debacle by allowing Jewish, Kurdish, and Bahai NGOs to be excluded from a February 2001 meeting held in preparation for the conference in Iran.[14] What happened at Durban naturally followed. A UN-accredited NGO distributed anti-Semitic caricatures similar to Nazi hate literature of the 1930s; another flyer at a Durban rally considered that if Hitler had won the Second World War, Israel would not have come into existence.[15] Thus the UN, which was born in the shadow of the Holocaust in 1945, was now giving protective cover to the very anti-Semitism that its founders had tried to combat; its so-called conference against racism supported racial and religious discrimination.

If Israel is a particular target in the UN, this is not Israel's problem alone. Rather, many member states are vulnerable as a result of the UN's broader system failure. Many peoples who cannot exercise political clout in the UN—and who cannot marshal majorities in their behalf—have been the victims of terrible crimes. The UN, as noted, did not take the lead in helping the Iraqi Kurds after the 1991 Gulf War—the United States and Britain did. The same was true for the Shiite Muslims of Iraq. For years, Christian communities have been brutalized in Lebanon, Indonesia, and Sudan, and yet no offers of international protection have been provided. Tibetan Buddhists have also been sacrificed.

More recently, the Sudanese government with the assistance of "Janjaweed" Arab militias launched an ethnic cleansing campaign that forced 1.2 million residents of the Darfur region in western Sudan from their homes. At a minimum, according to UN estimates, 30,000 people had been slaughtered in Darfur by mid-2004. And Amnesty International reported that the Janjaweed were systematically using rape as a weapon of war in Darfur. At least 100,000 refugees made their way to Chad after facing aerial bombardment and ground attacks. One refugee in Chad who had anticipated intervention commented in exasperation, "The United Nations has left us here to die."[16]

The sentiment was warranted. UN secretary-general Kofi Annan would not visit Darfur until July 2004—some sixteen months after the conflict broke out. More telling, in April 2004, the very same Sudan was elected to a three-year term to the UN Human Rights Commission in Geneva. Worse, in June, the UN Security Council failed to adopt a resolution criticizing Sudan; Algeria, Pakistan, and China successfully opposed the measure.[17] At the same time, the African Union was protecting Sudan from charges of genocide before international organizations. The morally twisted bloc voting of the UN's Third World states was helping legitimize and thus sustain the murder of innocent Africans, Buddhists, Christians, non-Arab Muslims, and Israelis.

## THE ROAD AHEAD

The debate about the future of American foreign policy has mainly focused on this question: Should the United States "go it alone" and use its superior military strength unilaterally, or should it still work through the UN? But as the Kosovo and Iraq cases reveal, there is a third option: working with allies outside of the UN framework.

Clearly, the UN cannot serve as the ultimate protector of international peace and security. It just doesn't work. The experience of the 1990s shows that we cannot rely on UN peacekeeping forces in the world's trouble spots. An internal UN report on peacekeeping issued in 2000, prepared by Lakhdar Brahimi, admitted that peacekeepers cannot remain impartial when the parties to a dispute are not "moral equals"; in some cases, the report acknowledged, there are "obvious aggressors and victims."[18] Of course, using UN forces to take sides and coerce one of the parties to comply with its commitments changes peacekeeping to what diplomats call "peace enforcement." That would require the UN to have larger and far more potent military forces under its control.

In response to the Brahimi Report, Secretary-General Kofi Annan backed the idea of "robust peacekeeping." He advocated new roles for his UN peacekeepers in dangerous situations. For example, in 2002 he recommended dispatching UN peacekeepers to the West Bank and the Gaza Strip, where they would undoubtedly be vulnerable to the same kinds of attacks that struck peacekeeping forces in Lebanon in 1983 and UN workers in Iraq in 2004.

In embracing the notion of peace enforcement, Annan over-looked the fact that in many of the world's unresolved conflicts, the UN can actually undermine international peace and security. Indeed, reading the Brahimi Report can easily lead one to arrive at the opposite conclusion from the one Annan reached: Keep the UN out of conflict areas requiring substantial military muscle. In fact, some had reached this conclusion well before the Brahimi Report was issued. Back in 1995, Senator Nancy Kassebaum, Kansas Republican, and Congressman Lee Hamilton, Indiana Democrat, concluded that the UN should have nothing to do with peace enforcement. Even Annan's predecessor, Boutros Boutros-Ghali, admitted near the end of his term as secretary-general, "Enforcement is beyond the power of the U.N."[19]

So what should be done to protect and enforce international peace?

The biggest problem to be addressed is the UN's lack of any cohesive sense of purpose or values common to all members. George F. Will, a vocal critic of the UN, has rightly observed that the term "international community" is an oxymoron, since the word "community" denotes unity based on shared political interests and values.[20] After all, when most UN member states have governments that are not democratically elected, and when many are authoritarian regimes that torture their own citizens, the UN can hardly be considered the ultimate source of international legitimacy. To solve this problem requires a two-track approach on the part of the United States and its Western allies: first, going outside the UN entirely to deal with immediate threats to American and international security, and second, working within the UN to address, in the long term, the organization's crippling flaws.

Before long-term changes can be achieved, the United States and its allies must, of course, deal with pressing threats—and that means bypassing the UN's anti-Western majority entirely. It would make sense to form an organization of democracies committed to the same common values and strategic purpose. Bill Clinton's secretary of state, Madeleine Albright, went partway to this goal when she convened the first meeting of the Community of Democracies in June 2000. The meeting's attendees set out to "collaborate on democratic-related issues in existing international and regional institutions . . . aimed at the promotion of democratic government." More than a hundred countries tried to join the Community of Democracies, but some had to be denied full membership because they did not meet all democratic standards. Secretary of State Colin Powell continued the initiative in the Bush administration, making it a bipartisan effort. In November 2002, in Seoul, South Korea, a second meeting of the Community of Democracies was held, at which 110 governments adopted an "action plan" committing members to preserving political freedom in their own countries and spreading it to their neighbors.[21]

The reason the Community of Democracies is only a partial solution is that at its meeting in Seoul, the organization affirmed the need to establish a Caucus of Democratic States within the UN General Assembly. In other words, the Community of Democracies has not been envisioned as a *replacement* for the UN; rather, member states hope to form a bloc within the UN framework to fight for democratic principles. The bloc of democracies could serve as a counterweight to the power of the Nonaligned Movement, which includes more than a hundred Third World states and authoritarian regimes.

Of course, the problems the United States encountered in building its coalition against Saddam Hussein had nothing to do with nondemocratic regimes. Indeed, France and Germany—both strong Western democracies—were among Washington's harshest opponents in the buildup to the Iraq War. What is needed to deal with the new security challenges the world is facing is not a revival of the UN but rather the refashioning of the Western alliance.

Recent events have demonstrated that the most effective guarantor of world order has been the emergence of new coalitions that are bound together by shared democratic values *and* by a common perception of the threats that they all face together. That is how the UN started, the presence of the Soviet Union notwithstanding. Remember, the UN was founded as a coalition of allies. By definition, allies don't get confused about who is the enemy, about who is the aggressor and who is the defender. Alliances stand for shared principles. When Roosevelt and Churchill met on the HMS *Prince of Wales* in 1941 and issued the Atlantic Charter, they had few doubts about what they stood for. Of course, alliances are not always easy to manage. States can be allies in one area of the world and rivals in another region. During the 1950s, for example, the United States stood against the residual elements of British and French imperialism in the Middle East. But effective diplomacy can ameliorate these kinds of disagreements.

The United States and its Western allies won the Cold War but obviously no longer have the common goal of containing Soviet expansionism as the glue holding together a coalition. Still, a coalition of allies could start with neutralizing the greatest threat to international peace today: global terrorism, another threat that the UN has failed to counter effectively. Despite the doubts that have been voiced about the reasons for going to war in Iraq, official reports released by the U.S. and British governments in 2004 back one of the war's principal justifications: terrorist groups desperate for deadly weapons could have gotten nonconventional weapons capabilities in Iraq. Even critics of the prewar intelligence on Iraq, like David Kay, have forcefully argued that the threat was real and that the U.S. military action prevented Iraq from becoming a major "marketplace" for weapons of mass destruction. To neutralize this type of threat on a global scale will require a new coalition response—especially since the UN proved it was unwilling to respond in the Iraqi case. Such a coalition might include states as diverse as the United States, Australia, Britain, Italy, Poland, Kenya, Turkey, Israel, the Philippines, Singapore, Thailand, and India. The issue of terrorism relates to a number of other concerns common to all of these nations: the spread of weapons of mass destruction, the proliferation of sensitive military technologies, terrorist financing and money laundering, and the incitement of ethnic hatred and violence in national media as well as in educational institutions.

Their commitment to curtailing these threats would lead democracies around the world to join together and take action. After all, in many cases governments are already sharing intelligence and military expertise to help counter the threats to global security. These arrangements are usually bilateral understandings, set up on an ad hoc basis, but they could become the basis for a multilateral framework.

Of course, there are those in France who want to turn the European Union into a bloc to counterbalance the power of the United States. In the current UN, the power of the EU is considerable, since non-EU states from Japan to Argentina frequently adjust their voting patterns on international issues according to EU preferences. A new democratic coalition would offer many friends of the United States, especially in Eastern Europe, an alternative multilateral body in which to coordinate their positions. As its strength grows, even those EU states antagonistic to Washington might change their position and join. The UN just exacerbates that antagonism. For a state like France, the veto power it enjoys on the Security Council is the strongest evidence of its continuing great power status. This tempts the French to adopt a policy of "I veto, therefore I am." This temptation is removed in coalitions outside the UN and could lead to an improvement in Franco-American relations.

Such a democratic coalition would be far more representative of the national will of each country's citizens than the UN currently is. Oddly, by going outside the UN, these countries would be recommitting themselves to the principles on which the UN was originally founded. They would embrace the principles laid out in the UN Charter and insist that members of the coalition fully adhere—not just give lip service—to a basic code of international conduct. States subscribing to these principles might gain distinctive economic advantages, while states refusing to adhere to these fundamental prerequisites for global security would not receive the same benefits British prime minister Tony Blair, who called for continuing American leadership to protect world order in a July 2003 address before a joint session of Congress, stated that UN members must be told, "If you engage in the systematic and gross abuse of human rights in defiance of the UN Charter, you cannot expect to enjoy the same privileges as those that conform to it." Unfortunately, that does not happen in the UN.

Blair was absolutely right when he called out to Americans,

"Don't ever apologize for your values." Those values were precisely what the UN was supposed to defend. Because the UN has lost the moral clarity of its founders, the United States and its allies must take the lead. The world will follow in time. If more than one hundred nations wanted to join the Community of Democracies, the democratic ideal must be powerful.

Only outside the UN can real progress toward global security be made in the short term. Yet the second track of the two-track approach should indeed be developing a long-term solution to the UN's critical problems. And ultimately the UN's biggest problem is that it no longer establishes any firm standards of behavior for UN member states. That lack of standards is why a dictatorship like Libya, with a long history of human rights abuses and support for terrorism, could be chosen to head the UN Human Rights Commission in Geneva; it is why Syria, another state sponsor of terrorism, could be elected to the Security Council, which is supposed to safeguard international peace and security. These states are given a superior status in the UN but are not expected to alter their behavior at all. It is a case of *noblesse* with no *oblige*.

Working within the UN, the United States and its allies must fundamentally alter the voting patterns of UN General Assembly member states. Here, the same grouping of democratic allies can also serve as a caucus for change and reform of the UN. They need to create the kind of international community based on the shared values that the UN's founders envisioned. Achieving this will involve breaking the Nonaligned Movement, a Cold War relic that sustains international rules for the benefit of dictatorships that persecute their own peoples. Many African and Asian states would certainly rather associate with a community of Democracies than hear Soviet-style speeches at summit meetings of the Nonaligned Movement. These nations need to be led and not abandoned.

Some states might be reluctant to make such a substantial diplomatic investment for the sake of a "debating society" that cannot adopt binding resolutions. But even if the General Assembly does not create binding international law, it can have a profound impact on international behavior, because it generates a global code of conduct that nations eventually follow. The United States and its allies can affect how other nations behave by, for instance, making clear that it matters how those states vote in the UN General Assembly— that their votes have negative consequences, as Blair suggested. The most direct means of showing that UN voting patterns matter is by downgrading bilateral relations with states that continue to undercut the principles for which the United States and the West stand. But diplomacy can involve the carrot as well as the stick: Western diplomats must lobby fellow ambassadors and expose them to a cogent defense of democracy and freedom. They can and should make the case for their values—the same values that Tony Blair said should not be apologized for.

The United States understood the importance of laying out clear principles of behavior—even if nonbinding—when it concluded the Helsinki Final Act with the Soviet Union in the 1970s. The Helsinki Final Act was just a declaration, not a binding treaty. But it became the rallying cry for millions behind the Iron Curtain seeking the protection of their basic human rights. It also set standards for Soviet international behavior: If Moscow wanted to benefit from East-West trade, it would have to bring its behavior in line with Helsinki.

If the UN is to have any relevance in the future, it must become a global Helsinki.

But as important as this transformation may be, realistically it will take many years to complete it. That is why effecting change within the UN can only do so much, and why going outside the UN is crucial. And until the UN is transformed, it must not be empowered. In the debate over the spread of democracy to the Arab world, critics frequently point out that premature democratic structures in a country like Saudi Arabia would lead to the election of Osama bin Laden as prime minister. States must first create a democratic political culture and a civil society with political parties before they can take the plunge to full-scale democracy. The mistake of the UN's architects was that they prematurely empowered its members to have a voice, even if those members represented values that were inimical to the UN itself.

It is a mistake to make serious aspects of global security dependent on the UN's decisions. The UN cannot take the lead in protecting states' vital national security interests. To be sure, some UN specialized agencies are successful at humanitarian work. The World Food Program, for example, fed 90 million people around the world in 2000, many of whom would have come close to starvation without its assistance, and the World Health Organization saved millions of lives by orchestrating the international response to the outbreak of SARS in the Far East and North America.[22] So let the UN give out tents and blankets when international disaster strikes; it simply cannot bear the burden of preventing wars and neutralizing aggression.

This book has outlined how the UN has dropped the ball repeatedly when it was expected to defend peoples who relied on its flag for their protection. A related problem is that when states assume the UN is involved in resolving an international problem, they have no reason to mobilize and handle the crisis: NATO might have gone into Bosnia two years earlier if it had known what the result of the UN's intervention would be. Similarly, the UN's involvement in Afghanistan in the 1990s offered an excuse for the United States and its allies not to take action; when asked what Washington was doing about the problems in Afghanistan, State Department officials often cited the "Six Plus Two" talks that were occurring under UN auspices (the group featured Afghanistan's six neighbors plus two other countries, Russia and the United States).

This deficiency in the UN is hard for many to admit. The UN is protected by a very high wall of political correctness that makes criticism of it tantamount to an attack on all of mankind. But it is time to recognize that it has utterly failed to achieve its founders' goals: to halt aggression and assure world order. With determined leadership, the United States can lead its allies in creating a safer and freer world. Perhaps in the long term they can reinvigorate the UN and make the organization's system of collective security a viable option. But that day is a long way off.

# The Real Oil-for-Food Scandal

The United Nations remains a disaster. The evidence of its mishandling—and even neglect—of some of the greatest global crises in our time is simply overwhelming.

By 2005, three years after the UN failed to take the lead in the Iraq crisis, the organization's failures were more apparent than ever. And more and more groups were calling the UN on its endemic problems. In June, a congressionally mandated bipartisan task force on UN reform, led by former House speaker Newt Gingrich and former senator George Mitchell, concluded, "Until and unless it changes dramatically, the United Nations will remain an uncertain instrument, both for the governments that comprise it and to those who look to it for salvation."[1]

The UN was in deep trouble. It had not brought the mass killings in Sudan's Darfur region to a halt. The U.S. State Department determined that the attacks by Arab Janjaweed militias and the Sudanese armed forces against the black non-Arab residents of Darfur constituted genocide—a significant determination in that signatories to the Genocide Convention are legally compelled to seek immediate UN action in cases of genocide. But the UN itself refused to reach the same conclusion, so no action was taken.[2] Stories of sexual abuse by UN peacekeeping forces continued, including revelations of hungry young girls in the Democratic Republic of the Congo providing sexual favors to UN soldiers for a banana or a piece of cake.[3]

Even where the UN seemed to advance the cause of global peace and security—by forcing the Syrian withdrawal from Lebanon—its true contribution was only partial. On September 2, 2004, the UN Security Council adopted Resolution 1559, which called on "all remaining foreign forces" to withdraw from Lebanon. Syria wasn't mentioned by name, but it was the clear target of the resolution, which was drafted just as the Syrians clumsily sought to amend the Lebanese constitution so that their hand-picked pro-Syrian president, Emile Lahoud, could extend his term of office.

And when several months later Syria appeared to be linked to the murder of former Lebanese prime minister Rafiq Hariri, it sparked a massive outpouring of rage by Lebanese citizens and the beginnings of a new democracy movement. One of the movement's leaders, Walid Jumblatt, the head of the Lebanese Druze community, did not credit the UN for the anti-Syrian unrest: "It's strange for me to say it, but this process of change has started because of the American invasion of Iraq."[4] This was the same war that UN Secretary General Kofi Annan said was illegal.

## THE UN STAINED BY "OIL FOR FOOD"

Probably no other revelations damaged the UN's reputation more than those associated with the "oil for food" scandal. As noted in previous chapters, oil-for-food was supposed to be purely a humanitarian UN program, allowing Saddam Hussein's government, which was under UN sanctions, to pump enough oil so that it could at least buy food and humanitarian supplies for the Iraqi people. But now it was clear that it had become a huge global scam dripping in corruption. The UN's own official investigation into the oil-for-food program was headed by former Federal Reserve chairman Paul Volcker. The Volcker panel charged in its first interim report, on February 3, 2005, that Benon Sevan, the UN official who was in charge of the UN's Iraq humanitarian assistance division from 1996 through 2003, was involved in Saddam Hussein's kickbacks scheme. Months earlier,

Charles Duelfer, head of the CIA's Iraq Survey Group, had estimated that Sevan had received thirteen million barrels of oil in special oil allocations from Saddam's regime.[5] But now a UN-appointed body was making the charge, not just the United States.

Kofi Annan suspended Sevan, but the secretary general could not escape the oil-for-food disclosures. Volcker's second interim report, issued on March 29, 2005, demonstrated how Annan's son, Kojo Annan, received a salary from Cotecna, the Swiss firm that won the UN contract to inspect all entry points into Saddam Hussein's Iraq. It had been believed that Kojo Annan's relationship with Cotecna, which began in 1996, was terminated in 1998, just as Cotecna sought the UN contract. But Volcker's report uncovered that Kojo Annan had earned a regular salary from the company via a noncompetition agreement until February 2004. Both Cotecna and Kojo Annan, according to the Volcker report, tried to conceal this financial relationship.

The real question is whether Secretary General Kofi Annan knew of his son's relationship with Cotecna and if somehow this affected the UN's connection with the inspection company. The secretary general issued a statement saying that the Volcker report had cleared him of any "wrongdoing." Yet the report criticized Annan for failing to order a thorough independent investigation of the Cotecna inspection contract, in light of allegations that the company had made illicit payments to Benazir Bhutto's family to try to secure a contract in Pakistan. The report added, "Had there been such an investigation of these allegations, it is unlikely that Cotecna would have been awarded renewals of its contract with the United Nations."[6]

Even before these oil-for-food details came out, a U.S. senator chairing a panel that was probing the UN scandal called for Annan's resignation. In November 2004, Senator Norm Coleman, Minnesota Republican, argued that Annan must be held accountable for allowing Saddam Hussein to abuse the UN program and accumulate $21 billion through bribes, kickbacks, and political manipulations. His accusations seemed vindicated by mid-2005 when two UN investigators revealed that half of the 4500 companies that took part in the oil-for-food program paid kickbacks or illegal surcharges to Iraq.

Kofi Annan's position seemed to become even more compromised in June 2005, when a memo was uncovered describing a late November 1998 conversation between the secretary general and a Cotecna representative in Paris. According to the memo, Michael Wilson, a Cotecna vice president, who was also Kofi Annan's close friend, wrote after a discussion with Annan and his entourage that he had been told "we could count on their support."[7] The timing was important: Cotecna won its UN contract on December 11, 1998, just weeks later. Nor had the Paris encounter been Annan's first meeting with Cotecna officers. Volcker discovered that Annan had also met with Elie Massey, the owner of Cotecna, on two occasions.

Worse still, through oil-for-food, Saddam Hussein tried to bribe states that sat on the UN Security Council. Benon Sevan was a tiny player in the overall oil-for-food scandal; Saddam ultimately was trying to buy international influence. And his biggest clients, according to the CIA's Iraq Survey Group, just so happened to be the three permanent members of the Security Council that consistently defended Iraq from the Americans and the British: Russia, France, and China. (Russia received 30 percent of Saddam's vouchers; France, 15 percent; China, 10 percent.) It could not be proven whether Saddam's schemes affected the policies of these states, but the revelations certainly tainted the credibility of their statements about the Iraq situation.

The oil-for-food program also undermined the UN sanctions that were intended to keep Iraq from developing weapons of mass destruction. Those sanctions did in fact degrade the industries that produced Iraq's weapons of mass destruction, but the corruption of the UN oil-for-food program proved critical to their revival. Although UN defenders seized on the failure to find large stocks of Iraqi weapons of mass destruction to argue that the UN sanctions had essentially worked and that military action had been unnecessary, they did not consider whether Iraq had retained a "breakout capability" that would have allowed it to reconstitute its weapons of mass destruction quickly.

And on this critical question, the Iraq Survey Group's Charles Duelfer concluded that with the flow of "illicitly diverted" oil-for-food money after 1996, Iraq's chemical industry surged while new funding went to employees of the Iraqi nuclear program. Duelfer's report reveals that in 1999 Saddam Hussein actually inquired how long it would take to build a production line for chemical weapons; he was told that more simple chemicals could be produced in six months. Maintaining the kind of large stockpiles of chemical and biological weapons that the West thought Saddam possessed made little sense, since impurities made them unstable and limited their shelf life.

Had the United States and coalition forces not intervened, Iraq would have been well positioned to restore the production of weapons of mass destruction, particularly if UN sanctions were lifted. Thus, as the oil-for-food program became more corrupt, it undermined the UN's main goal in Iraq since 1991: to deny Saddam Hussein future chemical, biological, and nuclear weapons capabilities.

## EMBOLDENING TERRORISTS

The revelations coming out of oil-for-food investigations were shocking, but an equally important story was the UN's failure to deal with the most urgent security threat of the present period—the ongoing problem of international terrorism. For years the UN could not come up with an agreed definition of terrorism, which was a prerequisite for the UN's taking any effective action in the future. The UN's own Counter-Terrorism Executive Directorate explained why this was still a problem for the UN, even after 9/11: "An unequivocal definition of terrorism would remove the political distinction some make between the action of so-called freedom fighters and terrorists."[8]

Then, on December 2, 2004, the UN High-Level Panel on Threats, Challenges, and Change concluded that the General Assembly needed to formulate a "consensus definition" of terrorism because of that body's "unique legitimacy" in setting the normative standards in international affairs. Kofi Annan did not put forward a definition of terrorism until March 2004, as part of his proposals for UN reform. Presenting the High-Level Panel's recommendation, Annan offered this definition of terrorism: "any action constitutes terrorism if it is intended to cause death or serious bodily harm to civilians or noncombatants with the purpose of intimidating a population or compelling a government or an international organization to do or abstain from doing any act."[9]

But considerably more action was still necessary. As the Gingrich-Mitchell report suggested, such a definition must become the basis for a clear international convention against international terrorism through action of the UN General Assembly. Given the UN's ugly record of not standing up to—and of ultimately emboldening—terrorists, such decisive action seems unlikely to occur. Unfortunately, certain UN officials continue to take soft positions on political movements that rely on terrorist tactics to advance their causes.

## THE UN HONORS THE ARAFAT LEGACY

Just after the November 2004 death of PLO leader Yasser Arafat, CNN broadcast a profile about the deceased Palestinian leader on its *People in the News* program. The show included a rare interview in which an unidentified Western reporter challenged Arafat on, for example, the PLO's September 1970 hijacking of three international airliners. "The taking of civilian lives, the hijacking of airlines," the reporter said, "these are deemed to be terrorist acts." Arafat's reply to this probing reporter revealed exactly how he came to conclude that his use of violence was completely legitimate: "You are mentioning the hijacking. You are neglecting the crux of the whole issue. We are under occupation and according to the United Nations Charter and resolution[s] and decisions, we have the right to resist against occupation."[10]

Never mind that Arafat's Fatah faction began to actively use terrorism in 1964, three years before Israeli forces captured the West Bank and Gaza Strip. The interview revealed that Arafat—the man who more than any other leader had popularized international terrorism in the last century—felt that the UN had legitimized his use of terrorism as a political tool. His comment plainly showed how he was invoking UN General Assembly resolutions to defend his actions. So the General Assembly, which had "unique legitimacy" in setting the normative standards for international diplomacy, according to UN spokesmen, did indeed have an impact—but it was a lethal impact.

Arafat, more than any other figure, represented the nexus between the United Nations and the growth of international terrorism. As seen in Chapter 1, within four years of the "Black September" hijackings, he was invited to address the UN General Assembly. In the years that followed, Arafat and his entourage developed connections to the worst international terrorist groups, many of which had concerns that went beyond his struggle with the state of Israel, thus indicating how Arafat's group never had second thoughts about its support of terrorism.

In fact, the head of Hizballah's overseas operations, Imad Mughniyah, came out of the Palestinian unit known as Force-17, which acted as Arafat's personal bodyguards in Beirut in the early 1980s. By April 1991, Arafat would visit Sudan to join a new Islamist *internationale* that included the Muslim Brotherhood, Hamas, and Osama bin Laden.[11] His ongoing connections with Saddam Hussein's Iraq enabled the PLO to receive oil-for-food vouchers and support. And finally, Arafat used his connections with Iran to purchase explosives and rockets for the *Karin A* weapons ship that Israel intercepted in 2002. The Israeli military uncovered, at this time, incriminating documents bearing Arafat's own signature in Arabic, in which he authorized payments to those engaged in suicide bombings against Israeli civilians.[12]

Despite this legacy, when Arafat died two years later, the UN still would not renounce the Palestinian leader or his miserable record. The UN, in fact, paid tribute to him with a special memorial session of the General Assembly and by lowering the UN flag to half-mast at its Manhattan headquarters.[13]

## PARTNERSHIP WITH TERROR

Yasser Arafat was by no means the only political leader compromised by a direct association with terrorism whom the UN emboldened.

For example, in October 2004, the Arab International Forum for Rehabilitation and Development in the Occupied Palestinian Territory held a conference in Beirut under the auspices of the UN's Economic and Social Commission for Western Asia (ESCWA). The conference announced a joint initiative between ESCWA and the Coalition of Goodness, an organization led by a cleric who was viewed as a spiritual head of the Muslim Brotherhood, Sheikh Yusuf Qaradhawi. This same individual, a year earlier, had appeared in Sweden and spoken in favor of suicide operations against Israeli civilians. And two months before the Beirut conference, he had signed a communiqué calling on Muslims to support the forces fighting the United States in Iraq.[14] Indeed, on July 7, 2004, BBC2 TV broadcast an interview in which he said that Islam justifies suicide bombings in Iraq against the U.S. military and in Israel against women and children.[15] Either someone at the UN was not doing his homework or his judgment about terrorism was so skewed that Qaradhawi's pronouncements didn't raise an eyebrow.

In some cases, UN agencies actually provided financial support for terrorist groups. In 2003 and 2004, the Israel Defense Forces captured documentation showing how the United Nations Development Program (UNDP) was regularly funding two Hamas front organizations: the Tulkarm Charity Committee and the Jenin District Committee for Charitable Funds (also known by its shorter name, the Jenin Charity Committee). The donations varied—sometimes $4,000, sometimes $10,000. Receipts and even copies of thank-you notes to UNDP were discovered. What UNDP was doing in the West Bank flew in the face of its declared mission: "to insure the most effective use of UN and international aid resources." It was effectively supporting international terrorism.

The UN should have exercised considerable caution with transfers of this sort, considering that in 2002, Yasser Arafat's Fatah movement described Jenin as "the capital of the suicide bombers." The Tulkarm Charity Committee had already been identified in 2002 as a Hamas front that had received significant funding from Saudi charities.[16]

Beyond all this public information, the UN had also received specific warnings that these were actually Hamas front groups. In June 2003, the Office of the Coordinator of the Activities of the Israel Defense Forces in the West Bank and Gaza Strip asked UNDP to stop all assistance to the Jenin District Committee because of its Hamas connection. Israel knew that Hamas operatives ran the charity; its deputy director had been a member of the Izz ad-Din al-Qassam Brigades, the elite terrorist unit of Hamas. UNDP was not persuaded; Timothy Rothermel, UNDP's special representative in Jerusalem, turned down the Israeli request. Writing on June 25, 2003, Rothermel stated only that "I have taken note of the reported political affiliation of the head of a *zakat* committee in the Jenin area." He said he hoped that UN "cash assistance" through these committees would no longer be necessary someday when the Palestinians' economic situation improved.

When these charges against UN support of Hamas fronts were first made by this author, the UN's undersecretary general for communications and public information, Shashi Tharoor, countered in the *Wall Street Journal* by stating that Rothermel had "acknowledged" the Israeli military's concern in his June 25 letter. Implying some sort of agreement with Israel on the matter, Tharoor, in his next sentence, wrote, "As a result, no further payments were made by the U.N." But Tharoor was wrong, for in fact, the UN did not stop payments to Hamas fronts after June 25, 2003. For example, Israeli forces subsequently found a UNDP bank transfer request—on UNDP stationery—for the payment of $6,000 to the Jenin Charity Committee, dated September 11, 2003. Another UNDP letter to the Jenin Charity Committee, dated October 3, 2003, requested that the $6,000 that had been transferred be given to the Tulkarm Charity Committee.

These disclosures proved highly embarrassing to the UN. As the *New York Sun* pointed out, UNDP, at the time of the transfers, was headed by Mark Maloch Brown, who later became Kofi Annan's chief of staff.[17] Brown's predecessor as chief of staff, Iqbal Riza, had left the UN in a cloud of scandal, accused of having shredded many of the files in Annan's possession that could have shed light on the oil-for-food affair. Brown's greatest asset to Annan had been his clean reputation. Revelations about UNDP assistance to terrorist groups under Brown's watch were not what Kofi Annan needed in 2005.

Another disturbing revelation from captured documents was the support the UN Relief and Works Agency (UNRWA) provided to the Koran and Sunna Society of the West Bank town of Kalkilya. As documented in Chapter 9, UNRWA has been heavily penetrated by Hamas for years; Hamas members dominate many of its unions, including the teachers union. But this new link represented a further deterioration in the UN's connections, for the Koran and Sunna Society defines itself as *salafi*—it adopts doctrines from militant Islam. Indeed, the Koran and Sunna Society, which has six branches in the West Bank, distributes pamphlets published in Saudi Arabia that are often written by radical Wahhabi clerics. References to the value of martyrdom and jihad are not uncommon in these materials. One of the Society's schools, called the Martyrs of the Al-Aqsa Intifada, received payments from UNRWA for educating children of Palestinian refugees in March and June of 2004.

The UN in New York may have been warning of the dangers of international terrorism, but this post-9/11 stance had not permeated downward to UN-affiliated organizations around the world, and especially in the Middle East. Back on September 28, 2001, the UN Security Council had adopted Resolution 1373, which forbids all states "from providing any forms of support, active or passive, to entities or persons involved in terrorist acts." Yet here, in 2004 and 2005, the UN continued to maintain links with, and even to prop up, individuals and groups that openly supported the murder of civilians.[18]

## OIL FOR TERRORISM

The UN scandals on terrorism and Iraq intersected, as it became increasingly clear that money from the oil-for-food program wound up in the hands of terrorist groups. The first indication of this activity came on January 25, 2004, when the Iraqi daily *Al-Mada* published 270 names of individuals and organizations that were beneficiaries of Saddam Hussein's oil vouchers. According to the *Al-Mada* list, among the recipients were the PLO, the Syrian-based Popular Front for the Liberation of Palestine, and Abu al-Abbas, who headed the pro-Iraqi Palestine Liberation Front in Baghdad.

It was the Palestine Liberation Front that hijacked the Italian cruise liner *Achille Lauro* in 1985 and murdered Leon Klinghoffer, an elderly American citizen who was confined to a wheelchair. The organization was still very much active. In the fall of 2001, Israeli forces captured a fifteen-man Palestine Liberation Front unit in the West Bank that had been trained by Iraqi officers at the al-Quds military camp outside of Baghdad and enjoyed close ties with Iraqi intelligence. Could the charge that oil-for-food vouchers went to the Palestine Liberation Front to support such operations be proven? A former undersecretary at the Iraqi Ministry of Petroleum, Abd al-Saheb Salman Qutb, confirmed that the *Al-Mada* list was indeed authentic.[19]

But the actual money trail showing precisely how the UN's oil-for-food dollars went to support terrorism became evident only much later. To understand how the funds flowed, it is important to realize that the Iraqi oil vouchers were actually only one part of how Iraq manipulated the oil-for-food program. For example, since the program built into the price of Iraqi oil a large profit margin, Iraq was able to demand a surcharge for each barrel of oil it sold. According to one estimate, Iraq earned $228.6 million by using such surcharges. Iraq also derived illegal income from kickbacks that the suppliers of commodities to Iraq were forced to pay. Estimates of this illegal income reach $1.5 billion.[20]

UN modifications of the oil-for-food program in the late 1990s allowed Saddam Hussein to spend his oil income on many commodities other than humanitarian goods—in particular, on equipment to revamp Iraq's oil infrastructure.[21] This helped Iraq expand oil output and facilitated oil smuggling through neighboring states like Turkey, Jordan, and Syria, which created yet another source of illicit income. To hide all these sources of illegal income, Iraq used foreign banks in Lebanon and Jordan. One critical bank for Saddam Hussein was the Jordanian branch of Iraq's al-Rafidain Bank, which, according to the CIA's Iraq Survey Group, "was established purely for use of the Iraqi government."[22] In fact, it was owned by the Iraqi Finance

Ministry. From 1999 onward, al-Rafidain's Amman branch also managed Iraqi government funds abroad. These included accounts that Saddam's regime "used for earnings from the ten per cent kickback scheme and oil surcharges payments" in the oil-for-food program, according to the CIA.[23] Using al-Rafidain, the Iraqi regime could move money all around the Middle East and circumvent sanctions. As al-Rafidain's branch manager in Beirut, Saeed Ahmad, boasted to *Bloomberg News,* "The UN is no problem."[24]

The Iraqi governmental figure responsible for managing the oil-for-food program from Baghdad was Taha Yasin Ramadan, Iraq's vice president. Ramadan was also the senior Iraqi official responsible for the operations of an organization called the Arab Liberation Front and for the Ba'ath Party in the areas under the control of the Palestinian Authority. The Arab Liberation Front was founded in 1969, and the Palestinians themselves regarded it as part of the Iraqi Ba'ath Party.[25] Like the Ba'ath, the Arab Liberation Front had a pan-Arab ideology. While it was a secular organization, it had no problem financing the attacks of Islamist groups like Hamas. Its key figure on the ground in the West Bank was general secretary Rakad Salem, a Palestinian who held Iraqi citizenship. Salem was also part of the Nationalist and Islamic Forces, an umbrella organization for coordinating Hamas, Fatah, and Islamic Jihad. He was arrested by Israeli security services, and from his interrogation it became clear that he was the main conduit for financing the families of Palestinian suicide bombers. He claimed to have distributed $15 million in Iraqi funds.

Salem confessed to how the money moved to the West Bank. The funds came from the notorious Jordanian branch of the al-Rafidain Bank and were transferred to the Amman branch of the Palestine Investment Bank. All of the money came to the Palestinians in hard currency—U.S. dollars. Since Iraq was under UN sanctions, Saddam Hussein's regime had limited opportunities to earn dollars and could not get at its foreign currency reserves abroad. According to U.S. sources, Taha Yasin Ramadan admitted after his capture that the main source for Iraqi dollars was the oil-for-food program. The CIA's Iraq Survey Group reached a similar conclusion: "The former regime managed to collect significant hard currency revenues by illicitly exploiting the OFF [oil for food] contracting process."[26] The Arab Liberation Front didn't need oil vouchers. It needed cash to pay off the families of suicide bombers. The UN oil-for-food program provided that cash.

Simply put, the oil-for-food was not just a source for illicit income for Saddam Hussein. It became a source for funding terrorism as well.

It is important to remember that the Iraqi-Palestinian connections were only a portion of the overall Iraqi effort to back international terrorism. For example, Charles Duelfer reported that the Iraqi Intelligence Service had a branch known as MI4 that trained not only Palestinians but also Iraqis, Syrians, Yemenis, Lebanese, Egyptians, and Sudanese in explosives and foreign operations.[27] While the Iraqi financial transfers to Palestinian terrorist organizations have been documented in detail, one cannot rule out Iraqi assistance to other terrorist groups in the Middle East.

Reports indicated, for instance, that in October 2002, notorious terrorist Abu Musab al-Zarqawi transferred two Iraqi payments, of $10,000 and $30,000, to operatives in Jordan through the al-Rafidain Bank to finance terrorist attacks, including the assassination of the U.S. diplomat Lawrence Foley.[28] The 9/11 Commission Report disclosed that an al-Qaeda delegation visited Iraq to meet with Iraqi intelligence in early 1998.[29] A senior member of Iraqi intelligence told U.S. officials that Iraqi intelligence actually made a payment of $300,000 to Ayman al-Zawahiri's Egyptian Islamic Jihad just prior to its merger with al-Qaeda and his establishing himself as Osama bin Laden's number two.[30] The CIA reported that al-Zawahiri visited Baghdad on February 3, 1998, and met with Taha Yasin Ramadan.[31] Where did these Iraqi dollars come from?

In short, the documented Iraqi support for the Arab Liberation Front could well have been just the tip of the iceberg.

The UN probably did not know these details, but it should have. It assigned dozens of officials to Baghdad to deal with Saddam Hussein's regime, beyond its weapons inspection teams. The UN approved the contracts of Iraqi oil sales and its commodity purchases. The whole purpose of having UN oversight on Iraqi oil-for-food contracts was to get UN officials to raise a red flag when the Iraqi regime engaged in suspect activities.

But this clearly didn't happen. For example, as journalists Marc Perelman and Claudia Rosett have noted, the UN approved the sale of Saddam's oil to Galp International Trading Corp., which had suspicious links to a shell company called ASAT Trust in Liechtenstein and Bank Al Taqwa in the Bahamas. Both ASAT Trust and Bank Al Taqwa were designated on the UN's own terror-watch list as entities "belonging to or affiliated with Al Qaeda."[32] Nevertheless, the oil sale went through.

Furthermore, as Rosett has noted, when the United States and Britain actually slowed down the processing of Iraqi contracts at the UN in order to scrutinize them more closely, Kofi Annan publicly criticized them, voicing his "serious concern."[33]

How did the UN let the corruption, the kickbacks, the terrorist funding, and everything else continue unchecked? Some critics have suggested that the UN Security Council alone was responsible for oil-for-food oversight and hence that the UN member states were at fault. But that claim is simply wrong. Oversight responsibility was formally shared between the Security Council, through its sanctions committee for Iraq, and the Office of the Iraq Program, which was created through the UN Secretariat. In fact, the day-to-day micro-management of Iraqi contracts fell mostly on the Office of the Iraq Program. And who headed the Office of the Iraq Program? It was no less than Benon Sevan, who has, of course, been fingered as a recipient of Saddam Hussein's oil vouchers. Kofi Annan had appointed Sevan to this post in 1997.

The oil-for-food saga reveals how desperately the UN needs to have independent oversight. Many commentators believe that the problems of the UN can be remedied through UN reform. For example, there are now suggestions to expand the Security Council from fifteen members to twenty-three. But these structural changes have little to do with the UN's most glaring flaws, which have helped spread chaos throughout the international system.

The problems at the UN are substantive. What values does the UN stand for? Are they the values supported largely by the likes of Syria,

Iran, Sudan, or Zimbabwe? Unless the democracies totally revamp UN resolutions, beginning by offering a firm definition of terrorism, then there will continue to be UN officials who are blind to the activities of terrorist groups, the suffering of peoples whose basic human rights are denied, and efforts of dictatorial regimes to acquire weapons of mass destruction in order to threaten their neighbors. In short, the UN will continue to betray the vision of its founders.

# The Paper Trail

The UN has proven itself to be singularly unsuited to preserving global order. The organization's record over the past half century reflects one shocking failure after another. The 1990s brought the UN's flaws into sharper focus, and they have only grown more glaring in recent years. The following pages present stark evidence of how the UN has ignored mass murder, propped up dictators, emboldened terrorists, and otherwise betrayed its mission to protect the world's security.

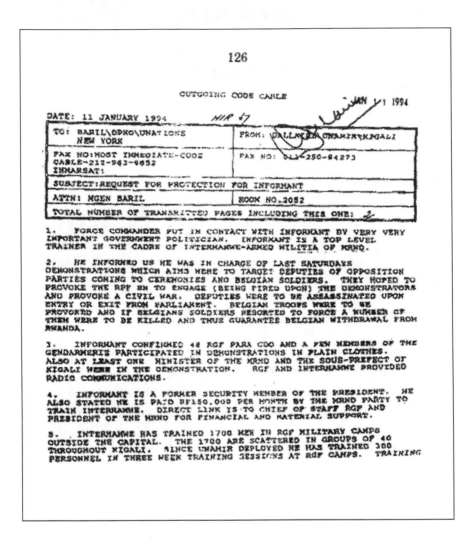

126

OUTGOING CODE CABLE

DATE: 11 JANUARY 1994                     MIR 17                            JAN 11 1994

| TO: BARIL\DPKO\UNATIONS NEW YORK | FROM: DALLAIRE\UNAMIR\KIGALI |
| FAX NO:MOST IMMEDIATE-CODE CABLE-212-963-9852 INMARSAT: | FAX NO: 011-250-84273 |
| SUBJECT:REQUEST FOR PROTECTION FOR INFORMANT | |
| ATTN: MGEN BARIL | ROOM NO.2052 |
| TOTAL NUMBER OF TRANSMITTED PAGES INCLUDING THIS ONE: 2 | |

1. FORCE COMMANDER PUT IN CONTACT WITH INFORMANT BY VERY VERY IMPORTANT GOVERNMENT POLITICIAN. INFORMANT IS A TOP LEVEL TRAINER IN THE CADRE OF INTERAHAMWE-ARMED MILITIA OF MRND.

2. HE INFORMED US HE WAS IN CHARGE OF LAST SATURDAYS DEMONSTRATIONS WHICH AIMS WERE TO TARGET DEPUTIES OF OPPOSITION PARTIES COMING TO CEREMONIES AND BELGIAN SOLDIERS. THEY HOPED TO PROVOKE THE RPF BN TO ENGAGE (BEING FIRED UPON) THE DEMONSTRATORS AND PROVOKE A CIVIL WAR. DEPUTIES WERE TO BE ASSASINATED UPON ENTRY OR EXIT FROM PARLIAMENT. BELGIAN TROOPS WERE TO BE PROVOKED AND IF BELGIANS SOLDIERS RESORTED TO FORCE A NUMBER OF THEM WERE TO BE KILLED AND THUS GUARANTEE BELGIAN WITHDRAWAL FROM RWANDA.

3. INFORMANT CONFIRMED 48 RGF PARA COD AND A FEW MEMBERS OF THE GENDARMERIE PARTICIPATED IN DEMONSTRATIONS IN PLAIN CLOTHES. ALSO AT LEAST ONE MINISTER OF THE MRND AND THE SOUS-PREFECT OF KIGALI WERE IN THE DEMONSTRATION. RGF AND INTERHAMWE PROVIDED RADIO COMMUNICATIONS.

4. INFORMANT IS A FORMER SECURITY MEMBER OF THE PRESIDENT. HE ALSO STATED HE IS PAID BF150,000 PER MONTH BY THE MRND PARTY TO TRAIN INTERAHAMWE. DIRECT LINK IS TO CHIEF OF STAFF RGF AND PRESIDENT OF THE MRND FOR FINANCIAL AND MATERIAL SUPPORT.

5. INTERAHAMWE HAS TRAINED 1700 MEN IN RGF MILITARY CAMPS OUTSIDE THE CAPITAL. THE 1700 ARE SCATTERED IN GROUPS OF 40 THROUGHOUT KIGALI. SINCE UNAMIR DEPLOYED HE HAS TRAINED 300 PERSONNEL IN THREE WEEK TRAINING SESSIONS AT RGF CAMPS. TRAINING

*Blind eye to genocide:* On January 11, 1994, the commander of UN peacekeeping forces in war-torn Rwanda, Major General Romeo Dallaire, sent this coded cable to UN headquarters. It warns of a reliable report from a "top level" informant that an extremist militia being trained in the Rwandan army's camps is planning the "extermination" of the minority Tutsi ethnic group. In the cable, Dallaire asks permission to seize the militia's weapons caches to try to prevent the slaughter. But the UN's Department of Peacekeeping Operations—headed by Kofi Annan, later to become UN secretary-general—denied Dallaire's request, not wanting to compromise the UN's impartiality in the Rwandan conflict. Three months later, the genocide began; more than 800,000 Rwandans were killed.

127

2/2

FOCUS WAS DISCIPLINE, WEAPONS, EXPLOSIVES, CLOSE COMBAT AND
TACTICS.

6.   PRINCIPAL AIM OF INTERHAMWE IN THE PAST WAS TO PROTECT
KIGALI FROM RPF. SINCE URAMIR MANDATE HE HAS BEEN ORDERED TO
REGISTER ALL TUTSI IN KIGALI. HE SUSPECTS IT IS FOR THEIR
EXTERMINATION. EXAMPLE HE GAVE WAS THAT IN 30 MINUTES HIS
PERSONNEL COULD KILL UP TO 1000 TUTSIS.

7.   INFORMANT STATES HE DISAGREES WITH ANTI-TUTSI EXTERMINATION.
HE SUPPORTS OPPOSITION TO RPF BUT CANNOT SUPPORT KILLING OF
INNOCENT PERSONS.  HE ALSO STATED THAT HE BELIEVES THE PRESIDENT
DOES NOT HAVE FULL CONTROL OVER ALL ELEMENTS OF HIS OLD
PARTY\FACTION.

8.   INFORMANT IS PREPARED TO PROVIDE LOCATION OF MAJOR WEAPONS
CACHE WITH AT LEAST 135 WEAPONS. HE ALREADY HAS DISTRIBUTED 110
WEAPONS INCLUDING 35 WITH AMMUNITION AND CAN GIVE US DETAILS OF
THEIR LOCATION.  TYPE OF WEAPONS ARE G3 AND AK47 PROVIDED BY RGF.
HE WAS READY TO GO TO THE ARMS CACHE TONIGHT-IF WE GAVE HIM THE
FOLLOWING GUARANTEE.  HE REQUESTS THAT HE AND HIS FAMILY (HIS
WIFE AND FOUR CHILDREN) BE PLACED UNDER OUR PROTECTION.

9.   IT IS OUR INTENTION TO TAKE ACTION WITHIN THE NEXT 36 HOURS
WITH A POSSIBLE H HR OF WEDNESDAY AT DAWN (LOCAL).  INFORMANT
STATES THAT HOSTILITIES MAY COMMENCE AGAIN IF POLITICAL DEADLOCK
ENDS.  VIOLENCE COULD TAKE PLACE DAY OF THE CEREMONIES OR THE DAY
AFTER.  THEREFORE WEDNESDAY WILL GIVE GREATEST CHANCE OF SUCCESS
AND ALSO BE MOST TIMELY TO PROVIDE SIGNIFICANT INPUT TO ON-GOING
POLITICAL NEGOTIATIONS.

10.  IT IS RECOMMENDED THE INFORMANT BE GRANTED PROTECTION AND
EVACUATED OUT OF RWANDA.  THIS HQ DOES NOT HAVE PREVIOUS UN
EXPERIENCE IN SUCH MATTERS AND URGENTLY REQUESTS GUIDANCE.  NO
CONTACT HAS AS YET BEEN MADE TO ANY EMBASSY IN ORDER TO INQUIRE
IF THEY ARE PREPARED TO PROTECT HIM FOR A PERIOD OF TIME BY
GRANTING DIPLOMATIC IMMUNITY IN THEIR EMBASSY IN KIGALI BEFORE
MOVING HIM AND HIS FAMILY OUT OF THE COUNTRY.

11.  FORCE COMMANDER WILL BE MEETING WITH THE VERY VERY IMPORTANT
POLITICAL PERSON TOMORROW MORNING IN ORDER TO ENSURE THAT THIS
INDIVIDUAL IS CONSCIOUS OF ALL PARAMETERS OF HIS INVOLVEMENT.
FORCE COMMANDER DOES HAVE CERTAIN RESERVATIONS ON THE SUDDENNESS
OF THE CHANGE OF HEART OF THE INFORMANT TO COME CLEAN WITH THIS
INFORMATION.  RECCE OF ARMED CACHE AND DETAILED PLANNING OF RAID
TO GO ON LATE TOMORROW.  POSSIBILITY OF A TRAP NOT FULLY
EXCLUDED, AS THIS MAY BE A SET-UP AGAINST THE VERY VERY IMPORTANT
POLITICAL PERSON.  FORCE COMMANDER TO INFORM SRSG FIRST THING IN
MORNING TO ENSURE HIS SUPPORT.

13.  PEUX CE QUE VEUX.  ALLONS-Y.

*CLN982  2/6*

## RENCONTRE ENTRE LE GENERAL JANVIER ET LE GENERAL MLADIC
### Commandant en chef les Forces serbes de Bosnie
### Bosnie le 4 Juin 1995

## 1. ARGUMENTAIRE DU FORCE COMMANDER.

L'approche a été effectuée en suivant quatre grands pôles de discussion : les otages de l'ONU détenus , le ravitaillement des enclaves de l'Est, les emprises des Nations-Unies et l'espace aérien serbe.

### 11. Les otages de l'ONU détenus.

La situation présente est inacceptable, elle est assortie d'une scandaleuse gesticulation médiatique, il faut libérer immédiatement les otages que vous détenez et nous retourner leurs matériels majeurs ainsi que leurs équipements.

Par votre attitude, vous vous placez de facto au ban de la Communauté Internationale. Une conséquence directe et irréversible de vos actions dirigées contre les soldats de l'ONU consiste en l'arrivée prochaine d'une brigade multinationale chargée en particulier d'augmenter la sécurité des casques bleus. Cette force sera sous mes ordres, force de théâtre, elle pourra intervenir par exemple en Croatie pour éviter que ne se reproduise un nouveau secteur Ouest. Il n'est plus en mon pouvoir de refuser cette brigade ; elle pourrait même être suivie d'une autre brigade très puissante.

Détenir des otages vous place dans une impasse politique et déconsidère le peuple serbe qui agit à la manière des Irakiens de Sadam Hussein. Cette attitude n'est pas digne de soldats. En outre, la valeur des otages diminue de jour en jour ; certains gouvernements, humiliés par vos procédés et leur exploitation médiatique, ne supporteront plus très longtemps cette situation et prendront des risques quelles qu'en soient les conséquences. Certains hommes politiques ont déjà fait part du caractère intolérable de la situation présente.

Paradoxalement, les frappes aériennes, loin de bloquer complètement une situation marquée par l'absence d'initiative politique, vous ouvrent une fenêtre, étroite il est vrai, qui peut vous permettre de tirer profit de la crise. Si vous avez la volonté d'aller vers la paix, ne négligez pas cette ouverture qui peut vous permettre de revenir en interlocuteur crédible au sein de la Communauté Internationale.

*A deal with the devil?:* Why didn't UN peacekeepers prevent Europe's worst massacre since World War II? This UN report (in French, with English translation at right) reveals that in a secret June 4, 1995, meeting, the commander of the Bosnian Serb Army offered a deal to the UN commander in the former Yugoslavia, France's General Bernard Janvier: If the UN halted air strikes, the Serbs would release UN hostages (mostly French troops) and leave peacekeepers alone in the future. Did Janvier accept the offer? This UN account doesn't say so, but just three days later the Serbs began releasing the hostages. And when the UN "safe area" of Srebrenica fell on July 11, Janvier refused to authorize timely air attacks to stop the Serbs. More than 7,000 Bosnian Muslims were ultimately slaughtered.

## MEETING BETWEEN GENERAL JANVIER
## AND GENERAL MLADIC, Commander and Chief of the Serbian
## forces of Bosnia, 4 June 1995

### 1. CONSIDERATIONS OF THE FORCE COMMANDER

The discussion followed four major themes: the detained hostages of the UN, the supply of the enclaves of the East, the areas under the control of the United Nations, and the Serbian airspace.

### 11. The detained UN hostages

The present situation is unacceptable; it is accompanied by a scandalous media event; it is necessary to immediately liberate the hostages whom you are detaining and to return to us their heavy equipment as well as their gear.

By your attitude, you place yourself beyond the law of the International Community. One direct and irreversible consequence of your actions against the soldiers of the United Nations consists of the coming arrival of an international brigade especially charged with the task of improving the security of the UN forces. This force will be under my orders; . . . it will be able to intervene in Croatia, for example, to prevent the replication of a new Western sector. It is no longer in my power to refuse this brigade; it may also be followed by another very powerful brigade.

Detaining the hostages places you in a political dead end and discredits the Serbian people, who are acting like the Iraqis of Saddam Hussein. This attitude is not worthy of soldiers. Besides, the value of the hostages declines by the day. Certain governments which were humiliated by your conduct and their exploitation in the media will not put up with this situation for a long time and will take risks without regard to the consequences. Certain political figures have already spoken about the intolerable nature of the present situation.

Paradoxically, the air strikes, far from completely blocking a situation marked by the absence of political initiative, offer you an opening—a narrow one, it is true—which could afford you the opportunity to draw an advantage from the crisis. If you have the will to move in the direction of peace, do not ignore this opening which permits you to return as a credible speaker in the midst of the International Community.

2

*C2N947 3/6*

12. Le ravitaillement des enclaves de l'Est.

Les enclaves de l'Est ont un besoin très urgent de ravitaillement. La situation n'est plus tolérable ; les soldats qui s'y trouvent ont besoin de nourriture et de carburant.

Si vous continuez d'empêcher les convois de ravitailler les enclaves, nous allons être obligés d'effectuer ce ravitaillement par hélicoptères ; vous imaginez aisément les risques de provocation et d'escalade que ce procédé impliquerait.

L'image que vous donnez à la Communauté Internationale est désastreuse, c'est elle qui nous poussera à ravitailler de force les soldats de l'ONU. Là encore, par votre attitude, vous n'avez pas de crédibilité auprès de la Communauté.

Le régime de fonctionnement des enclaves n'est pas satisfaisant et doit être discuté ; avant toute chose, il faut effectuer un premier ravitaillement d'urgence de ces enclaves en nourriture et en carburant. Considérant la situation très tendue en Bosnie centrale, et à condition que les autorités de Belgrade en soient d'accord, ce ravitaillement d'urgence pourrait s'effectuer en passant par le territoire de la R.F.Y.

L'urgence est telle, qu'une avancée significative doit se produire au plus tard dans deux ou trois jours ; passé ce terme nous entrerons dans la spirale que nous cherchons à éviter profitant de la courte pause qui s'offre à nous.

13. Les emprises des Nations-Unies.

Aujourd'hui, vous occupez ou vous encerclez des emprises des Nations-Unies, il vous faut remédier à cela. Vous devez évacuer les postes et les points que vous occupez.

Un problème particulier est constitué par les Sites de regroupement d'armes lourdes (WCPs) dans la région de Sarajevo. Je sais que vous avez prélevé les armes des sites que vous occupez et que cette situation est irréversible ; ces armes doivent sortir de la zone d'exclusion des 20 km.

14. L'espace aérien serbe.

Il ne faut rien faire qui puisse entraîner vers la guerre. En abattant cet appareil américain de l'OTAN vous avez fait un pas de plus ; si vous détenez, comme vous le prétendez, le pilote, au lieu de basculer de nouveau dans la logique habituelle et d'être désigné comme le fauteur de troubles, libérez ce pilote sans l'humilier en montrant des images aux télévisions du monde entier, comportez vous en grands seigneurs, tout le mérite vous en reviendra ; ainsi, vous pourrez reprendre pied dans la Communauté Internationale.

### 12. The supply of the enclaves of the East

The enclaves of the East have a very pressing need for supplies. The situation is no longer bearable. The soldiers who are there need food and motor fuel.

If you hinder the convoys from supplying the enclaves, we will be obliged to bring in supplies with helicopters. You can easily imagine the risks of provocation and of escalation that this conduct would imply.

The image that you convey to the International Community is disastrous; it is this which will force us to supply the soldiers of the UN. There again, because of your attitude, you do not have credibility in the Community.

The regime of the functioning of enclaves is not at all satisfactory and should be discussed; above all it is necessary to carry out a first urgent supply of these enclaves to provide them with food and motor fuel. Considering the very strained situation in central Bosnia, and on condition that the authorities in Belgrade were in agreement [with the proposition], this emergency provision of supplies could be carried out by passing through the territory of the R.F.Y. [Federal Republic of Yugoslavia].

It is very important that a significant improvement take place at the latest in two or three days; after this time, we will enter into the cycle [of events] that we seek to avoid, taking advantage of the short pause it affords us.

### 13. The areas under the control of the United Nations

Today, you occupy and encircle the areas under the control of the United Nations. You must remedy this. You must evacuate the [out]posts and points which you occupy.

One particular problem consists of the locations for regrouping heavy weapons (WCPs) in the Sarajevo region. I know that you have taken the weapons of the sites you occupy and that the situation is irreversible. These weapons should be outside of the 20-km zone of exclusion.

### 14. The Serbian airspace

One should do nothing that would lead to war. By shooting down the American plane of the NATO forces you have taken one more step; if you detain the pilot as you claim, instead of slipping anew into the habitual logic of being designated as a troublemaker, [you should] free the pilot without humiliating him and showing televised images all over the world; behave nobly, you will [thus] do yourself credit; in this way, you will be able to return to the International Community.

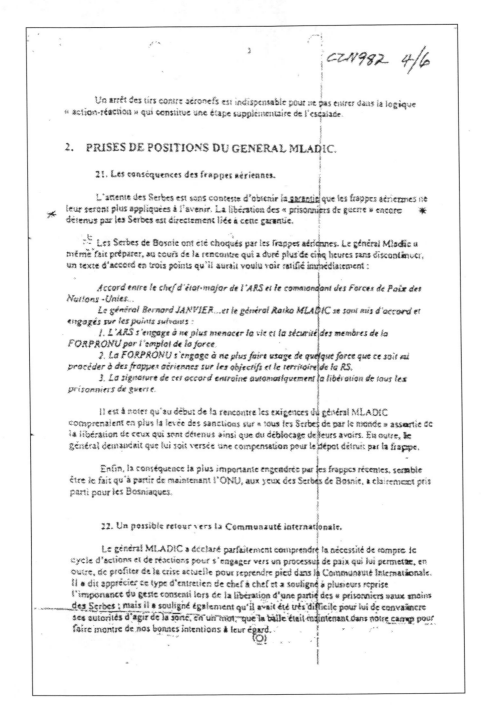

CZN982 4/6

Un arrêt des tirs contre aéronefs est indispensable pour ne pas entrer dans la logique « action-réaction » qui constitue une étape supplémentaire de l'escalade.

## 2. PRISES DE POSITIONS DU GENERAL MLADIC.

21. Les conséquences des frappes aériennes.

L'attente des Serbes est sans conteste d'obtenir la garantie que les frappes aériennes ne leur seront plus appliquées à l'avenir. La libération des « prisonniers de guerre » encore détenus par les Serbes est directement liée à cette garantie.

Les Serbes de Bosnie ont été choqués par les frappes aériennes. Le général Mladic a même fait préparer, au cours de la rencontre qui a duré plus de cinq heures sans discontinuer, un texte d'accord en trois points qu'il aurait voulu voir ratifié immédiatement :

*Accord entre le chef d'état-major de l'ARS et le commandant des Forces de Paix des Nations-Unies...*
*Le général Bernard JANVIER...et le général Ratko MLADIC se sont mis d'accord et engagés sur les points suivants :*
*1. L'ARS s'engage à ne plus menacer la vie et la sécurité des membres de la FORPRONU par l'emploi de la force.*
*2. La FORPRONU s'engage à ne plus faire usage de quelque force que ce soit ni procéder à des frappes aériennes sur les objectifs et le territoire de la RS.*
*3. La signature de cet accord entraîne automatiquement la libération de tous les prisonniers de guerre.*

Il est à noter qu'au début de la rencontre les exigences du général MLADIC comprenaient en plus la levée des sanctions sur « tous les Serbes de par le monde » assortie de la libération de ceux qui sont détenus ainsi que du déblocage de leurs avoirs. En outre, le général demandait que lui soit versée une compensation pour le dépôt détruit par la frappe.

Enfin, la conséquence la plus importante engendrée par les frappes récentes, semble être le fait qu'à partir de maintenant l'ONU, aux yeux des Serbes de Bosnie, a clairement pris parti pour les Bosniaques.

22. Un possible retour vers la Communauté internationale.

Le général MLADIC a déclaré parfaitement comprendre la nécessité de rompre le cycle d'actions et de réactions pour s'engager vers un processus de paix qui lui permette, en outre, de profiter de la crise actuelle pour reprendre pied dans la Communauté Internationale. Il a dit apprécier ce type d'entretien de chef à chef et a souligné à plusieurs reprise l'importance du geste consenti lors de la libération d'une partie des « prisonniers aux moins des Serbes ; mais il a souligné également qu'il avait été très difficile pour lui de convaincre ses autorités d'agir de la sorte, en un mot, que la balle était maintenant dans notre camp pour faire montre de nos bonnes intentions à leur égard.

A ceasefire against air traffic is indispensable in order not to enter into the logic of "action and reaction" which constitutes an additional stage of escalation.

## 2. POSITIONS OF GENERAL MLADIC

### 21. The consequences of the air strikes

The expectation of the Serbs is to obtain without a contest the guarantee that air strikes will not be used against them in the future. The liberation of the "prisoners of war" which the Serbs still hold is directly linked to the guarantee.

The Serbs of Bosnia were shocked by the air strikes. General Mladic in the course of this meeting, which lasted five hours without a break, had also prepared the text of an agreement, based on three points, which he would have liked to see immediately ratified:

> *Agreement between the Chief of Staff of the ARS [Army of the Republika Srpska] and the Commander of the Peace forces of the United Nations . . .*
> *General Bernard Janvier . . . and General Ratko Mladic have entered into agreement and have committed themselves to the following points:*
> *1. The ARS [Army of the Republika Srpska] undertakes not to menace any longer the life and security of the members of the UNPROFOR by the use of force.*
> *2. The UNPROFOR undertakes not to use any kind of force any longer nor carry out air strikes on the targets and the territory of the RS [Republika Srpska].*
> *3. The signing of this accord will automatically bring about the liberation of all the prisoners of war.*

It should be noted that at the beginning of the meeting the demands of General Mladic included in addition the lifting of sanctions on "all the Serbs in the world" along with the liberation of those who are detained as well as the unfreezing of their assets. In addition, the general demanded that he should be compensated for the depot [warehouse], which was destroyed by the strike.

Finally, the most important consequence that resulted from the recent strikes appears to be the fact that from now on the United Nations in the eyes of the Serbs of Bosnia has clearly taken the side of the Bosniaks [Muslim inhabitants].

### 22. A possible return to the International Community

General Mladic declared that he understands perfectly the need to break the cycle of actions and reactions in order to make a commitment to a peace process that would permit him to benefit as well from the present crisis in order to recover his position in the International Community. He said that he appreciated this type of conversation between commanders and he emphasized several times the importance of a [previously] agreed upon gesture at the time of the liberation of one part of the "prisoners" to the hands of the Serbs; but he emphasized equally that it was very difficult for him to convince the authorities to act in this way and, in a word, that it was now up to us to show our good intentions with regard to them.

*CZN 982 5/6*

Les Serbes de Bosnie semblent attentifs aux possibilités qui pourraient s'offrir à eux de pouvoir sortir de « l'isolement politique, médiatique et économique » qui est le leur. Ils demandent à être traités sur un pied d'égalité avec les autres parties.

C'est avec une certaine frénésie que le général MLADIC, après avoir épuisé rappels historiques connus et propositions irréalistes, s'est enfin décidé à proposer d'engager au plus vite des négociations au niveau des chefs militaires des parties en conflit.

Cette proposition, qui semblait préparée puisque pour l'expliquer le général a eu recours à ses notes, était assortie des remarques suivantes :

a.) Le but général de ces négociations serait d'obtenir un accord de cessation définitive des hostilités. Après avoir dit qu'un cessez-le-feu ne serait qu'une mesure partielle et dilatoire très contre-productive, le général a admis que la première étape devrait être constituée par un cessez-le feu.

b.) Le cessez-le-feu serait signé par les chefs militaires des parties sur les bases actuelles d'occupation du terrain. (pas de retour à des positions antérieures en préalable aux négociations.)

c.) Le Force Commander réunirait les chefs militaires des forces adverses dans un espace neutre qui pourrait être Paris (sic).

d.) Cet accord permettrait de donner aux diplomates un espace de négociations en vue de la résolution des différends.

23. L'attitude des Serbes de Bosnie face au problème des enclaves.

Le général MLADIC : « le fait de faire intervenir de nouvelles forces sur le territoire ne va pas faciliter les choses, cette présence ne nous fait pas peur mais en exagérant son volume vous prenez vous même le parti d'entrer dans cette spirale de guerre dont vous parliez. Les forces qui vont arriver ne tarderont pas à être considérées comme des forces d'occupation.

Le problème de ravitaillement de vos enclaves est directement lié à cette présence et aux restrictions que nous subissons du fait de la surveillance de la Drina. Il n'est pas raisonnable d'attendre quelque chose de notre part si aucun signe d'assouplissement n'intervient quant à l'attitude et à la présence de vos forces et quant à l'application des sanctions.

Nous devons ressentir la bonne volonté de la Communauté Internationale après le premier pas que nous avons fait. Il faut suspendre ou adoucir la Résolution 924 qui traite de la Drina... »

The Bosnian Serbs seemed aware of the possibilities that were open to them to get out of their "political, media, and economic isolation." They demand to be treated on an equal footing with the other parties.

It is with a certain frenzied haste that General Mladic, after having exhausted the known historical arguments and unrealistic propositions, finally made up his mind to propose to engage in negotiations as quickly as possible on the level of military commanders of the sides in conflict.

This proposal, which seemed to have been prepared in advance, because the general consulted his notes, was accompanied by the following remarks:

a) The general purpose of these negotiations will be to obtain an agreement for the definitive end of hostilities. After having said that a cease-fire would only be a partial measure, dilatory and very counterproductive, the general admitted that the first step should be a cease-fire.
b) The cease-fire would be signed by the military commanders on the basis of current occupation of territory.
c) The Force Commander would convene the military heads of forces in a neutral location, which could be Paris (*sic*).
d) This location will afford the diplomats the possibility to negotiate for the purpose of resolving their differences.

**23. The attitude of the Serbs of Bosnia in view of the problem of the enclaves.**

General Mladic: "The fact of causing new forces to intervene in the territory will not make things easier. This presence does not cause us fear, but in overdoing its extent, you personally share in this cycle of war of which you were speaking. The forces which will come will quickly be considered as forces of occupation.

"The problem of supplying your enclaves is directly linked to this presence and to the restrictions we suffer, which result from the fact of the surveillance of the Drina [River]. It is not reasonable to expect anything of us if there is no sign of relief with regard to the presence of your forces and with regard to the application of sanctions.

"We should feel the good will of the International Community after the first step we have taken. One must suspend or soften Resolution 924, which applies to the Drina. . . ."

CZN992 6/6

Le général MLADIC, devant une urgence qu'il mesure d'autant mieux qu'il était en possession des chiffres actualisés des réserves de vivres et de carburant dans les enclaves, s'est dit prêt à faire un geste en permettant le ravitaillement proposé transitant par la RFY, sous réserve d'acceptation de cette dernière. Il a alors donné des points de rendez-vous très précis dans chacune des enclaves de l'Est pour mettre au point ce ravitaillement. (contact mardi 6 juin à 12h00.)

24. Divers.

Le général MLADIC, après avoir remercié le Force Commander pour ses conseils quant à l'attitude à adopter face au problème de la détention du pilote américain abattu, a déclaré qu'il n'avait plus rien à dire à ce sujet au chef des forces militaires de l'ONU, ce problème restant à traiter entre lui et l'OTAN, voire même entre lui et les Américains.

General Mladic, taking note of the urgency which he was able to calculate all the better because he had updated figures of the reserves of provisions and fuel in the enclaves, declared himself ready to make a gesture in permitting the supply proposed crossing [by] the RFY on condition of the acceptance of the last. He also gave very precise meeting points in each of the enclaves of the East to finalize this supply. (contact Tuesday, 6 June at 12:00 hours).

**24. Miscellaneous**

General Mladic, after having thanked the Force Commander for his advice on the attitude to take with regard to the problem of the detention of the American pilot who was shot down, declared that he would have nothing to say on this subject to the chief of the UN military forces, this problem remaining to be dealt with between himself and NATO, or even between himself and the Americans.

UNITED NATIONS     NATIONS UNIES

### INTERNAL AUDIT DIVISION
### OFFICE OF INTERNAL OVERSIGHT SERVICES

Reference:    AUD-7-1:31 ( 0487 /03)        08 April 2003

To:      Mr. Benon Sevan, Executive Director
       Office of the Iraq Programme

From:     Esther Stern, Director
       Internal Audit Division, OIOS

Subject:    **OIOS Audit No. AF2002/23/1: Management of the contract for the provision of independent inspection agents in Iraq**

1.     I am pleased to present herewith the final report on the subject review, which was conducted from July through October 2002.

2.     We note from your response to the draft report that OIP has generally accepted the recommendations. Based on the response, we are pleased to inform you that we have closed recommendations 2, 9, 12, 14 to 16, 18 to 22 and 25 in the IAD recommendation database. OIOS has also withdrawn recommendations 3 and 17. In order for us to close out the remaining recommendations-recommendations 1, 4 to 8, 10, 11, 13, 23 and 24 we request that you provide us with additional information as indicated in the text of the report and a time schedule for implementing each of the recommendations. Please refer to the recommendation number concerned to facilitate monitoring of the implementation status.

3.     IAD is assessing the overall quality of its audit process and kindly requests that you consult with your managers who dealt directly with the auditors and complete the attached client satisfaction survey form.

4.     I take this opportunity to thank the management and staff of OIP for the assistance and cooperation provided to the auditors in connection with this assignment.

Copy to:
UN Board of Auditors
Ms. H Thorup-Hayes
D. Knutsen
J. Prasad

Best regards.

---

*Oil for weapons:* Saddam Hussein's Iraqi regime pocketed billions of dollars from the UN's oil-for-food program, which was supposedly a humanitarian initiative. This internal UN audit confirms that the oil-for-food program was not being monitored adequately. In particular, the independent inspectors the UN hired were derelict in the area of import controls, which would help explain how the Iraqis used the oil-for-food program to fund an arms buildup. The CIA's special adviser on Iraq's weapons of mass destruction, Charles Duelfer, told Congress in March 2004 that the Iraqis "imported banned military weapons technology" through oil-for-food and diverted money to the Military Industrialization Commission, increasing its budget nearly a hundredfold from 1996 to 2003.

# United Nations
## OFFICE OF INTERNAL OVERSIGHT SERVICES
### Internal Audit Division

# Audit Report

| | |
|---|---|
| **Audit subject:** | Management of the contract for the provision for independent inspection agents in Iraq |
| **Audit No.:** | AF2002/23/1 |
| **Report date:** | 08 April 2003 |
| **Audit team:** | Jayanti Prasad, Auditor-in-charge<br>Anna Halasan, Auditing Assistant |

**Audit of the management of the contract for the provision of
independent inspection agents in Iraq
(AF2002/23/1)
Executive Summary**

Between July and October 2002, OIOS conducted an audit of the management of the contract for the provision of independent inspection agents in Iraq between the United Nations and Cotecna Inspection S.A. (the Contractor). The focus of the audit was on administrative, contractual and management aspects of the Contract.

OIOS' overall conclusion is that management of the Contract has not been adequate and certain provisions of the Contract had not been adhered to. In addition, the incorporation of additional costs, such as rehabilitation of camps, in the man-day-rate was an uneconomical arrangement. Also, the Contract had been amended prior to its commencement, which was inappropriate. OIP needs to strengthen its management of contracts and the Procurement Division (PD) should ensure that the basis of payment is appropriate in order to avoid additional costs to the Organization.

**Results in brief:**

Monitoring contractors performance and payments

- The Contractor had not fully performed its contractual duties in relation to goods procured by the Inter-agency Humanitarian Programme in North Iraq. As a result, under the 13 per cent account for goods imported by the UN agencies, there were huge differences between the figures for goods reported to have arrived by the UN agencies and the Contractor. The Contractor also did not provide convoy control services in relation to the 13 per cent account goods at Zakho. This service was provided by UNOHCI resulting in additional cost to the Organization.

- Contract payments are based entirely on man-days worked, however, there was no verification of attendance records of the Contractor, which forms the basis for the payments. Furthermore, the Contractor had sometimes maintained lower staff strengths than those required by the Contract. While OIP had been aware of this, no action to correct it had been taken. If lower staff numbers than those provided for in the Contract were considered adequate by OIP, consideration should have been given to amending it and reducing costs.

- Though required under the Contract to provide 24-hour services at all specified locations in Iraq, the Contractor was not doing so at Zakho and Trebil. Despite OIP being aware of this, no remedial action was taken to ensure this or, if this requirement was satisfactory to OIP, to effect a reduction in contract price for reduced hours of duty.

Contract issues

❑ Despite the Contract being "all inclusive", the per-man day fee of the original contract was inappropriately increased from $499 to $600 on account of rehabilitation of camps, communication charges, and fee for retention of agents. In addition, the decision of OIP/PD to pay for camps' rehabilitation at a cost of $320,000 by merging it with the per-man-day fee of $600 instead of paying for it as a one-time lump sum, led to an avoidable expenditure of approximately $700,000.

❑ Even before the Contractor started providing services under the Contract from 01 February 1999, OIP/PD amended the Contract by authorizing additional communication cost of $206,000 and operating cost of $150,000, which was approved by the Headquarters Committee on Contracts (HCC) four days after the signing of the initial Contract. The amendment, even prior to start of services, could be viewed as a modification to the original Request for Proposal (RFP), and therefore negotiating it with only one bidder was not appropriate. Furthermore, $95,000 was not recovered from the Contractor by way of the residual value of the equipment as provided for in the Contract.

❑ The present Contract had no linkage with the actual volume of work being performed as the contract price was based on the number of agents. Furthermore, the Contract specified a fixed number of agents at the four locations. OIP had not assessed whether it may have been more economical for the contract price to include a variable charge component to reflect the actual volume of work and to have more flexibility in the number of agents at specific locations based on the workloads.

Major recommendations:

OIP should:

❑ Reconcile and analyse the reasons for variation in the figures reported by the Contractor and those provided by UN agencies for the 13 per cent account goods. Determine if the Contractor has not provided services as required under the contract for certain portion of the 13 per cent account goods and deduct a proportional amount from the payments to the Contractor.

❑ Recover an appropriate amount from the Contractor for not providing services pertaining to convoy control and passport collection for the 13 per cent account goods as required.

❑ Re-assess the requirement for the 24-hour operation at all sites based on ground realities, and if reduced working hours is acceptable to OIP, amend the Contract and effect an appropriate reduction in Contract price.

❑ Recover $95,000 from the Contractor provided for in Amendment of the Contract.

## TERRORIST OPERATIVES EDUCATED IN SCHOOLS RUN BY UNRWA

| No. | Name | Organization | Relation to UNRWA | Terrorist Activity | Remarks |
|---|---|---|---|---|---|
| 1 | Ali Al-Amudi | Hamas | Received scholarship from UNRWA for his high grades in engineering studies in Qalandia institute. | Took part in shooting toward IDF soldiers in the area of Hebron and in murder of ISA (Israel Security Agency) agent. | Born in Hebron (1975). Arrested in 1994. Sentenced to 439 years in prison. |
| 2 | Ibrahim Maqadma | Hamas | Studied in schools run by UNRWA in Jebalia refugee camp. | Established in 1983 the military wing of the Muslim Brotherhood. Considered a senior and radical leader of Hamas. Took part in formulating the terrorist policy of the Hamas movement. | Born in 1950. Killed on 8 March 2003 during Israeli operation in the Gaza Strip. |
| 3 | Abd Muneem Abu Hameid | Hamas | Studied in schools run by UNRWA in Al-Amari refugee camp in Ramallah. | Murdered ISA's agent, Noam Cohen, on 13 April 1994 in Ramallah. | Born in 1969 in Ramallah. Arrested several times by Israeli security forces because of his involvement in terrorist activity. |

*Breeding terrorists:* The UN has not stood up to terrorism. In fact, it seems that UN organizations have been penetrated by terrorist groups. In its ongoing role in the Israeli-Palestinian conflict, the UN Relief and Works Agency (UNRWA) is supposed to provide humanitarian aid to Palestinians in refugee camps. But it has extensive links to terrorist groups. For example, UNRWA workers' homes have been found

| | | | | | |
|---|---|---|---|---|---|
| 4 | Suhaib Tirmaz | Hamas | Studied in secondary and junior schools run by UNRWA in Jebalia refugee camp. | Committed suicide attack with booby-trapped truck adjacent to Kefar Darom. | Born in Jebalia in 1980. Started his activity in the Hamas movement during his high school studies. |
| 5 | Iyad Al-Akhras | Hamas | Studied in secondary and junior schools run by UNRWA in Shaboura refugee camp in Rafah. | Took part in terrorist attacks against Israeli settlers in the Gaza Strip, which included launching mortar bombs at Israeli communities in 19 different events. | Born in 1972 in Rafah. Killed on 16 October 2001 when a mortar bomb exploded prematurely. |
| 6 | Abc Al-Rahim Ahmad Faraj | Hamas | Studied in secondary and junior schools run by UNRWA in Jenin. | Committed terrorist attacks against Israeli targets. Took part in Palestinian ambush that killed 13 Israeli soldiers in Jenin. | Born in 1979. Killed on 8 April 2002 during the fighting in Jenin refugee camp (April 2002). |

plastered with posters praising suicide bombers. Worse, UNRWA has been a willing accomplice to the hatred taught in Palestinian schools that has spawned some of the most dangerous terrorist operatives. As shown in this chart, numerous graduates of UNRWA schools have gone on to leading roles in Hamas, Islamic Jihad, and the al-Aqsa Martyrs Brigades of Fatah.

| No. | Name | Organization | Relation to UNRWA | Terrorist Activity | Remarks | |
|---|---|---|---|---|---|---|
| 7 | Mahmoud Hassan Al-Abed | Hamas | Educated in a kindergarten run by UNRWA. His father worked as a teacher for UNRWA's school. | Took part in terrorist attacks against Israeli settlers in the Gaza Strip. | Born in 1979. Killed during exchanges of fire with Israeli forces on 15 June 2002. Videotaped with his mother before setting off to his suicide mission. His encouraging mother became a symbol in Palestinian society to mothers willing to sacrifice their sons for the sake of Islam and the liberation of Palestine. | |
| 8 | Mahmoud Ali Al-Hallawa | Hamas | Studied in a secondary school run by UNRWA in Jenin. | Took part in terrorist attacks against Israeli settlers. Headed the military wing of Hamas in the area of Jenin. | Born in 1971. Killed during the fighting in Jenin refugee camp (April 2002). | |
| 9 | Salah Taleb Nassar | Hamas | Studied in schools run by UNRWA. | Took part in terrorist attacks against Israeli settlers in the Gaza Strip. Manufactured explosive charges and Qassam rockets. | Born in 1967. Died of his wounds on 8 November 2002 caused by an explosion that occurred during manufacturing explosives charges. | |

| # | Name | Org | Education | Activities | Fate |
|---|------|-----|-----------|------------|------|
| 10 | Salah Mustafa Shehada | Hamas | Studied in a secondary school run by UNRWA. | Established the military wing of Hamas. Returned to command the military wing after released from Israeli jail in 2000. Was responsible for formulating the terrorist policy of Hamas and for the murdering of scores of Israeli citizens. | Killed in Israeli air force attack in Gaza on 22 July 2002. |
| 11 | Mohanad Yussof Abu Beed | Hamas | Studied in secondary and junior schools run by UNRWA in Jebalia refugee camp. | Took part in terrorist attacks against Israeli settlers including shooting, placing explosive charges, launching mortar bombs and Qassam and anti-tank rockets. | Born in 1982 in Jebalia refugee camp. Killed on 8 June 2003 while attacking Israeli outpost with two other operatives from the Islamic Jihad and Fatah. |
| 12 | Mohamad Abd Al-Jawad Mcheesan | Hamas | Studied in secondary and junior schools run by UNRWA in Jebalia refugee camp. | Joined the military wing of Hamas at the end of 2000. Took part in terrorist attacks against Israeli targets in the Gaza Strip. Launched mortar bombs at Israeli communities. Manufactured explosive charges and hand grenades. | Killed on 25 June 2003 while committing suicide attack inside the Israeli Erez industrial area. |

| No. | Name | Organization | Relation to UNRWA | Terrorist Activity | Remarks |
|-----|------|--------------|-------------------|--------------------|---------|
| 13 | Mahmoud Abu Suraya | Hamas | Studied in a secondary school run by UNRWA in Jenin refugee camp. | Stabbed to death an Israeli officer on 30 January 1996. | Judged to lifetime sentence and ten additional years. |
| 14 | Iyad Khalil Musa | Hamas | Studied in a secondary school run by UNRWA in Jenin refugee camp. | Joined the military wing of Hamas in 2000. Committed terrorist attacks that included shooting and placing explosive charges against Israeli targets in the area of Jenin. | Born in 1981 in Jenin refugee camp. Killed on 31 January 2003 during exchanges of fire with Israeli forces in Jenin. |
| 15 | Riyad Hussein Abu Zeid | Hamas | Studied in a school run by UNRWA. | Took part in killing an Israeli soldier in 1990 and sending suicide bombers in 2000 to their missions. Considered a senior leader in the military wing of Hamas. Was close associate of Salah Shehadeh. | Born in 1970 in Al-Bureij refugee camp. Killed on 17 February 2003 during an operation conducted by Israeli special forces in the Gaza Strip. |
| 16 | Munir Issa Wishahi | Hamas | Studied in secondary and junior schools run by UNRWA in Jenin refugee camp. | Was responsible for throwing explosive charges and hand grenades at Israeli forces, which operated in Jenin refugee camp (April 2002). | Born in 1983. Killed during the fighting in Jenin refugee camp (April 2002). |

| | | | | |
|---|---|---|---|---|
| 17 | Mohamad Hassan Al-Faid | Hamas | Studied in secondary and junior schools run by UNRWA in Jenin refugee camp. | Took part in terrorist attacks against Israeli targets. Manufactured, with his brother, explosive charges. | Born in 1983 in Jenin. Killed during the fighting in Jenin refugee camp (April 2002). |
| 18 | Imad Musa Mahmoud Abu Aiysh | Islamic Jihad | Studied in secondary and junior schools run by UNRWA. | Committed terrorist attacks against Israeli targets. | Born in 1982. Killed on 22 July 2002 on his way to infiltrate an Israeli community in attempt to commit suicide attack against Israeli settlers. |
| 19 | Islam Mohamad Harb | Islamic Jihad | Studied in a school run by UNRWA. Received scholarship from UNRWA for achieving high grades in his studies. | Preached to the Jihad against the Jews. | Born in 1972. Killed on 29 December 1990 during violent clashes between Palestinians and Israeli forces. |
| 20 | Mahmoud Khawaja | Islamic Jihad | Worked for UNRWA. | Took part in establishing the Islamic Jihad. Committed terrorist attacks against Israeli targets. Was responsible for sending suicide bombers to their missions. | Born in 1960. Killed on 22 June 1995 during an operation carried out by Israeli special forces. |

| No. | Name | Organization | Relation to UNRWA | Terrorist Activity | Remarks |
|-----|------|--------------|-------------------|--------------------|---------|
| 21 | Yussuf Al-Sawitat | Islamic Jihad | Studied in schools run by UNRWA in Jenin. | Committed suicide attack with Nidal Al-Jibali in Hadera on 27 October 2001. | |
| 22 | Nidal Al-Jibali | Islamic Jihad | Studied in schools run by UNRWA in Jenin. | Committed suicide attack with Yussuf Al-Sawitat in Hadera on 27 October 2001. | |
| 23 | Mohamad Mahmoud Abd Al-Aziz Al-Sakafi | Islamic Jihad | Studied in schools run by UNRWA in Jenin. | Was member of the military wing of the Islamic Jihad. Killed on 11 April 2002 while committing terrorist attack in Eli Sinai community. | |
| 24 | Ahed Ali Al-Mubashir | Islamic Jihad | Studied in secondary and junior schools run by UNRWA in Shati refugee camp. | Was member of the military wing of the Islamic Jihad. Killed on 8 June 2002 when he tried to attack the Israeli community of Dugit. | |
| 25 | Taha Zubeidi | Islamic Jihad | Studied in schools run by UNRWA in Jenin. | Was member of the military wing of the Islamic Jihad. Took part in terrorist attacks against Israeli settlers. | Killed during the fighting in Jenin refugee camp (April 2002). |

| | | | |
|---|---|---|---|
| 26 | Hisham Ismail Hamed | Islamic Jihad | Studied in schools run by UNRWA in Jenin. | Was member of the military wing of the Islamic Jihad. Committed suicide attack with booby-trapped motorcycle adjacent to Nezarim on 11 November 1994. |
| 27 | Yussuf Mohamad Zrair | Islamic Jihad | Studied in secondary and junior schools run by UNRWA in Shouafat refugee camp. | Committed suicide attack in Israeli market in Jerusalem on 5 November 1998. |
| 28 | Mohamad Abd Al-Rahman | Islamic Jihad | Studied in schools run by UNRWA in Jenin. | Committed suicide attack with booby-trapped car on 2 November 1995. |
| 29 | Mostafa Faisal Abu Saraya | Islamic Jihad | Studied in schools run by UNRWA in Jenin. | Committed with Fatah operative a terrorist attack in Afula on 27 November 2001. |
| 30 | Salah Abd Al-Hamid Shaker | Islamic Jihad | Studied in a junior school run by UNRWA. | Committed suicide attack with Anwar Sukkar at Bet Lid junction on 22 January 1995. |

| No. | Name | Organization | Relation to UNRWA | Terrorist Activity | Remarks | |
|---|---|---|---|---|---|---|
| 31 | Ala Abd Al-Latif Mostafa Al-Haj Abd Al-Rahman Sais (Alam Quneiri) | Al-Aqsa Martyrs Brigades | Studied in secondary and junior schools run by UNRWA in Jenin refugee camp. | Committed terrorist attacks which included shooting and placing explosive charges against Israeli targets in the area of Jenin. | Killed during the fighting in Jenin refugee camp (April 2002). | |
| 32 | Ahmad Abu Khatla | Al-Aqsa Martyrs Brigades | Studied in schools run by UNRWA in Rafah. | Committed terrorist attacks which included shooting and placing explosive charges against Israeli targets in southern Gaza. Manufactured explosive charges. | Killed on 1 May 2002 during exchanges of fire with Israeli forces in Rafah. | |
| 33 | Kaid Al-Makiri | Al-Aqsa Martyrs Brigades | Studied in schools run by UNRWA in Balata refugee camp. | Committed terrorist attacks which included shooting and placing explosive charges against Israeli targets. Manufactured explosive charges. | Killed on 28 February 2002 during exchanges of fire with Israeli forces in Nablus. | |

| 34 | Shadi Ali Moutlaq Al-Najmi | Al-Aqsa Martyrs Brigades | Studied in schools run by UNRWA in Nablus. | Committed with Said Al-Batta a terrorist attack, which included shooting at Israeli civilians in Netanya on 9 March 2002. | |
|----|----------------------------|--------------------------|--------------------------------------------|-------------------------------------------------------------------------------------------------------------------------|---|
| 35 | Wisam Faiz Yussuf Hassan | Al-Aqsa Martyrs Brigades | Studied in schools run by UNRWA. | Committed terrorist attacks against Israeli targets in the Gaza Strip. Was responsible for detonation of an explosive charge directed at Israeli bus. | Killed on 26 January 2003 during exchanges of fire with Israeli forces in Zaytoon neighborhood in Gaza. |
| 36 | Ziad Ibrahim Id Amer | Al-Aqsa Martyrs Brigades | Studied in schools run by UNRWA. | Considered a senior member of the military wing of the Fatah movement. Committed terrorist attacks against Israeli targets in the area of Jenin. | Killed during the fighting in Jenin refugee camp (April 2002). |
| 37 | Imad Adnan Al-Hindi | Hamas | Studied in secondary and junior schools run by UNRWA. | Joined the military wing of Hamas in 2000. Committed terrorist attacks against Israeli targets in the Gaza Strip. | Killed on 9 April 2003 during Israeli military operation in the Gaza Strip. |

| No. | Name | Organization | Relation to UNRWA | Terrorist Activity | Remarks |
|-----|------|--------------|-------------------|--------------------|---------|
| 38 | Hissein Abu Naser | Hamas | Studied in schools run by UNRWA. | Committed suicide attack with booby-trapped truck adjacent to Nezarim on 25 May 2001. | |
| 39 | Hashem Abdallah Najjar | Hamas | Studied in secondary and junior schools run by UNRWA. | Committed suicide attack with an explosive belt in the Jordan Valley on 22 December 2000. | |
| 40 | Ahmad Hassan Marshoud | Hamas | Studied in secondary and junior schools run by UNRWA in Balata refugee camp in Nablus. | Considered a senior member of the military wing of the Hamas movement in Nablus. Was responsible for sending suicide bombers to their missions. | Born in 1972 in Nablus. Killed in car explosion on 15 October 2001. |

| | | | | |
|---|---|---|---|---|
| 41 | Mohamad Taleb | Hamas | Studied in secondary and junior schools run by UNRWA in Jenin refugee camp. | Committed terrorist attacks which included shooting and placing explosive charges against Israeli targets in the area of Jenin. | Killed during the fighting in Jenin refugee camp (April 2002). |
| 42 | Nidal Mohamad Ali Sawitat | Hamas | Studied in secondary and junior schools run by UNRWA in Jenin refugee camp. | Committed terrorist attacks which included shooting and placing explosive charges against Israeli targets in the area of Jenin. | Killed during the fighting in Jenin refugee camp (April 2002). |
| 43 | Sais Hussein Ahmad Awwad | Hamas | Studied in secondary and junior schools run by UNRWA in Tulkarem. | Considered a senior member of the military wing of the Hamas movement in the northern area of the West Bank. Manufactured explosive charges and Qassam rockets used in terrorist attacks against Israeli civilians. | Killed during an Israeli military operation on 5 April 2002. |

| No. | Name | Organization | Relation to UNRWA | Terrorist Activity | Remarks |
|---|---|---|---|---|---|
| 44 | Shadi Zakariya Tubasi | Hamas | Studied in secondary and junior schools run by UNRWA. | Committed suicide attack with an explosive belt in a restaurant in Haifa on 31 March 2002. | |
| 45 | Mazooz Dalal | Hamas | Studied in secondary and junior schools run by UNRWA in Qalqilia. | Was member of the military wing of the Hamas movement in the early '90's. | Died of health complications while he was in Israeli jail on 15 November 1994. |
| 46 | Fuad Ismail Mohamad Al-Horani | Hamas | Studied in secondary and junior schools run by UNRWA in Al-Aroob refugee camp. | Committed suicide attack with an explosive belt in "Moment" restaurant in Jerusalem on 9 March 2002. | |

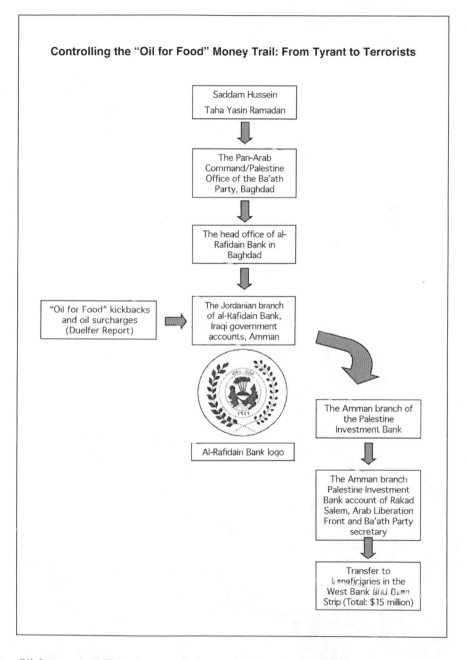

**Controlling the "Oil for Food" Money Trail: From Tyrant to Terrorists**

Saddam Hussein
Taha Yasin Ramadan

↓

The Pan-Arab
Command/Palestine
Office of the Ba'ath
Party, Baghdad

↓

The head office of al-
Rafidain Bank in
Baghdad

↓

"Oil for Food" kickbacks
and oil surcharges
(Duelfer Report) → The Jordanian branch
of al-Rafidain Bank,
Iraqi government
accounts, Amman

Al-Rafidain Bank logo

The Amman branch of
the Palestine
Investment Bank

↓

The Amman branch
Palestine Investment
Bank account of Rakad
Salem, Arab Liberation
Front and Ba'ath Party
secretary

↓

Transfer to
beneficiaries in the
West Bank and Gaza
Strip (Total: $15 million)

*Oil for terrorism:* This chart, exclusive to the paperback edition of *Tower of Babble,* shows precisely how Saddam Hussein's regime exploited the UN "oil-for-food" program to fund suicide bombing attacks in Israel. Iraq's clearly documented financial support for Palestinian terrorist organizations may have been just the tip of the iceberg when it came to its links to terrorism.

The Martyr Osama Mohammad 'Id Bahr

Al-Quds Dahiyat Al-Band [neighborhood]

بنك الاستثمار الفلسطيني
Palestine Investment Bank
A/C : 02-02-040-04199515
ID# 0
TEL : 0
899 - Albireh 20060078

Mohammad Hussein 'Id Bahr
fifteen thousand USD

Rakad Salem's Signature

22 January 2002

#20000078 #76#59902# 0#00#199511#

*Hard currency for suicide bombings:* After his arrest, Arab Liberation Front general secretary Rakad Salem claimed to have distributed $15 million in Iraqi funds to the families of Palestinian suicide bombers. This $15,000 check, signed by Salem, was payable to the father of Hamas suicide bomber Osama Bahr, who killed 11 people and wounded 188 others in a December 2001 attack in Jerusalem.

*Hamas honors its "martyrs":* Hamas offered this tribute to Osama Bahr (left) and his partner in the 2001 Jerusalem suicide attack, whose families were paid by Iraq for their terrorist operation.

*The UN funds terrorists:* Documents captured in 2003 and 2004 reveal that the UN Development Program (UNDP) was regularly funding two terrorist front organizations. This document from the Arab Bank, dated January 13, 2003, confirms that the bank received a UNDP check of $4,000 on behalf of the Tulkarm Charity Committee, a Hamas front identified as a terrorist entity.

# NOTES

## INTRODUCTION: THE ROOTS OF CHAOS

1. See, for example, U.S. Diplomatic Mission to Pakistan, Press Release: "State Dept. Report Cites Seven State-Sponsors of Terrorism," May 22, 2002, available at usembassy.state.gov/islamabad/wwwh02052203. html.

2. William G. Hyland, *Clinton's World: Remaking American Foreign Policy* (Westport: Praeger Publishers, 1999), p. 5.

3. "Confrontation in the Gulf: Transcript of President's Address to Joint Session of Congress," *New York Times*, September 12, 1990, p. A20.

4. "Remarks by the President in Address to the United Nations General Assembly, New York, New York," September 12, 2002, available at www.whitehouse.gov/news/releases/2002/09/20020912-1.html.

5. "Transcript of Bush U.N. Address," CNN.com, September 23, 2003, available at www.cnn.com/2003/US/09/23/sprj.irq.bush.transcript/.

6. David Rieff, "Up the Organization," *New Republic*, February 1, 1999.

7. Michael Barnett, *Eyewitness to Genocide: The United Nations and Rwanda* (Ithaca: Cornell University Press, 2002), p. 158.

8. Geoffrey Robertson, *Crimes Against Humanity: The Struggle for Global Justice* (New York: The New Press, 2002), p. 301

9. Javier Pérez de Cuéllar, *Pilgrimage for Peace: A Secretary-General's Memoir* (New York: St. Martin's Press, 1997), pp. 453–54. Pérez de Cuéllar writes, "While I had no sympathy for the Pol Pot regime, I was convinced that we were going to have to gain the cooperation of the Khmer Rouge (and their Chinese friends) in order to reach a settlement. Use of the word 'genocide' in any form would, I was certain, make this far more difficult."

10. Robert D. Kaplan, *The Coming Anarchy: Shattering the Dreams of the Post Cold War* (New York: Vintage Books, 2001), p. 178.

11. Richard Butler, *The Greatest Threat: Iraq, Weapons of Mass Destruction, and the Crisis of Global Security* (New York: Public Affairs, 2000), p. 177. See also A. M. Rosenthal, "On My Mind: Softening Saddam's Deal," *New York Times,* February 24, 1998.

12. Charles Krauthammer, "Kofi Annan's Offense," *Washington Post,* March 28, 2003.

13. Colum Lynch, "GAO: Iraq Oil Profits Understated," *Washington Post,* March 19, 2004.

14. Therese Raphael, "Saddam's Global Payroll," *Wall Street Journal,* February 9, 2004.

15. Susan Sachs, "Hussein's Regime Skimmed Billions from Aid Program," *New York Times,* February 29, 2004; Claudia Rosett, "Turtle Bay's Carnival of Corruption: Digging Deeper in the Scandalous Oil-for-Food Program," *National Review,* March 21, 2004.

16. See interview with Michael Soussan in David Rennie, "UN's 'Shameful Silence' over the Evils of Saddam," *Daily Telegraph,* June 14, 2004.

17. Maggie Farley, "U.N. Seeks to Curb Role in Spread of AIDS: World Organization Wages Campaign to Curtail International Peacekeepers' Involvement in Transmission of the Disease," *Los Angeles Times,* January 7, 2000; Betsy Pisik, "AIDS Being Spread by Its Peacekeepers," *Washington Times,* July 7, 2000.

18. News Briefs, UN Wire, August 24, 2001 — *Corriere Della Serra,* August 24, 2001.

19. The former first lady of Mozambique admitted that in her own country, soldiers from the UN Operation in Mozambique (ONUMOZ) recruited girls between the ages of twelve and eighteen into prostitution; a UN Commission of Inquiry confirmed the allegations. See Inter Press Service, July 26, 2002. On the dossier of Kathryn Bolkovac to the UN detailing the involvement of UN workers in the sex trade in Bosnia, see Daniel McGrory, "Woman Sacked for Revealing UN Links with Sex Trade," *Times* (London), August 7, 2002. For an interview with Madeleine Rees, the UN High Commissioner for Human Rights in Bosnia, who leveled charges about UN workers' involvement in child prostitution in Bosnia, see Dominic Hipkins, "Bosnia Sex Trade Shames UN," *Scotland on Sunday,* February 9, 2003. Rees charges the UN with a cover-up.

20. Shashi Tharoor, "Why America Still Needs the United Nations," *Foreign Affairs,* September/October 2003, p. 68.

21. James A. Baker, *The Politics of Diplomacy: Revolution, War, and Peace, 1989–1992* (New York: G. P. Putnam's Sons, 1995), p. 447.

22. Winston Churchill, "The Sinews of Peace," Speech at Westminster College, Fulton, Missouri, March 5, 1946, available at www.britannia.com/history/docs/sinews1.html.

23. Robertson, *Crimes Against Humanity,* p. 49.

24. Anne F. Bayefsky, "Israel and the United Nations' Human Rights Agenda: The Inequality of Nations Large and Small," *Israel Law Review,* Volume 29, Number 3, p. 451, n. 84.

25. "In Annan and Chirac's Words: 'Fork in the Road' and 'Call a Summit,' " *New York Times,* September 24, 2003.

26. Ruth Wedgewood, "The Fall of Saddam Hussein: Security Council Mandates and Preemptive Self-Defense," *American Journal of International Law,* Volume 97, July 2003.

27. William Shawcross notes that a senior UN official, Edward Mortimer, pointed out to him that only two wars in the hundreds that have taken place since the UN was created have been fought with Security Council authorization. See William Shawcross, *Allies: The U.S., Britain, Europe, and the War in Iraq* (New York: Public Affairs, 2004), p. 140. There are different legal opinions on whether UN authorization is needed before a state resorts to force. For example, Anne Marie Slaughter, the dean of the Woodrow Wilson School at Princeton University, argues, "The UN Charter demands that the use of force in any cause other than self-defense be authorized by the Security Council" (see Slaughter, "Good Reasons for Going Around the UN," *International Herald Tribune,* March 19, 2003).

28. Margaret Thatcher, *The Downing Street Years* (New York: HarperCollins, 1993), p. 821.

29. Charter of the United Nations, Chapter I, Article 2 (4).

30. Jane E. Stromseth, "Law and Force After Iraq: A Transitional Moment," *American Journal of International Law,* Volume 97, July 2003.

31. David Frum and Richard Perle, "U.N. Should Change—or U.S. Should Quit," *Los Angeles Times,* January 23, 2004.

32. United Nations Security Council, "The Role of the Security Council in the Pacific Settlement of Disputes," May 13, 2003, S/PV/4753. See testimony of Nabil Elaraby, p. 7.

33. Rosemary Righter, *Utopia Lost: The United Nations and World Order* (New York: The Twentieth Century Fund Press, 1995), p. 213.

34. Amir Taheri, "Motives in the U.N.," Townhall.com, September 28, 2003.

35. Michael Walzer, *Just and Unjust Wars: A Moral Argument* (New York: Basic Books, 1977), p. 107.

36. Richard A. Falk, "What Future for the UN Charter System of War Prevention?" *American Journal of International Law,* Volume 97, July 2003.

37. George F. Will, "The Emptiness of Desert Storm," *Washington Post,* January 12, 1992.

38. Michael Ignatieff, *The Lesser Evil: Political Ethics in the Age of Terror* (Princeton: Princeton University Press, 2004), p. 165.

39. United Nations General Assembly, A/RES/54/54, January 10, 2000.

40. Bayefsky, "Israel and the United Nations' Human Rights Agenda,"

p. 425; Anne F. Bayefsky, "The UN and the Assault on Israel's Legitimacy: Implications for the Roadmap," *Jerusalem Viewpoints*, No. 501, July 15–August 1, 2003, Jerusalem Center for Public Affairs.

41. Gil Loescher, *The UNHCR and World Politics* (Oxford: Oxford University Press, 2001), p. 301.

42. Daniel Bergner, "The Most Unconventional Weapon," *New York Times Magazine*, October 26, 2003, p. 48.

43. Jules Lobel, "American Hegemony and International Law: Benign Hegemony? Kosovo and Article 2(4) of the U.N. Charter," *Chicago Journal of International Law*, Spring 2000.

44. "Israeli Forces Enter Gaza, West Bank," CNN.com, January 30, 2004, available at www.cnn.com/2004/WORLD/meast/01/30/mideast/.

45. David Rieff, *A Bed for the Night: Humanitarianism in Crisis* (New York: Simon & Schuster, 2002), p. 150.

## CHAPTER 1: THE EROSION OF STANDARDS

1. Daniel P. Moynihan, *A Dangerous Place* (Boston: Little, Brown, 1975), p. 108.

2. William Safire, *Safire's Political Dictionary* (New York: Random House, 1978), p. 757.

3. Jon Meacham, *Franklin and Winston: An Intimate Portrait of an Epic Friendship* (New York: Random House, 2003), p. 228.

4. Townsend Hoopes and Douglas Brinkley, *FDR and the Creation of the U.N.* (New Haven: Yale University Press, 1997), p. 100.

5. Stanley Meisler, *United Nations: The First Fifty Years* (New York: The Atlantic Monthly Press, 1995), p. 3.

6. Conrad Black, *Franklin Delano Roosevelt: Champion of Freedom* (New York: Public Affairs, 2003), p. 1016.

7. Frederick H. Fleitz, *Peacekeeping Fiascoes of the 1990s: Causes, Solutions, and U.S. Interests* (Westport: Praeger Publishers, 2002), pp. 21–24.

8. Hoopes and Brinkley, *FDR and the Creation of the U.N.*, p. 100.

9. Ibid., p. 56.

10. Meisler, *United Nations*, p. 2.

11. Henry Kissinger, *Diplomacy* (New York: Simon & Schuster, 1995), p. 247.

12. Rosemary Righter, *Utopia Lost: The United Nations and World Order* (New York: The Twentieth Century Fund Press, 1995), p. 28.

13. Ibid.

14. Stephen C. Schlesinger, *Act of Creation: The Founding of the United Nations* (Boulder: Westview Press, 2003), pp. 103–106. Alger Hiss was not indicted for espionage because the charges against him exceeded the statute of limitations, but he was convicted of perjury for his testimony on his personal history. He dropped a lawsuit against a journalist who charged that he had worked for the Soviet Union.

15. Leland M. Goodrich, *The United Nations in a Changing World* (New York: Columbia University Press, 1974), p. 41.

16. Johannes Morsink, *The Universal Declaration of Human Rights: Origins, Drafting, and Intent* (Philadelphia: University of Pennsylvania Press, 1999), p. 21.

17. Mary Ann Glendon, *A World Made New: Eleanor Roosevelt and the Universal Declaration of Human Rights* (New York: Random House, 2001), pp. 61–63, 124–25, 132–33, 168.

18. Bat Yeor, *Islam and Dhimmitude: Where Civilizations Collide* (Madison and Teaneck: Farleigh Dickinson University Press, 2002), pp. 383–85.

19. Michael J. Glennon, "Why the Security Council Failed," *Foreign Affairs*, May/June 2003.

20. Linda Fasulo, *An Insider's Guide to the UN* (New Haven: Yale University Press, 2004), p. 146. Fasulo derives her data from the U.S. Department of State, *18th Annual Report on Voting Practices in the UN*, 2000, p. 2.

21. Robert Kagan, *Of Paradise and Power: America and Europe in the New World Order* (New York: Alfred A. Knopf, 2003), p. 79.

22. Madeleine Albright, *Madam Secretary: A Memoir* (New York: Miramax Books, 2003), pp. 134–35.

23. Geoffrey Robertson, *Crimes Against Humanity: The Struggle for Global Justice* (New York: The New Press, 2002), p. 74.

24. Ibid.

25. David W. Wainhouse, *Remnants of Empire: The United Nations and the End of Colonialism* (New York: Council on Foreign Relations/Harper & Row, 1964), pp. 10–19.

26. "Status of Goa," in Wolfgang Friedman, Oliver J. Lissitzyn, Richard Pugh, *International Law: Cases and Materials* (St. Paul: West Publishing Company, 1969), p. 467.

27. Adlai Stevenson, *Looking Outward: Years of Crisis at the United Nations* (New York: Harper & Row, 1961), p. xii.

28. Ibid., p. xix.

29. Meisler, *United Nations*, p. 138.

30. Nicolas Nyiri, *The United Nations' Search for a Definition of Aggression* (New York: Peter Lang, 1989), pp. 57–58.

31. Ibid., p. 87.

32. Ibid., p. 245.

33. UN General Assembly Resolution 3314 (XXIX) UNGAOR 29th Session, Supp. No. 31 (1974)—Definition of Aggression.

34. Julius Stone, "Hopes and Loopholes in the 1974 Definition of Aggression," *American Journal of International Law*, April 1977.

35. Robertson, *Crimes Against Humanity*, pp. 364–65.

36. See also Harris O. Schoenberg, *A Mandate for Terror: The United Nations and the PLO* (New York: Shapolsky Publishers, 1989), p. 209.

37. Alan M. Dershowitz, *Why Terrorism Works: Understanding the Threat, Responding to the Challenge* (New Haven: Yale University Press, 2002), p. 54.

38. "Agreed Definition of Terrorism Needed to Promote Cooperation on Its Elimination, Sixth Committee Told," Press Release L/2823, February 21, 1997, available at www.fas.org/nuke/control/nt/docs/1-2823.htm.

39. United Nations General Assembly, Fifty-third session, Agenda item 155, Measures to Eliminate International Terrorism, letter dated March 24, 1999, from the Permanent Representative of the Syrian Arab Republic to the United Nations addressed to the Secretary-General, A/53/876, S/1999/326, April 6, 1999.

40. "Future of the United Nations," CSPAN2, September 11, 2003.

41. Allan Gerson, *The Kirkpatrick Mission: Diplomacy Without Apology, America and the United Nations 1981–1985* (New York: The Free Press, 1991), pp. 249–52.

42. Michael Rubin, "U.N. Gives Aid and Comfort to Terrorists," *Wall Street Journal*, April 18, 2002.

43. Glendon, *A World Made New*, p. 209.

## CHAPTER 2: FAILURE FORESHADOWED

1. Trygve Lie, *In the Cause of Peace* (New York: Macmillan, 1954), p. 174.

2. Meron Medzini, ed., *Israel's Foreign Relations: Selected Documents, 1947–1974* (Jerusalem: Ministry for Foreign Affairs, 1976), p. 411.

3. Abba Eban, *Abba Eban: An Autobiography* (New York: Random House, 1977), p. 122.

4. Paul S. Riebenfeld, "The Legitimacy of Jewish Settlement in Judea, Samaria, and Gaza," in Douglas Feith et al., *Israel's Legitimacy in Law and History* (New York: Center for Near East Policy Research, 1993), p. 41. Riebenfeld was a Zionist delegate to the Permanent Mandate Commission of the League of Nations from 1937 to 1939.

5. Julius Stone, "Israel, the United Nations, and International Law: Memorandum of Law," John Norton Moore, ed. *The Arab-Israeli Conflict*, Volume IV, Part I. *The Difficult Search for Peace, 1975–1988* (Princeton: Princeton University Press, 1991), p. 790.

6. Wolfgang Friedman, Oliver J. Lissitzyn, and Richard C. Pugh, *International Law: Cases and Materials* (St. Paul: West Publishing Co., 1969), pp. 153–55, 164–65.

7. J. C. Hurewitz, *The Struggle for Palestine* (New York: Schocken Books, 1976), pp. 307–8.

8. Medzini, *Israel's Foreign Relations*, p. 141.

9. Marshall J. Breger and Thomas A. Idinopulos, *Jerusalem's Holy Places and the Peace Process* (Washington: The Washington Institute for Near East Policy, 1998), p. 12.

10. Henry Cattan, *Jerusalem* (London: Saqi Books, 2000), p. 38.

11. Eban, *Abba Eban,* p. 113.

12. Martin Gilbert, *Jerusalem in the Twentieth Century* (New York: John Wiley & Sons, 1996), p. 206.

13. Medzini, *Israel's Foreign Relations,* p. 224.

14. Stanley Meisler, *United Nations: The First Fifty Years* (New York: Atlantic Monthly Press, 1995), p. 51.

15. Medzini, *Israel's Foreign Relations,* p. 243.

16. Gil Loescher, *The UNHCR and World Politics: A Perilous Path* (Oxford: Oxford University Press, 2001), p. 39.

17. Ruth Lapidoth, "Legal Aspects of the Palestinian Refugee Question," *Jerusalem Viewpoints,* September 1, 2002, Jerusalem Center for Public Affairs, p. 2.

18. Cited by Benjamin Netanyahu, *A Place Among the Nations: Israel and the World* (New York: Bantam Books, 1993), p. 36. Memorandum to the Secretary of State, May 17, 1939, in *Foreign Relations of the United States, 1939,* Volume 4 (Washington: U.S. Government Printing Office, 1955), p. 757.

19. Loescher, *The UNHCR and World Politics,* p. 56. He writes, "At the insistence of the Arab states, Palestinians registered with UNRWA were purposely excluded from the competence of the UNHCR, both in its Statute and in the 1951 Refugee Convention."

20. Alan Dershowitz, *The Case for Israel* (New York: John Wiley & Sons, 2003), p. 86.

21. Ibid., p. 85.

22. Edward H. Buehrig, *The UN and the Palestinian Refugees* (Bloomington: Indiana University Press, 1971), p. 11.

23. Ibid., p. 134.

24. Efraim Karsh, "The Palestinians and the 'Right of Return,' " *Commentary,* May 2001.

25. Khaled al-Azm, *Memoirs* (Beirut: Al-Dar al Muttahida Lil-Nashr, 1972), Volume I, pp. 386–87, quoted in Chaim Herzog, *Who Stands Accused?: Israel Answers Its Critics* (New York: Random House, 1978), pp. 42, 43. Years later, even members of the PLO leadership concurred. Writing in *Falastin al-Thawra* in March 1976, PLO Executive Committee member Abu Mazen noted, "The Arab armies entered Palestine to protect the Palestinians . . . but, instead, they abandoned them, forced them to emigrate and to leave their homeland, imposed upon them a political and ideological blockade and threw them into prisons similar to the ghettos in which the Jews used to live in Eastern Europe." See Herzog, *Who Stands Accused?* p. 43. Abu Iyad also wrote in his memoirs that hundreds of thousands of Palestinians fled their homes under the mistaken assumption that they would soon be able to return in the wake of victorious Arab armies; he added, "I think my compatriots should have stood their ground." See Neil C. Livingstone and David Halevy, *Inside the PLO: Covert Units, Secret Funds, and the War Against Israel and the United States* (New York: William Morrow, 1990), p. 61.

26. Medzini, *Israel's Foreign Relations*, p. 367.

27. Sumit Ganguly, *Conflict Unending: India-Pakistan Tensions Since 1947* (New York: Woodrow Wilson Center/Columbia University Press, 2001), pp. 2–3.

28. Rosalyn Higgins, *United Nations Peacekeeping 1946–1967: Documents and Commentary*, Volume II: Asia (London: Royal Institute of International Affairs/Oxford University Press, 1970), pp. 315–16.

29. Memorandum of Conversation by the Secretary of State, October 13, 1949, in *Foreign Relations of the United States 1949*, Volume VI (Washington: U.S. Government Printing Office, 1977), p. 1750.

30. Josef Korbel, *Danger in Kashmir* (Princeton: Princeton University Press, 1954), p. 94.

31. Ganguly, *Conflict Unending*, p. 20.

32. Victoria Schofield, *Kashmir in Conflict: India, Pakistan, and the Unending War* (London: I. B. Tauris, 2003), p. 68.

33. C. Dasgupta, *War and Diplomacy in Kashmir: 1947–48* (New Delhi: Sage Publications, 2002), p. 111.

34. Ibid., p. 21.

35. Ibid., p. 131.

36. Higgins, *United Nations Peacekeeping 1946–1967*, p. 323. See footnote 19.

37. Ibid., p. 324.

38. Major General Akbar Khan, *Raiders in Kashmir* (Karachi: Pak Publishers, 1970), p. 11.

39. Dasgupta, *War and Diplomacy in Kashmir*, p. 39.

40. Ibid.

41. Josef Korbel, "The Kashmir Dispute and the United Nations," *International Organization*, Volume 3, Number 2, 1951, pp. 278–87.

42. United Nations, *The Blue Helmets: A Review of United Nations Peace-keeping* (New York: Department of Public Information, 1996), p. 134.

43. Ibid., p. 137.

44. Meisler, *United Nations*, p. 167.

45. Ganguly, *Conflict Unending*, p. 71.

46. United Nations, *The Blue Helmets*, p. 142.

47. Oscar Schacter, "The Right of States to Use Armed Force," *Michigan Law Review*, April/May 1984.

48. See appeal of the Tibetan government to the United Nations, November 11, 1950, in International Commission of Jurists, *The Question of Tibet and the Rule of Law* (Geneva: International Commission of Jurists, 1959), p. 95.

49. Letter from Tibetan leaders to Mr. Jawaharlal Nehru, summer 1958, in International Commission of Jurists, *The Question of Tibet and the Rule of Law*, p. 143.

50. Thomas Franck, "Of Gnats and Camels: Is There a Double Standard at the United Nations?" *American Journal of International Law*, October 1984.

51. Ibid.

## CHAPTER 3: THE COLD WAR FREEZE

1. Stanley Meisler, *United Nations: The First Fifty Years* (New York: Atlantic Monthly Press, 1995), p. 57.
2. David McCullough, *Truman* (New York: Simon & Schuster, 1992), p. 792.
3. Henry Kissinger, *Diplomacy* (New York: Simon & Schuster, 1994), pp. 475–76.
4. In criticizing General MacArthur's explicit statements about seeking to unite Korea on the basis of the new UN General Assembly resolution, Dean Acheson wrote, "General MacArthur once stripped from the resolution of October 7 its husk of ambivalence and gave it an interpretation that the enacting majority in the General Assembly would not have accepted." See Dean Acheson, *Present at the Creation: My Years in the State Department* (New York: W. W. Norton, 1987), p. 455.
5. Yehuda Z. Blum, *Eroding the United Nations Charter* (Dordrecht: Martinus Nijihaff Publishers, 1993), pp. 103–22.
6. Ibid., p. 121.
7. Leland M. Goodrich, *The United Nations in a Changing World* (New York: Columbia University Press, 1974), p. 128.
8. See Rosemary Righter, *Utopia Lost: The United Nations and World Order* (New York: Twentieth Century Fund, 1995), p. 377. It is important to note that the operative paragraph of UN Security Council Resolution 83 "recommends that the Members of the United Nations furnish such assistance to the republic of Korea as may be necessary to the repel the armed attack and restore international peace and security in the area."
9. Goodrich, *The United Nations in a Changing World*, p. 128.
10. Clay Blair, *The Forgotten War: America in Korea 1950–1953* (Annapolis: Naval Institute Press, 1987), pp. 327–28.
11. Acheson, *Present at the Creation*, p. 452. For the positions of the secretary-general and the British, see Blair, *The Forgotten War*, p. 328.
12. Nikita Khrushchev, *Khrushchev Remembers: The Last Testament*, Strobe Talbott, editor and translator (Boston: Little, Brown, 1974), p. 484.
13. Brian Urquhart, *Hammarskjold* (New York: Alfred A. Knopf, 1972), p. 48.
14. For details on the Hungarian Revolution and the UN, see ibid., pp. 231–35.
15. Ibid., p. 366.
16. Dino A. Brugioni, *Eyeball to Eyeball: The Inside Story of the Cuban Missile Crisis* (New York: Random House, 1991).
17. Meisler, *United Nations*, p. 145.
18. Louis Henkin, *How Nations Behave: Law and Foreign Policy* (New York: Columbia University Press, 1979), pp. 280–81, 291; Document 41, "Minutes of the 507th Meeting of the National Security Council," October 22, 1962, 3 P.M., in U.S. Department of State, *Foreign Relations of the United States, 1961–1963, Volume XI: Cuban Missile Crisis and*

*Aftermath*(Washington: U.S. Government Printing Office, 2001). Article 53 of the UN Charter stipulates that "no enforcement action shall be taken under regional arrangements or by regional agencies without the authorization of the Security Council." The United States argued, nonetheless, that the OAS did not initiate an "enforcement action" but only made a "recommendation." And since the Security Council did not challenge this recommendation, it provided implicit authorization. If this in fact was the legal reasoning of the time, then the Kennedy administration had even less UN backing for the Cuban quarantine than the Bush administration had in the Iraq War.

19. Brugioni, *Eyeball to Eyeball,* p. 329.
20. Ibid., pp. 333–34.
21. Ibid., pp. 425–29.
22. Michael R. Beschloss, *The Crisis Years: Kennedy and Khrushchev 1960–1963* (New York: HarperCollins, 1991), p. 502.
23. Meisler, *United Nations,* p. 148.
24. Document 87, "Memorandum of Telephone Conversation Between President Kennedy and Prime Minister Macmillan," October 26, 1962, in U.S. Department of State, *Foreign Relations of the United States.*
25. Ibid.
26. Document 107, "Telegram from the Mission to the United Nations to the Department of State," October 28, 1962, 9 P.M., in U.S. Department of State, *Foreign Relations of the United States.*
27. Brugioni, *Eyeball to Eyeball,* p. 485.
28. Ibid.
29. Ibid., p. 501.
30. Khrushchev, *Khrushchev Remembers,* p. 484.
31. Document 232, "Memorandum from Secretary of State Rusk to President Kennedy," Undated, Subject: The 17th General Assembly: A Summary Round-Up, in U.S. Department of State, *Foreign Relations of the United States, 1961–1963, Volume XXV: Organization of Foreign Policy; Information Policy; United Nations; Scientific Matters* (Washington: U.S. Government Printing Office, 2001), pp. 509–13.

## CHAPTER 4: IGNITING WAR, UNDERMINING PEACE

1. Lyndon Baines Johnson, *The Vantage Point: Perspectives of the Presidency 1963–1969* (New York: Holt, Rinehart, and Winston, 1971), p. 288.
2. Meron Medzini, ed., *Israel's Foreign Relations: Selected Documents, 1947–1974* (Jerusalem: Ministry of Foreign Affairs, 1976), p. 359.
3. Aryeh Shalev, *The Israel-Syria Armistice Regime: 1949–1955* (Tel Aviv: Jaffee Center for Strategic Studies, 1993), p. 211.
4. Medzini, *Israel's Foreign Relations,* p. 271.

5. Chaim Herzog, *The Arab-Israeli Wars: War and Peace in the Middle East* (New York: Vintage Books, 1984), p. 148.

6. Michael B. Oren, *Six Days of War: June 1967 and the Making of the Modern Middle East* (Oxford: Oxford University Press, 2002), p. 76.

7. Abba Eban, *Abba Eban: An Autobiography* (New York: Random House, 1977), p. 322.

8. Gideon Rafael, *Destination Peace: Three Decades of Israeli Foreign Policy* (New York: Stein and Day, 1981), p. 139.

9. Oren, *Six Days of War*, p. 70.

10. Ibid., p. 28.

11. Stanley Meisler, *United Nations: The First Fifty Years* (New York: Atlantic Monthly Press, 1995), p. 175.

12. Eban, *Abba Eban*, p. 376.

13. Rafael, *Destination Peace*, p. 149.

14. Eban, *Abba Eban*, p. 378.

15. Lyndon Baines Johnson, *The Vantage Point: Perspectives of the Presidency, 1963–1969* (New York: Holt, Rinehart, and Winston, 1971), p. 292.

16. Oren, *Six Days of War*, p. 104.

17. Ibid., pp. 140–41.

18. Document 39, "Nasser's Speech to Arab Trade Unionists," May 26, 1967, in Walter Laqueur and Barry Rubin, eds., *The Israel-Arab Reader: A Documentary History of the Middle East Conflict* (New York: Penguin Books, 1991), p. 176.

19. Herzog, *The Arab-Israeli Wars*, p. 149.

20. Oren, *Six Days of War*, p. 184.

21. Ibid., p. 184.

22. For the sequence of events, see ibid., pp. 186–87.

23. Herzog, *The Arab-Israeli Wars*, p. 153.

24. Eban, *Abba Eban*, p. 415.

25. Arthur Lall, *The UN and the Middle East Crisis, 1967* (New York: Columbia University Press, 1968), p. 103; Julius Stone, "Israel, the United Nations, and International Law," John Norton Moore, ed. *The Arab-Israeli Conflict*, Volume IV, Part I. *The Difficult Search for Peace, 1975–1988* (Princeton: Princeton University Press, 1991), p. 815.

26. Rafael, *Destination Peace*, p. 179.

27. Ibid., p. 179.

28. P. M. Dadant, "American and Soviet Defense Systems Vis-à-Vis the Middle East," in Willard Beling, ed., *The Middle East: Quest for an American Policy* (Albany: State University of New York Press, 1973), pp. 185–87.

29. Just prior to the Six-Day War, the Soviets were putting five to seven supply ships per month through the Suez Canal bound for North Vietnam. See Dadant, "American and Soviet Defense Systems Vis-à-Vis the Middle East," p. 181.

30. Eugene Rostow, "The Intent of UNSC Resolution 242—The View of Non-

Regional Actors," in Washington Institute for Near East Policy, *UN Security Council Resolution 242: The Building Block of Peacemaking* (Washington: The Washington Institute, 1993), pp. 15–16.

31. Shlomo Slonim, *Jerusalem in America's Foreign Policy, 1947–1997* (The Hague: Kluwer Law International, 1998), p. 193.

32. Stephen M. Schwebel, "What Weight to Conquest?" *American Journal of International Law,* Volume 64 (1970).

33. Eban, *Abba Eban,* p. 449.

34. Ibid.

35. Vernon Turner, in Washington Institute for Near East Policy, *UN Security Council Resolution 242,* p. 27.

36. Ibid., p. 27.

37. Rafael, *Destination Peace,* p. 189.

38. See Shabtai Rosenne, "On Multi-Lingual Interpretation—UN Security Council Resolution 242," January 1, 1971, available at www.mfa.gov.il/MFA/Peace+Process/Guide+to+the+Peace+Process/On+Multi-Lingual+Interpretation+-UN+Security+Counc.htm. Rosenne writes, "Many experts in the French language, including academics with no political axe to grind, have advised that the French translation is an accurate and idiomatic rendering of the original English text, and possibly even the only acceptable rendering into French. As an independent scholar of the law has recently written: 'The expression *"des territoires"* in [the French] translation may be viewed merely as an idiomatic rendering into French, not intended to depart . . . from the English.' . . . On the question of concordance, the French representative was explicit in stating that the French text was 'identical' with the English text." Rosenne is the former permanent representative of Israel to the United Nations Office at Geneva and member of the United Nations International Law Commission.

39. Meir Rosenne, "Legal Interpretations of UNSC 242," in Washington Institute for Near East Policy, *UN Security Council Resolution* 242.

40. Ovadia Soffer, *The UN as Peacemaker* (Irchester: Mark Saunders Books, 1971), p. 92.

41. On NBC's *Meet the Press* on July 12, 1970, Joseph Sisco, the assistant secretary of state for Near Eastern affairs, emphatically stated his understanding of Resolution 242 as follows: "That Resolution did not say 'withdrawal to the pre–June 5 lines.' "

42. Slonim, *Jerusalem in America's Foreign Policy, 1947–1997,* p. 202.

43. Soffer, *The UN as Peacemaker,* p. 191. Jarring's proposal was with reference to the Egyptian front alone, where Israel decided to fully withdraw seven years later in 1978. Yet Jarring did not reassure Israel that his proposal did not set a precedent for other fronts.

44. Ibid., p. 214.

45. For example, see "Resolution Adopted by the General Assembly," A/RES/ ES-10/5, March 20, 1998.
46. James Bennet, "Mideast Turmoil: The Overview: U.N. Chief Tells Israel It Must End 'Illegal Occupation,' " *New York Times,* March 13, 2002.
47. George P. Fletcher, "Annan's Careless Language," *New York Times,* March 21, 2002.


## CHAPTER 5: THE RETURN OF THE UN?

1. Stanley Meisel, *United Nations: The First Fifty Years* (New York: Atlantic Monthly Press, 1995), p. 257.
2. Ibid.
3. United Nations, Department of Public Information, *The United Nations and the Iraq-Kuwaiti Conflict: 1990–1996* (New York: United Nations Department of Public Information, 1996), p. 23.
4. Meisler, *United Nations,* p. 248.
5. Rosemary Righter, *Utopia Lost: The United Nations and World Order* (New York: The Twentieth Century Fund Press, 1995), pp. 80–81.
6. Javier Pérez de Cuéllar, *Pilgrimage for Peace* (New York: St. Martin's Press, 1997), p. 131.
7. Ibid., p. 132.
8. Chris Suellentrop, "Hans Blix: Incompetent Bureaucrat or Cowardly Diplomat?" *Slate,* November 22, 2002. See also Byron York, "Blix-krieg," *National Review,* October 1, 2002.
9. Richard Butler, *The Greatest Threat: Iraq, Weapons of Mass Destruction, and the Crisis of Global Security* (New York: Public Affairs, 2000), p. 11.
10. Samantha Power, *"A Problem from Hell": America and the Age of Genocide* (New York: Perennial Books, 2002), pp. 171–207; David McDowall, *A Modern History of the Kurds* (London: I. B. Tauris, 1996), p. 357.
11. McDowall, pp. 357–63.
12. Pérez de Cuéllar points out that Waldheim had made the mistake of appearing pro-Iraqi to the Iranians. In his autobiography, he makes it clear that he did not want to repeat this mistake.
13. David Wurmser, *Tyranny's Ally: America's Failure to Defeat Saddam Hussein* (Washington: American Enterprise Institute, 1999), p. 11.
14. Document 103, "Report on the Situation of Human Rights in Iraq Prepared by the Special Rapporteur of the Commission on Human Rights," February 18, 1992, in Department of Public Information, *The United Nations and the Iraq-Kuwait Conflict, 1990–1996* (New York: United Nations, 1996), pp. 407–408.
15. Righter, *Utopia Lost,* p. 336.

16. Gil Loescher, *The UNHCR and World Politics: A Perilous Path* (Oxford: Oxford University Press, 2001). p. 289.

17. Power, *"A Problem from Hell,"* p. 244.

18. United Nations, *UNMOVIC Quarterly Report to the UN Security Council,* May 30, 2003. See Appendix 1, "Destruction, Removal, or Rendering Harmless of Proscribed Items and Materials in Iraq, 1991 to 1998."

19. Butler, *The Greatest Threat,* p. 52.

20. Ibid., p. 65.

21. Ibid., p. 127.

22. Susan Sachs, "Hussein's Regime Skimmed Billions from Aid Program," *New York Times,* February 29, 2004; Claudia Rosett, "Turtle Bay's Carnival of Corruption: Digging Deeper in the Scandalous Oil-for-Food Program," *National Review,* March 21, 2004.

23. U.S. General Accounting Office, statement of Joseph A. Christoff, director, International Affairs and Trade, Testimony Before the Committee on Foreign Relations, U.S. Senate, "United Nations: Observations on the Oil-for-Food Program," April 7, 2004.

24. Therese Raphael, "Saddam's Global Payroll," *Wall Street Journal,* February 9, 2004.

25. Testimony to the U.S. Congress by Mr. Charles Duelfer, Director of Central Intelligence Special Advisor for Strategy Regarding Iraqi Weapons of Mass Destruction (WMD) Programs, March 30, 2004, available at www.odci.gov/cia/public_affairs/speeches/2004/tenet_testimony_03302004.html.

26. Christopher Wren, "Standoff With Iraq: The UN: No Need to Humiliate Iraq, the Secretary General Says," *New York Times,* February 11, 1998.

27. William Shawcross, *Deliver Us from Evil: Peacekeepers, Warlords, and World of Endless Conflict* (New York: Simon & Schuster, 2000), p. 267.

28. Butler, *The Greatest Threat,* p. 110.

29. Michael Gordon and Elaine Sciolino, "The Deal on Iraq: The Way It Happened: Fingerprints on Iraqi Accord Belong to Albright," *New York Times,* February 25, 1998.

30. Butler, *The Greatest Threat,* p. 98.

31. Ibid., p. 163.

32. Ibid., p. 176.

33. A. M. Rosenthal, "On My Mind: Annan's Bad Gamble," *New York Times,* February 27, 1998.

34. Terence Taylor, "Biological Weapons," in Roy Gutman and David Rieff, eds., *Crimes of War* (New York: W. W. Norton, 1999), p. 46.

35. Butler, *The Greatest Threat,* p. 118.

36. Ibid., p. 161.

37. "Iraq Says West Destroyed Seven Missile Plants," Reuters, February 3, 2000.

38. Butler, *The Greatest Threat,* p. 128.

39. UNMOVIC Working Document, "Unresolved Disarmament Issues: Iraq's Pro-scribed Weapons Programmes," March 6, 2003, p. 98.

40. Ibid., pp. 128–29.

41. Ibid., p. 118.

42. Richard Wolffe and Daniel Klaidman, "Judging the Case," *Newsweek,* February 17, 2003.

43. National Commission on Terrorist Attacks Upon the United States, "Overview of the Enemy," Staff Statement No. 15, available at www.9-11commission.gov/hearings/hearing12/staff_statement_15.pdf.

44. Cited by George Shultz, "An Essential War: Ousting Saddam Was the Only Option," *Wall Street Journal,* March 29, 2004.

45. UNMOVIC Working Document, "Unresolved Disarmament Issues: Iraq's Pro-scribed Weapons Programmes," March 6, 2003, p. 103.

46. Kenneth M. Pollack, "Spies, Lies, and Weapons: What Went Wrong," *Atlantic Monthly,* January/February 2004.

47. Excerpts from David Kay's testimony to the Senate Armed Services Committee, January 28, 2004, available at www.house.gov/gibbons/intelligence_davidkay.htm.

48. Con Coughlin, "Saddam's WMD Hidden in Syria," *Daily Telegraph,* July 19, 2004; Warren Hoge, "The Reach of War: Weapons Inspections: Suspect Items from Iraq Shipped Abroad, U.N. Says," *New York Times,* June 10, 2004.

49. Kay's testimony, January 28, 2004.

## CHAPTER 6: IMPARTIAL TO GENOCIDE

1. Frederick H. Fleitz Jr., *Peacekeeping Fiascoes of the 1990s* (Westport: Praeger Pub-lishers, 2002), p. 103.

2. William Shawcross, *Deliver Us from Evil: Peacekeeping, Warlords, and a World of Endless Conflict* (New York: Touchstone Books, 2000), pp. 124–29; see also Samantha Power, *"A Problem from Hell": America in the Age of Genocide* (New York: Perennial, 2002), pp. 329–41.

3. Cable To: Baril, DPKO, United Nations, From: Dallaire, UNAMIR, Kigali. See: www.pbs.org/wgbh/pages/frontline/shows/evil/warning/cable.html.

4. PBS interview with Iqbal Riza, available at www.pbs.org/wgbh/pages/frontline/shows/evil/interviews/riza.html.

5. Michael Barnett, *Eyewitness to Genocide: The United Nations and Rwanda* (Ithaca: Cornell University Press, 2002), p. 79.

6. Ibid., p. 90.

7. Romeo Dallaire, *Shake Hands with the Devil: The Failure of Humanity in Rwanda* (Toronto: Random House Canada, 2003), p. 146.

8. Shawcross, *Deliver Us from Evil,* p. 333.

9. L. R. Melvern, *A People Betrayed: The Role of the West in Rwanda's Genocide* (London: Zed Books, 2000), p. 93.
10. Power, *"A Problem from Hell,"* p. 238.
11. UN Security Council, *Report of the Independent Inquiry in the Actions of the United Nations During the 1994 Genocide in Rwanda,* S/1999/1257, p. 7.
12. Melvern, *A People Betrayed,* p. 89.
13. PBS Interview with Iqbal Riza.
14. UN Security Council, *Report of the Independent Inquiry in the Actions of the United Nations During the 1994 Genocide in Rwanda,* S/1999/1257, p. 14.
15. Ibid.
16. Barnett, *Eyewitness to Genocide,* p. 158.
17. David Rieff, *A Bed for the Night: Humanitarianism in Crisis* (New York: Simon & Schuster, 2002), p. 159.
18. Power, *"A Problem from Hell,"* p. 346.
19. PBS Interview with Iqbal Riza.
20. Barnett, *Eyewitness to Genocide,* pp. 98–99.
21. Ibid., p. 104.
22. Power, *"A Problem from Hell,"* p. 352.
23. Human Rights Watch, "Leave None to Tell the Story: Genocide in Rwanda," 1999, available at www.hrw.org/reports/1999/rwanda/ Geno15-8-01.htm#P88_24569.
24. Ibid.
25. For the story of the École Technique Officielle, see Power, *"A Problem from Hell,"* p. 353.
26. Geoffrey Robertson, *Crimes Against Humanity: The Struggle for Global Justice* (New York: The New Press, 1999), p. 78.
27. Melvern, *A People Betrayed,* p. 177.
28. Donatella Lorch, "Thousands of Rwanda Dead Wash Down to Lake Victoria," *New York Times,* May 21, 1994.
29. Ibid., p. 181.
30. Ibid.
31. Based on the account by Philip Gourevitch, *We Wish to Inform You That Tomorrow We Will Be Killed with Our Families* (New York: Farrar, Straus & Giroux, 1998), excerpted by PBS. See www.pbs.org/wgbh/pages/frontline/shows/ evil/readings/french.html.
32. Melvern, *A People Betrayed,* p. 211.
33. Ibid.
34. Boutros Boutros-Ghali, *Unvanquished: A U.S.-U.N. Saga* (New York: Random House, 1999), p. 130.
35. See Human Rights Watch Report on Rwanda, p. 2, available at www.hrw.org/reports/1999/rwanda/Geno1-3-05.htm.
36. Melvern, *A People Betrayed,* p. 179.

37. Madeleine Albright, *Madam Secretary: A Memoir* (New York: Miramax Books, 2003), p. 154.

38. Melvern, *A People Betrayed,* p. 233.

39. UN Security Council, *Report of the Independent Inquiry in the Actions of the United Nations During the 1994 Genocide in Rwanda,* S/1999/1257, p. 9.

40. Belgian Senate, Parliamentary Commission of Inquiry Regarding the Events in Rwanda, December 6, 1997. See www.senate.be/english/rwanda.htm#4 (see chapter 4, section 4).

41. Ibid.

42. Fleitz, *Peacekeeping Fiascoes of the 1990s,* p. 154.

43. James C. McKinley, "General Tells Rwanda Court Massacre Was Preventable," *New York Times,* February 28, 1998.

44. Barnett, *Eyewitness to Genocide,* pp. 179–80.

45. Michael Ignatieff, *The Warrior's Honor: Ethnic War and the Modern Conscience* (New York: Owl Books, 1997), pp. 77–78.

### CHAPTER 7: "SCENES FROM HELL"

1. United Nations General Assembly, "Report of the Secretary-General Pursuant to General Assembly Resolution 53/35: The Fall of Srebrenica," November 15, 1999, A/54/549, p. 6.

2. Ibid., pp. 8–9.

3. The Bosnian Serb Army (BSA) was how the international community described what was officially titled the Ármy of Republika Srpska. See ibid.

4. David Rohde, *Endgame: The Betrayal and Fall of Srebrenica: Europe's Worst Massacre Since World War II* (Boulder: Westview Press, 1998), pp. xiv–xv.

5. Jan Willem Honig and Norbert Both, *Srebrenica: Record of War Crime* (London: Penguin Books, 1997), p. 6.

6. United Nations General Assembly, "Report of the Secretary-General Pursuant to General Assembly Resolution 53/35: The Fall of Srebrenica," p. 6.

7. Rohde, *Endgame,* p. 164.

8. A Dutch general, Brigadier General Cees Nicolai, who was chief of staff of UN forces in Bosnia, is quoted as saying that "the Dutchbat [Dutch battalion] had received the instruction 'to assist' in the deportation, because 'to participate in ethnic separation is better that watching ethnic murder.' " *NRC Handelblad,* August 13, 1998, cited by Gerstenfeld, "Srebrenica," p. 7.

9. *NRC Handelsblad,* July 13, 1996, cited by Gerstenfeld, "Srebrenica," p. 2.

10. Rohde, *Endgame,* p. 325.

11. Ibid., pp. 202–3.

12. The Dutch historian who said Karremans was pro-Serbian was Ed Ribbnik, cited in the Dutch daily *NRC Handelsblad,* August 17, 1998. See Manfred Ger-

stenfeld, "Srebrenica: The Dutch Sabra and Shatilla," *Jerusalem Viewpoints,* July 15, 2001, Jerusalem Center for Public Affairs, p. 6.

13. Frederick H. Fleitz, Jr., *Peacekeeping Fiascos of the 1990s: Causes, Solutions, and U.S. Interests* (Westport: Praeger Publishers, 2002), p. 80.

14. Ibid., pp. 92–93 (see endnote 16).

15. Ibid., p. 140.

16. Roy Gutman, "UN's Deadly Deal: How Troop-Hostage Talks Led to the Slaughter of Srebrenica," *Newsday,* May 29, 1996. See also Jacques Julliard, "Should Janvier Be Held Accountable for the Events at Srebrenica," *Le Nouvel Observateur,* October 3–9, 1996.

17. Ambrose Evans-Pritchard, "Chirac in Secret Deal with Serb General," *Daily Telegraph,* July 11, 2003. Interestingly, Western intelligence intercepts turned over to the International War Crimes Tribunal recorded December 1995 conversations between the former Yugoslav president Zoran Lilic and the head of the Yugoslav armed forces that Chirac had given guarantees to protect Mladic from extradition in exchange for French airmen.

18. Rohde, *Endgame,* p. 360.

19. Ibid., p. 23.

20. Richard Holbrooke, *To End a War* (New York: Random House, 1998), p. 70.

21. Honig and Both, *Srebrenica,* p. 127.

22. William Shawcross, *Deliver Us from Evil: Peacekeepers, Warlords, and a World of Endless Conflict* (New York: Touchstone Books, 2000), p. 154.

23. Rohde, *Endgame,* p. 26.

24. Honig and Both, *Srebrenica,* pp. 141–59.

25. Ibid., p. 361.

26. Netherlands Institute for War Documentation Report, Part III, Chapter III, The Fall of Srebrenica, Part 5, "The Report on the Meeting with Janvier and Mladic," available at http://194.134.65.21/srebrenica/.

27. Ibid., pp. 359–61.

28. David Rieff, *Slaughterhouse: Bosnia and the Failure of the West* (New York: Touchstone Books, 1995), p. 127.

29. Honig and Both, *Srebrenica,* pp. 132–33.

30. Phillip Corwin, *Dubious Mandate: A Memoir of the UN in Bosnia, Summer 1995* (Durham: Duke University Press, 1999), pp. ix–xxii.

31. Rohde, *Endgame,* pp. 364–67.

32. Akashi made these statements during staff meetings in Zagreb. Ibid., p. 194.

33. Shawcross, *Deliver Us from Evil,* p. 162.

34. Ibid., p. 162. See also Rohde, *Endgame,* p. 23.

35. Gutman, "UN's Deadly Deal."

36. United Nations General Assembly, "Report of the Secretary-General Pursuant to General Assembly Resolution 53/35: The Fall of Srebrenica," p. 53.

37. Corwin, *Dubious Mandate,* p. 212.

38. Manfred Gerstenfeld, "Anti-Semitism and Hypocrisy in Dutch Society" (forthcoming). Gerstenfeld cites *NRC Handelsblad,* November 21, 2002.

39. Shawcross, *Deliver Us from Evil,* pp. 168–69. See also Rohde, *Endgame,* pp. 268–69.

40. Netherlands Institute for War Documentation Report, Part IV, Chapter V, The Debriefings in Zagreb, Part 8, "Couzy, The Group of 55 and the Media," available at http://194.134.65.21/srebrenica/.

41. Ibid.

42. John Sweeny, "UN Cover-Up of Srebrenica Massacre," *The Observer,* August 10, 1995.

43. See www.pbs.org/wnet/cryfromthegrave/massacre/time_line.html.

44. Netherlands Institute for War Documentation Report, Part IV, Chapter V, The Debriefings in Zagreb, Part 8, "Couzy, The Group of 55 and the Media," available at http://194.134.65.21/srebrenica/.

45. Ibid., Part 10, "Why Was the KTO Group Not Debriefed."

46. Madeleine Albright, *Madam Secretary: A Memoir* (New York: Miramax Books, 2003), p. 186.

47. Netherlands Institute for War Documentation, Part IV, Chapter V, The Debriefings in Zagreb, Part 17, "Investigations Among Displaced Persons."

48. Samantha Power, *"A Problem from Hell": America and the Age of Genocide* (New York: Perennial Books, 2002), p. 417.

49. Bassir Pour Afsane, "Yasushi Akashi's Replacement Is Well Received," *Le Monde,* October 12, 1995.

50. Nedzib Sacirbey, "The Genesis of Genocide: Reflections on the Yugoslav Conflict," *Brown Journal of World Affairs,* Winter/Spring 1996, p. 350.

51. Ibid.

52. Rohde, *Endgame,* p. 377.

53. Rieff, *Slaughterhouse,* p. 193.

54. Rohde, *Endgame,* p. 326.

55. United Nations General Assembly, "Report of the Secretary-General Pursuant to General Assembly Resolution 53/35: The Fall of Srebrenica," p. 107.

56. Holbrooke, *To End a War,* p. 99.

## CHAPTER 8: INSTITUTIONALIZED MORAL EQUIVALENCE

1. See the International Criminal Court website: www.un.org/law/icc/general/overview.htm.

2. Geoffrey Robertson, *Crimes Against Humanity: The Struggle for Global Justice* (New York: The New Press, 2002), p. 346. See also William A. Schabas, *An Introduction to the International Criminal Court* (Cambridge: Cambridge University Press, 2001).

3. For information about the Rome Conference, see www.un.org/icc/index.htm.

4. Alessandra Stanley, "Conference Opens on Creating Court to Try War Crimes," *New York Times*, June 15, 1998.

5. "Human Rights Watch Condemns United States' Threat to Sabotage International Criminal Court," Common Dreams Newswire, July 9, 1998.

6. Robertson, *Crimes Against Humanity*, p. 346.

7. Alessandra Stanley, "U.S. Dissents, but Accord Is Reached on War-Crime Court," *New York Times*, July 18, 1998.

8. Lee A. Casey, "Assessments of the United States Position: The Case Against the International Criminal Court," *Fordham International Law Journal*, March 2002.

9. Lee A. Casey, Eric J. Kadel Jr., David B. Rivkin Jr., and Edwin D. Williamson, "The United States and the International Criminal Court: Concerns and Possible Courses of Action," February 8, 2002—Paper Prepared for the Federalist Society, available at www.fed-soc.org/Publications/Terrorism/ICC.pdf.

10. Allan Gerson, *The Kirkpatrick Mission: Diplomacy Without Apology: America at the United Nations 1981–1985* (New York: The Free Press, 1991), pp. 258–63.

11. Casey, "Assessments of the United States Position."

12. International Criminal Court: Letter to UN Secretary General Kofi Annan, May 6, 2002, available at www.state.gov/r/pa/prs/ps/2002/9968pf.htm.

13. John R. Bolton, "Courting Danger," *National Interest*, Winter 1998/1999, Issue Number 54.

14. Jeremy Rabkin, "The International Kangaroo Court," *Weekly Standard*, April 25, 2002. Rabkin argues that the Belgian case points to the dangers inherent in the ICC: "We don't need to rest on speculation about where the trend is heading. There has already been a dry run. Embarrassed at pulling their troops from Rwanda in 1994, leaving 800,000 Tutsis to be slaughtered, the Belgians gave their courts 'universal jurisdiction' to try any perpetrator, anywhere, of a crime against humanity."

15. Malvina Halberstam, "Belgium's Universal Jurisdiction Law: Vindication of International Justice or Pursuit of Politics?," *Cardozo Law Review*, November 2003.

16. Halberstam, "Belgium's Universal Jurisdiction Law."

17. Ibid.

18. "On the Legitimacy of the International Criminal Court," *Wall Street Journal*, March 7, 2003.

19. Steven Edwards, "Try U.S., Britain for Bombings in Iraq, War Crimes Court Urged," *Ottawa Citizen*, January 27, 2004.

20. Severin Carrell, "Blair Waged War Illegally, Says Panel of Lawyers," *Independent* (London), November 2, 2003.

21. Arnold Beichman, "The Get Is In: The International Criminal Court at Work," *National Review* Online, April 25, 2003.

22. Lee A. Casey and David B. Rivkin Jr., "What Israeli Illegality? The Yassin Assassination Was Perfectly Lawful," *National Review,* March 25, 2004.

23. Abraham D. Sofaer, "Responses to Terrorism: Targeted Killing Is a Necessary Option," *San Francisco Chronicle,* March 26, 2004.

24. Ibid.

25. See remarks by Mary Whelan of Ireland, who spoke on behalf of the European Union at the UN Commission on Human Rights in Geneva. United Nations, "Commission Approves Special Sitting on Situation in Occupied Palestine Following Assassination of Sheikh Yassin," Press Release, Commission on Human Rights, March 23, 2004.

26. The ICC seemed to be careful with its appointments at the outset. For example, it chose as its first prosecutor Luis Moreno-Ocampo of Argentina, who had prosecuted members of Argentina's former military junta and had served as a visiting law professor in the United States. And it picked a former U.S. federal prosecutor, Christine Chung, to lead its first investigation, against Ugandan warlords accused of abducting children to serve as rebel soldiers and sex slaves. See Robert Lane Greene, "Fleeing Prosecution," *New Republic,* August 12, 2003; Marlise Simons, "Argentine Is Expected to Be Prosecutor for War Crime Court," *New York Times,* March 23, 2003; Jess Bravin, "International Criminal Court Picks US Lawyer to Lead First Case," *Wall Street Journal,* January 30, 2004.

27. See the International Criminal Court website: www.un.org/law/icc/general/overview.htm.

28. Testimony of Professor Jeremy Rabkin before the U.S. House of Representatives Committee on International Relations, February 28, 2002.

## CHAPTER 9: THE UN BACKS TERRORISM

1. See Richard Armitage, press conference in Brussels, September 5, 2002, available at www.useu.be.

2. Eric Lesky, "Ending Hezbollah—Now," *National Review,* May 28, 2003.

3. Dan Eggen and Vernon Loeb, "U.S. Indicts 14 Suspects in Saudi Arabia Blast," *Washington Post,* June 22, 2001.

4. Reuven Erlich, *Hezbollah: Profile of the Lebanese Shiite Terrorist Organization of Global Reach Sponsored by Iran and Supported by Syria* (Tel Aviv: Intelligence and Terrorism Information Center, Center for Special Studies, 2000), pp. 77–78.

5. Joint Inquiry into Intelligence Community Activities Before and After the Terrorist Attacks of September 11, 2001, *Report of the U.S. Senate Select Committee on Intelligence and U.S. House Permanent Select Committee on Intelligence* (Washington: U.S. Government Printing Office, December 2002), p. 229.

6. "18 in N.C. Accused of Hezbollah Aid," Associated Press, July 21, 2000; John

Mintz, "FBI Focus Increases on Hamas, Hezbollah," *Washington Post*, May 8, 2003.

7. Erlich, *Hezbollah*, p. 143.

8. Jeffrey S. Helmreich, "Beyond Political Terrorism: The New Challenge of Transcendent Terror," *Jerusalem Viewpoints*, Number 466, November 15, 2001, p. 4.

9. Ibid., p. 26.

10. UN Security Council, "Letter Dated 24 July 2000 from the Secretary-General Addressed to the President of the Security Council," July 24, 2000, S/2000/731.

11. UN Security Council Resolution 1337 (2001), January 30, 2001, S/RES/1337 (2001).

12. Danna Harman, "Annan: Hizbullah Should Not Be Ignored," *Jerusalem Post*, June 22, 2000.

13. Nicholas Blanford, "How Hizballah Captured Three Members of the IDF," *Daily Star*, October 11, 2002.

14. United Nations, "Report of the Fact-Finding Investigation Relating to the Abduction of Three Israeli Soldiers on 7 October 2000 and Subsequent Related Events," August 2, 2001.

15. Amos Harel, Yossi Verter, and Shlomo Shamir, "UN Admits It Has a Videotape of Soldier's Kidnap," *Haaretz*, June 6, 2001.

16. "UN Sweats Over Intelligence Video," Australian Broadcasting Corporation Online, July 12, 2001.

17. David Rudge, "MIA Families See UNIFIL Videos," *Jerusalem Post*, January 18, 2002.

18. Efrat Avraham, "The Record of the Meeting Between the Families of the Kidnapped Soldiers and UN Representatives," available at images. maariv.co.il/cache/cachearchive/24012002/ART239677.html.

19. Nicholas Blanford, "Lebanon's 'A-Team of Terrorists' Valued for Social Services," *Christian Science Monitor*, May 19, 2003. See also Nicholas Blanford, "Hizbullah Defiant at US Warning—Resistance Says It Will Not Abandon Its Aims," *Daily Star* (Lebanon), May 5, 2003. Blanford writes, "While US officials continue to call for the dismantling of Hizbullah and for the deployment of Lebanese troops to the frontier with Israel, a senior UNIFIL official said that Hizbullah's ability to help maintain the present calm in the South 'cannot be ignored.' "

20. David Rudge, "Hizbullah Reinforcing Its Positions on Lebanese Border," *Jerusalem Post*, July 23, 2002.

21. Douglas Davis, "Janes Sees Hizbullah Opening Front with Israel," *Jerusalem Post*, April 25, 2002.

22. "Major Events Along the Israel-Lebanon Border Since the IDF's Pullout on 24/5/00," Israel Defense Forces website, file://C:DOCUME~1\office1\ LOCALS'1\Temp\06KAIR15.htm.

23. Reuven Paz, "Rantisi vs. the United States: A New Policy of a New Leader of Hamas?" Intelligence and Terrorism Center, Center for Special Studies, available at www.intelligence.org.il/eng/g_j/rp_e_11_03.htm.

24. Dore Gold, *Hatred's Kingdom: How Saudi Arabia Supports the New Global Terrorism* (Washington: Regnery Publishing, 2004) (paperback edition).

25. Brigadier General Eival Giladi, "Why Arafat Went to War: The Wrong Lessons from Lebanon and Kosovo," *Jerusalem Issue Brief* (Jerusalem Center for Public Affairs), Volume 2, Number 1, June 19, 2002, available at www.jcpa.org/art/brief1-24.htm.

26. "Jenin: The Capital of the Palestinian Suicide Terrorists," Intelligence and Terrorism Information Center, Center for Special Studies, available at www.intelligence.org.il/eng/bu/jenin/jenin_e.htm.

27. Mohammed Assadi, "Palestinians Urge UN Probe into Jenin Killings," Associated Press, April 11, 2002.

28. Stephanie Nebehay, "Annan Wants International Force to Stem Violence," Associated Press, April 12, 2002.

29. "Bush Throws Support Behind Israel," Agence France-Presse, April 18, 2002.

30. T. Christian Miller, "Israel Faulted for Ignoring Victims," *Los Angeles Times,* April 19, 2002.

31. Paul Martin, "Jenin 'Massacre' Reduced to Death Toll of 56," *Washington Times,* May 1, 2002.

32. Lieutenant Colonel Yonathan D. Halevy, "The Battle for the Jenin Refugee Camp—The Palestinian Perspective," September 2003, Intelligence and Terrorism Center, Center for Special Studies, available at www.intelligence.org.il/sp/jenin/jen_y.htm.

33. Israel Defense Forces, Central Command, April 2002 briefing.

34. Martin, "Jenin 'Massacre' Reduced to Death Toll of 56."

35. Yagil Henkin, "Urban Warfare in Jenin: Lessons for the War on Terror," *Azure,* No. 15, Summer 5763/2003, p. 45.

36. "Israeli Army Says Hundreds of Casualties in Jenin," Reuters, April 12, 2002.

37. Israel Foreign Ministry, press release, April 20, 2002.

38. *Jerusalem Post* Internet Staff and Associated Press, "Annan Names Team to Investigate Jenin," *Jerusalem Post,* April 22, 2002; Charles Krauthammer, "Red Cross Snub," *Washington Post,* March 24, 2000.

39. Isabel Kershner, "The Refugees' Choice: Another Look at UNRWA," *Jerusalem Report,* August 2002.

40. Intelligence and Terrorism Information Center, Center for Special Studies, January 2004, available at www.intelligence.org.il/sp/sib_1_04/amb_01_04.htm.

41. "Israel: Gunmen Used UN Ambulances to Carry Remains," Reuters, May 14, 2004.

42. Charles A. Radin, "Do UNRWA Schools Foster Violence?" *Boston Globe,* July 8, 2002.

43. *Filastin al-Muslima* (Lebanon), July 2003, available at www.fm-m.com/2003/jul2003/pdf/p5.pdf.

44. *Al-Watan* (Kuwait), June 11, 2003, available at www.al-watan.com/data/20030611/index.asp?content=outstate2.

45. *Filastin al-Muslima* (Lebanon), July 2003, available at www.fm-m.com/2003/jul2003/pdf/p5.pdf.

46. "School Notebook in Kalandia Refugee Camp Reflects the Glorification of Violence as Propagated in UNRWA Schools in Palestinian Territories," Intelligence and Terrorism Information Center, Center for Special Studies, available at www.intelligence.org.il/eng/edu_en.htm.

47. *Al-Bayan* (United Arab Emirates), July 31, 2002, available at www.albayan.co.ae/albayan/alarbea/2002/issue143/axis/1.htm.

48. United Nations General Assembly, "Report of the Secretary-General Prepared Pursuant to General Assembly Resolution ES-10/10," July 30, 2002, A/ES-10/186.

49. Anne Bayefsky, "The UN Is Unable to Recognize Terrorism," *Jerusalem Post,* September 21, 2003.

50. Jeffrey Gettleman, "The Struggle for Iraq: Unrest: A Young Radical's Anti-U.S. Wrath Is Unleashed," *New York Times,* April 5, 2004.

51. Nathan Guttman, "U.S. Sources Claim Hezbollah Sending Combatants to Iraq," *Haaretz,* June 20, 2004.

### CONCLUSION: FROM MORAL EQUIVALENCE TO WORLD ORDER

1. E. H. Carr, *The Twenty Years' Crisis, 1919–1939: An Introduction to the Study of International Relations* (New York: Palgrave, 2001), p. 8.

2. Ibid., p. 216.

3. Bernard Lewis, "Iraq, India, Palestine," *Wall Street Journal,* May 12, 2004.

4. William Malley, "The UN and Afghanistan: 'Doing Its Best' or 'Failure of Mission'?" in William Malley, ed., *Fundamentalism Reborn?: Afghanistan and the Taliban* (New York: NYU Press, 2001), p. 195.

5. Human Rights Watch, "Failure to Protect: Anti-Minority Violence in Kosovo, March 2004," July 2004, available at hrw.org/english/docs/2004/07/27/serbia9136_txt.htm.

6. Per Ahlmark, "UN Chief's Career Clouded," *Australian,* May 3, 2004, available at www.theaustralian.news.com.au/common/story_page/0,5744,9450605%255E2703,00.html.

7. Colum Lynch, "GAO: Iraq Oil Profits Understated," *Washington Post,* March 19, 2004.

8. See, for example, Claudia Rosett, "The Oil-for-Food Scam: What Did Kofi Annan Know, and When Did He Know It?," *Commentary,* May 2004. Rosett writes, "By 2002, the sixth year of the program, it was no longer credible that

the UN Secretariat could be clueless about Saddam's systematic violations and exploitation of the humanitarian purpose of Oil-for-Food. On May 2, in a front-page story by Alix M. Freedman and Steve Stecklow, the *Wall Street Journal* documented in detail Saddam's illicit kickbacks on underpriced oil contracts. . . . A mere fortnight later, on May 14, 2002, the Security Council passed a resolution cutting itself out of the loop entirely on all Oil-for-Food contracts deemed humanitarian, and giving direct power of approval to the Secretary-General. . . . On June 2, Annan approved a newly expanded shopping list by Saddam that the Secretariat dubbed 'Oil-for-Food Plus.' "

9. *Meet the Press,* NBC, May 2, 2004.
10. Claudia Rosett, " 'We Have Other Priorities': Why Won't the U.N. Answer Questions About Its Iraq Scandal?," *Wall Street Journal,* May 5, 2004.
11. Ahlmark, "UN Chief's Career Clouded."
12. Ibid.
13. Irwin Cotler, "Discrimination Against Israel in the International Arena: Undermining the Cause of Human Rights at the United Nations," in Manfred Gerstenfeld, *Europe's Crumbling Myths: The Post-Holocaust Origins of Today's Anti-Semitism* (Jerusalem: Jerusalem Center for Public Affairs, 2004), p. 219.
14. Tom Lantos, "The Durban Debacle: An Insider's View of the World Racism Conference at Durban," *The Fletcher Forum of World Affairs,* Winter/Spring 2002, Vol. 26:1, p. 5.
15. Ibid., p. 16
16. Dina Temple-Raston, "Sudan: A Lucky One Tells His Story," *New York Sun,* May 11, 2004.
17. James Traub, "Never Again, No Longer?" *New York Times Magazine,* July 18, 2004.
18. Frederick H. Fleitz, *Peacekeeping Fiascoes of the 1990s: Causes, Solutions, and U.S. Interests* (Westport: Praeger Publishers, 2002), p. 162.
19. Townsend Hoopes and Douglas Brinkley, *FDR and the Creation of the U.N.* (New Haven: Yale University Press, 1997), p. 219.
20. George F. Will, "U.N. Absurdity," *Washington Post,* March 13, 2003.
21. Max M. Kampelman, "A Caucus of Democracies: How to Reform the U.N.," *Wall Street Journal,* January 6, 2004.
22. Linda Fasulo, *An Insider's Guide to the UN* (New Haven: Yale University Press, 2004), p. 183.

## AFTERWORD FOR THE PAPERBACK EDITION:
## THE REAL OIL-FOR-FOOD SCANDAL

1. Task Force on the United Nations, *American Interests and UN Reform: Report of the Task Force on the United Nations* (Washington, D.C.: United States Institute for Peace, 2005), p. 4.

2. The Crisis in Darfur, Secretary Colin L. Powell, Testimony Before the Senate Foreign Relations Committee, Washington, D.C., September 9, 2004, available at www.state.gov/secretary/former/powell/remarks/36042.htm. In contrast, see the Report of the International Commission of Inquiry on Darfur to the United Nations Secretary-General Pursuant to Security Council Resolution 1564, January 25, 2005. This report stated: "The Commission concluded that the government of Sudan has not pursued a policy of genocide." See www.unsudanig.org/emergencies/darfur/reports/data/missions/commission -of-inquiry-report.pdf.

3. Kate Holt, "DR Congo's Shameful Sex Secret," BBC News World Edition, June 3, 2004.

4. David Ignatius, "Beirut's Berlin Wall," *Washington Post,* February 23, 2005.

5. Judith Miller, "Panel Pegs Illicit Iraq Earnings at $21.3 Billion," *New York Times,* November 16, 2004.

6. Paul Volcker, chairman, *Independent Inquiry Committee into the United Nations Oil-for-Food Program,* Second Interim Report, March 29, 2005, available at www.iic-offp.org.

7. Judith Miller, "Memo Seems to Link Annan to Contract of Son's Company," *New York Times,* June 14, 2005.

8. United Nations Counter-Terrorism Executive Directorate, "Frequently Asked Questions about UN Efforts to Combat Terrorism," January 2005, available at www.un.org/News/dh/infocus/terrorism/CTED_FAQs.pdf.

9. United Nations, *In Larger Freedom: Towards Development, Security, and Human Rights for All,* Report of the Secretary General, available at www.un.org/largerfreedom/contents.htm.

10. CNN, *People in the News: Profiles of Scott Peterson, Yasser Arafat,* November 13, 2004.

11. Giles Kepel, *Jihad: The Trail of Political Islam* (Cambridge: Harvard University Press, 2002), p. 184.

12. In a memorandum captured in Operation Defensive Shield, the secretary general of the Fatah office in Tulkarm requested that Arafat provide $2,000 to each of fifteen specifically named "Fighting Brethren" of the Tanzim military wing of Fatah. According to Israeli military sources, each of the "fighters" was involved in the planning or execution of suicide attacks. With his own signature in Arabic, Arafat authorized the payment of $800 to each of the "fighters" on April 5, 2001.

13. UN News Center, "Annan, UN Bodies Pay Tribute to Arafat, Pledging Support for a Palestinian State," November 11, 2004, available at www.un.org/apps/news/story.asp?NewsID=12516&Cr=palestin&Cr1=.

14. MEMRI Special Dispatch Series No. 794, "Reactions to Sheikh Al-Qaradhawi's Fatwa Calling for the Abduction and Killing of American Civilians in Iraq," available at memri.org/bin/articles.cgi?Page=archives&Area=sd&ID=SP79404.

15. Ibid.

16. Dore Gold, *Hatred's Kingdom: How Saudi Arabia Supports the New Global Terrorism* (Washington, D.C.: Regnery Publishing, 2003), pp. 199-201.
17. Benny Avni, "Despite Israeli Alerts, U.N. Transfers Thousands to Hamas Affiliates," *New York Sun,* January 28–30, 2005.
18. True, the resolution gave many states an escape clause since there was no agreed definition of a "terrorist act." Then, too, the UN could argue that it was not formally a state. Nevertheless, it was clear that by its actions, the UN was essentially violating its own resolution and weakening the U.S.–led war on terrorism.
19. Nimrod Raphaeli, "The Saddam Oil Vouchers Affair," MEMRI Inquiry and Analysis—No. 164, available at memri.org/bin/articles.cgi?Page=countries&Area=iraq&ID=IA16404.
20. Central Intelligence Agency, *Comprehensive Report of the Special Advisor to the DCI on Iraq's WMD,* September 30, 2004—Volume 1, Regime Finance and Procurement, pp. 34–36, available at www.odci.gov/cia/reports/iraq_wmd_2004/index.html.
21. Claudia Rosett, "Blame Game," *New Republic,* February 21, 2005.
22. Central Intelligence Agency, *Comprehensive Report,* Volume 1.
23. Ibid., p. 46.
24. "Saddam Hussein's Banker in Lebanon Says United Nations Sanctions Don't Get in His Way," *Bloomberg News,* February 20, 2003.
25. Palestinian National Authority—The Official Website, available at www.pna.gov.ps/Government/gov/Arab_Liberation_Front.asp.
26. Central Intelligence Agency, *Comprehensive Report,* Volume 1, p. 57.
27. Douglas Jehl, "Inspector's Report Says Hussein Expected Guerilla War," *New York Times,* October 8, 2004.
28. Jean-Charles Brisard, *Zarqawi: The New Face of Al-Qaeda* (New York: Other Press, 2005), p. 86. In October 2002, Zarqawi was in Iraq. The money in question was sent to Salem Saad Salem Ben Suwaid, Foley's assassin, who was in Jordan.
29. *The 9/11 Commission Report: Final Report of the National Commission on Terrorist Attacks on the United States* (New York: W. W. Norton, 2004), p. 66.
30. Stephen Hayes, *The Connection: How al Qaeda's Collaboration with Saddam Hussein Has Endangered America* (New York: HarperCollins, 2004), pp. 103–104.
31. Ibid.
32. Claudia Rosett, "Oil-for-Terror?" *National Review,* April 18, 2004.
33. Rosett, "Blame Game."

# ACKNOWLEDGMENTS

This project grew out of the efforts of several close friends and associates. I owe a special debt of gratitude to my friend and mentor Ronald S. Lauder, a former ambassador and Pentagon official with years of experience in foreign policy, who always stressed to me the importance of the struggle of ideas in keeping societies secure and free. Allen Roth specifically felt that it was vital at this time for a former ambassador to the UN to look into the roots of what made this organization so dysfunctional right from its earliest days.

I also owe special thanks to my agent, Richard Pine, who spent hours with me discussing the growing perception of many in the late 1990s that a new world-order crisis was at hand, leading me to rethink the role of the UN in its emergence. As I completed earlier drafts of this work, Dr. Bernard Salick offered a detailed critique that I incorporated into the final text. His insights, personal encouragement, and regular telephone calls were absolutely invaluable to me during the long months of my writing.

Books of this sort require tremendous amounts of research. I would like to acknowledge the extraordinary research skills of Zachary K. Goldman, who, as a student at Harvard University, demonstrated both his dedication and intellectual powers in gathering and summarizing large amounts of legal and historical materials. Just as in my previous book, *Hatred's Kingdom,* it was Lieutenant Colonel (res.) Jonathan D. Halevi who performed an invaluable service in bringing together the materials I needed on international terrorism from original Arabic sources.

Intellectually, I am particularly grateful for the discussions I had with the chairman of the board of the Jerusalem Center, Manfred Gerstenfeld, who introduced me to the subject of Srebrenica and helped with materials written in Dutch. Similarly, Joel S. Fishman used his analytical and language skills to help me navigate through the Dutch parliamentary investigation of Srebrenica as well as the documents collected in the French parliamentary investigation.

As in the past, through the preparation and writing of this book, Jeffrey Helmreich offered me indispensable advice. Since we worked together at the UN in New York, he was prepared to provide me with critical feedback and made important suggestions of his own. Gene and Nadia Kleinhendler also shared their impressions from reading much of the text, as did Ariel Kleinhendler, who made an important contribution to the title.

The preparation of this book for publication would have been impossible without the hard work of Rachel Elrom. I would also like to express appreciation to the entire staff of the Jerusalem Center for Public Affairs and our director-general, Chaya Herskovic, for their patience and support while this book was being prepared.

The production of readable nonfiction on current affairs requires close teamwork between an author and his publisher. Jed Donahue, at Crown Forum, spent hours refining the text and sharing new ideas for its improvement. Let me also add my appreciation for Toni Rachiele, who provided detailed copyediting as well.

Finally, the hours of research and writing by an author are felt most by his family. If my wife, Ofra, had not had such faith in this project, and if my children, Yael and Ariel, had not been so excited about it, I would have found it extremely difficult to complete this work. I am indebted to them for their constant support.

# INDEX